*The Face in the Mirror*

*(John F. Kennedy Library)*

# THE FACE IN THE MIRROR

*Hemingway's Writers*

## Robert E. Fleming

*The University of Alabama Press*

*Tuscaloosa and London*

Library of Congress Cataloging-in-Publication Data

Fleming, Robert E. (Robert Edward), 1936–
The face in the mirror : Hemingway's writers / Robert E. Fleming.
p.  cm. (alk. paper)
Includes bibliographical references (p.) and index.
ISBN 0-8173-0703-6
1. Hemingway, Ernest, 1899–1961—Characters—Authors.
2. Authorship in literature.   3. Authors in literature.   4. Self in
literature.   I. Title.
PS3515.I37Z5936   1994
813'.52—dc20
93-13245

British Library Cataloguing-in-Publication Data available

*To Kathleen Fleming, who has taught me about being a parent while being a writer.*

*And to the memory of Edward S. Bogusch, who was much on my mind as I worked on this book.*

" 'I said I was a different man. . . . ' Looking into
the mirror he saw that this was quite true."

—"The Sea Change"


"He looked at the mirror and it was someone else he saw."

—*The Garden of Eden*

# Contents

# *Acknowledgments*

EXTRACTS FROM THE unpublished Ernest Hemingway papers are copy-right © 1993 by and used by permission of the Ernest Hemingway Foundation. Because of unsettled copyright questions I have not quoted manuscript materials related to any of the published works of the author.

Quotations from *The Garden of Eden* are reprinted with permission of Charles Scribner's Sons, an imprint of Macmillan Publishing Company, from THE GARDEN OF EDEN by Ernest Hemingway. Copyright © 1986 by Mary Hemingway, John Hemingway, Patrick Hemingway, and Gregory Hemingway.

Quotations from *To Have and Have Not* are reprinted with permission of Charles Scribner's Sons, an imprint of Macmillan Publishing Company, from TO HAVE AND HAVE NOT by Ernest Hemingway. Copyright 1934, 1937 by Ernest Hemingway; renewal copyrights © 1962, 1965 by Mary Hemingway.

Quotations from *Islands in the Stream* are reprinted with permission of Charles Scribner's Sons, an imprint of Macmillan Publishing Company, from ISLANDS IN THE STREAM by Ernest Hemingway. Copyright © 1970 by Mary Hemingway. Permission also granted for use of quotations from *Islands in the Stream* by HarperCollins Publishers Limited, who hold copyright in the United Kingdom.

Quotations from *A Moveable Feast* are reprinted with permission of Charles Scribner's Sons, an imprint of Macmillan Publishing Company, from A MOVEABLE FEAST by Ernest Hemingway. Copyright © 1964 by Mary Hemingway.

Portions of Chapter 2 originally appeared as "Portrait of the Artist as a Bad Man" in *North Dakota Quarterly*, Volume 57, no. 1 (Winter 1987). Reprinted with permission of the publisher.

Portions of Chapter 2 first appeared as "Perversion and the Writer in

'The Sea Change' " in *Studies in American Fiction*, Volume 14, no. 2 (Autumn 1986). Reprinted with permission of the publisher.

Portions of Chapter 5 were published in "The Endings of Hemingway's *The Garden of Eden*." *American Literature*, Volume 61, copyright © 1989 Duke University Press. Reprinted with permission of the publisher.

# Introduction: An Unliterary Writer

ERNEST HEMINGWAY is atypical of modern writers of fiction in his disinclination to use the problems of the writer himself as a major topic. Twentieth-century authors, unlike those of the nineteenth century, whose protagonists might be soldiers or businessmen, rakes or clergymen, frontiersmen or whalers or scholars, have frequently turned to the subjects they know the best: the problems of the awakening artist and the conflicts between the worlds of commerce and art.

James Joyce explored the coming of age of the writer with his autobiographical Stephen Dedalus in *A Portrait of the Artist as a Young Man*; D. H. Lawrence used his early life and his struggles to overcome a hostile environment and become an artist as the background for his story of Paul Morel, *Sons and Lovers*. American authors Sherwood Anderson, Floyd Dell, Thomas Wolfe, and James T. Farrell created protagonists such as George Willard, Felix Fay, Eugene Gant, George Weber, and Danny O'Neill, whose struggles with small-town narrow-mindedness or first-generation immigrant provincialism are the precursors of later artistic careers. Even authors less dependent on autobiographical material in their fiction have often treated the theme of the life of the artist: Theodore Dreiser's Eugene Witla (*The "Genius"*) is a painter whose struggles for acceptance by the art world parallel Dreiser's own conflicts with the literary world, and John Dos Passos's Camera Eye segments in *USA* closely parallel the early experience of the young Dos Passos.[1]

In contrast, Hemingway frequently created protagonists who were men of action: soldiers, boxers, matadors, and fishermen. When casual readers think of Hemingway's works, they are likely to recall characters such as Manuel Garcia of "The Undefeated," Jack Brennan of "Fifty Grand," Harry Morgan of *To Have and Have Not*, and Santiago of *The Old Man and the Sea*. At times Hemingway went so far as to suggest that he personally might have been happier if he had not been a writer at all, as when he wrote to his wartime friend and confidant Colonel Charles T. "Buck" Lanham: "I was, and am, absolutely homesick for the regiment and I miss you badly Buck. I don't give a damn about writing."[2] But if there were times when he felt that other roles—soldier, fighter, journalist—might have been simpler, for Hemingway the greatest pleasure to be derived from life was achieved by writing.[3]

Despite his avowed enthusiasm for his work, Hemingway did not find writing a source of unalloyed pleasure. Over a career spanning nearly forty years, he frequently considered the unique problems the writer faces, both the practical problems of finding a congenial place to write and a comfortable method of working and the ethical problems of reconciling one's personal roles as father, son, and husband with one's professional role as writer. He talked and wrote rather freely about the practical problems and his solutions to them, and any student of his work can easily learn about his routines, his simple adages, and his respect for his craft. However, the ethical topic dealt with more intimate information than the type of paper he preferred; these problems could not be solved with generalizations such as the necessity of beginning to write with "one true sentence." To treat that ethical problem meant depending on his own emotions and inner experiences for the raw material of his fiction. Although he was slow to approach this latter theme in his fiction, his nonfiction from the early 1930s to the end of his career documents his concern.[4]

This book treats a limited portion of the Hemingway canon. Although it might be argued that nearly any work by Hemingway addresses the craft of writing metaphorically—that one can see in the art of the matador or of the fisherman parallels to the writer's art—I have chosen to work with only those texts in which a writer or artist is a significant figure. Thus, I discuss *The Sun Also Rises*, which emphasizes the literary and personal foibles of Robert Cohn and his associates, but not *The Old Man and the Sea*, in which Hemingway obviously drew and emphasized metaphorical correspondences between an aging fisherman and aging writers. As a result, some major texts in the Hemingway canon—*A Farewell to Arms*, *For Whom the Bell Tolls*, and *The Old Man and the Sea*, to name but a few—have been omitted from this study. Conversely, some novels and stories that have been less popular with critics—for example, *To Have and Have Not*, *The Fifth Column*, *Islands in the Stream*, "Mr. and Mrs. Elliot," and "The Gambler, the Nun, and the Radio"—have been discussed at length because they shed light on Hemingway's thoughts and on his exploration of questions about the inner life of the literary artist.

Such a selective reading of the Hemingway canon exposes a theme that has been systematically ignored, a theme that may offer new perspectives on Hemingway's art. Since Wyndham Lewis tagged Hemingway with the appellation "the dumb ox" in 1934,[5] many critics have been content to classify the novelist as anti-intellectual or primitive. Nothing could be further from the truth. As a modernist who learned his craft from Ezra Pound and Gertrude Stein, Hemingway was a highly self-conscious writer who addressed his art openly in his nonfiction and—more subtly—from behind a number of masks in his fiction itself.

Hemingway's openness about the workaday problems of the writer as craftsman perhaps explains the critics' failure to look for subtlety in his fictional treatment of authors. His frank discussion of his own habits has provided a guide for many would-be writers. In "Monologue to the Maestro," an *Esquire* account of a budding author who sought him out for advice, Hemingway stresses the importance of resting the conscious mind when the writing is done for the day so that the subconscious mind may take over to prepare the writer for the next day's work,[6] while in *Death in the Afternoon* he affirms the value of the writer's getting his work done no matter what else is happening around him; Hemingway insists that it is the writer's job not to save the world but just to produce literature.[7] Late in his career, perhaps as a self-exculpatory way to account for his unsuccessful struggles to finish *The Garden of Eden* or *Islands in the Stream*, he told readers that he was resolved never to be distracted from that same mission of getting his work done—no more cooperation with film companies or ventures into journalism.[8] These comments treat the day-to-day concerns of the writer, as mundane as sharpening his pencils before beginning work. But even in the nonfiction, where he is less introspective than in his fiction, and in interviews, Hemingway recognizes darker problems that disturb the life of the writer.

In *Green Hills of Africa*, for example, the Papa persona that Hemingway created to represent himself tells Kandisky why America has produced no truly great writers whose careers have endured. Something strange always happens to American writers, Papa says: caught up by the money their craft produces, they set up establishments that require an ever-increasing income; they become ensnared by ambition and write even when they have nothing to say; perhaps worst of all, they listen to the critics who judge their work and thus develop masterpiece complexes that will not allow them simply to write as truthfully as they can. Finally, their careers end in impotence.[9] While Papa is speaking of other writers— Fitzgerald comes immediately to mind, as do several nineteenth-century novelists with truncated careers—by the middle of the 1930s he had experienced several of these traps at first hand. Wed to a wealthy wife, he had seen his own "establishment" on Whitehead Street in Key West grow to alarming proportions. He had written self-indulgent "letters" to *Esquire* even when he had little to say. And if the masterpiece complex and the creative impotence were still beyond the horizon, they were waiting for his career to overtake them.

This tragic vision of the plight of the American writer becomes even darker in Hemingway's later nonfiction, where it causes the author to become so subjective that the boundary between fiction and nonfiction is obscured. In an apparently heartfelt section of *A Moveable Feast* Hemingway recalls the jealousy of acquaintances, friends, and even family toward the working writer. Acquaintances and friends who are also writers feel reproached by a writer who succeeds in getting his work done; they try to distract him so that they will not feel guilty for their own lack of progress.[10] A spouse, resentful of the withdrawal that accompanies the writer's deep concentration on his work, may similarly seek to distract him or to draw his attention away from the work by making him jealous, as Zelda Fitzgerald did to Scott, according to Hemingway's biased interpretation. Nor did his observations avoid his own life: in the same book Hemingway cites, as evidence that a writer doing difficult work is a poor companion for a spouse, his own experience in Schruns, Austria, while he was rewriting *The Sun Also Rises*.[11] The writer's need for solitude could become excessive, however, so that the artist could find himself cut off from humanity permanently, like one of Nathaniel Hawthorne's outcasts.

In talking to interviewers, too, Hemingway expressed his concern with the special problems of the writer. Uneasy while being interviewed, Hemingway often sought to put interviewers off by speaking in metaphors or by making deliberately enigmatic or misleading statements; nevertheless his comments over the years provide some index to his thoughts about the role of the writer. Like his nonfiction, the interviews seem to be most straightforward when they are dealing with the safest topics—mere commonplace reports on the actual mechanics of writing: his best time for writing (early in the morning); his best manner of writing (longhand, except when dialogue was going particularly well, sitting at a table early in his career and standing at a writing board in later years); his habit of reading over several previous days' work before starting his daily writing stint; his emphasis on rewriting until he was satisfied with a passage; and his refusal to talk about a work in progress.

From time to time, however, Hemingway approached more philosophical questions about writing. His responses to these more abstruse questions always raise doubts about his honesty: is he really telling the interviewer what is in his heart, or is he deliberately projecting his carefully conceived public persona? Nearly all of Hemingway's interviews date from the 1930s or later, and as John Raeburn has shown, by 1932, when *Death in the Afternoon* was published, Hemingway had perfected the image that he wanted his public to see.[12] But whatever he might have concealed, Hemingway was always specific about the absolute necessity of being honest in one's writing and of always giving one's best, as when he spoke to a reporter for the *Kansas City Times* in 1940 and said that he had never written for the market but had written what he felt that he had to write.[13]

(Here Hemingway was conveniently forgetting his "letters" to *Esquire*, penned just a few years before.) Similarly, for *Time* in 1950, he summed up his credo as "to write as well as he can about things that he knows and feels deeply about."[14] Concomitant with the need to write one's best was the occasional need to throw bad work away, as Hemingway maintained he had always done.[15] Yet as the publication of *Across the River and Into the Trees* shows, he was not always capable of recognizing his bad work or of compelling himself to throw it away.

In a 1934 interview with the *New York Herald Tribune*, Hemingway maintained that the writer should not exploit the personalities of friends in his fiction,[16] and he said much the same thing about using family members as raw material when he was interviewed for a *New Yorker* article in 1947.[17] He also insisted more than once that, while writers might know each others' weak points, they should not speak or write in such a way as to discredit each other.[18] Yet these rules were more often honored in the breach than in strict observance. Hemingway frequently disregarded his own stricture against the use of friends, family members, and other authors because he stressed inventing out of his own knowledge, making a careful distinction between the "photographic" or "naturalistic" depiction of a real person and the use of that person to create a literary character. For example, white hunter Phillip Percival was the basis for Pop in *Green Hills of Africa* and for Robert Wilson in "The Short Happy Life of Francis Macomber"; in the first work he was treated naturalistically, while in the second, the character was created out of what Hemingway knew of the real man plus what he added as a writer of fiction. In spite of that seemingly precise distinction, however, Hemingway appears to have wondered at times whether he had gone too far in invading the privacy of those closest to him. To his credit, he did occasionally suppress stories that would have reflected badly on recognizable sources. For example, although he used his children as subjects—as in "A Day's Wait"—he did not always publish the stories that resulted. Two instances of apparent attempts to protect a child are the stories "I Guess Everything Reminds You of Something" and "Great News from the Mainland," which appeared posthumously in the Finca Vigía edition of the short stories.[19]

Two other motifs emerge from the interviews: the nature of the challenge a writer faces and Hemingway's love for the difficult life he had chosen. He made it clear in his Nobel Prize acceptance speech that one of his goals was to measure himself against great writers of the past and to try to surpass their work, a notion that had surfaced in an earlier interview as well.[20] He also told Harvey Breit in 1950 that it was important to him to go beyond his own best work, an effort that sometimes led him either to surpass the critics' ability to comprehend him or to fail in some of his experiments, as when he moved from "arithmetic" to "calculus" in going from his early work to *Across the River and Into the Trees*.[21] Of course it is possible that Hemingway merely used the idea of trying to surpass his previous accomplishment as a convenient excuse for failing to finish several of the works that he attempted after World War II.

Despite his awareness of the difficulties a writer faces, Hemingway's love for writing is well documented in interviews. He said that the actual process of writing and revision was pleasurable for him and that, compared with that pleasure, "money, honors and success" were small rewards.[22] In later years, the pleasure of writing could become such a narcotic that the time to publish the manuscript never came. For example, a relatively simple journalistic assignment such as reporting on the *mano a mano* bullfight series between Luis Miguel Dominguín and Antonio Ordóñez for *Life* grew from its originally planned 10,000 words to an elephantine 120,000-word manuscript that Hemingway could not bring himself to cut.[23] When the pleasure factor was complicated by artistic problems and by questions about how much of himself he wished to reveal in his fiction, the result would be artistic paralysis.

In spite of misleading statements and occasional outright lies, Hemingway's nonfiction and public utterances tell a good deal about how he regarded his vocation. But once he had become a "public writer," everything that Hemingway said must be weighed carefully to determine whether it was part of an act, a self-serving attempt to maintain his public image. Because of the importance Hemingway attached to his integrity as a writer, he was most honest and least guarded while writing fiction. In his fiction, he could discard the macho writer persona that he wore for the public and instead assume various literary personae that would enable him to explore various facets of philosophical questions regarding the literary life. Hemingway's fiction, then, contains the most interesting indications of his concepts of writing and his perceptions of the writer, and in general, writers become more prominent in his work as he matures. Therefore it seems logical to treat the works in this study more or less in the order in which they were written.

Even though Hemingway thought of his earliest autobiographical character as a writer, he skirted the actual problems peculiar to the writer or artist in the Nick Adams stories as they were published in his lifetime. Nick is identified as a writer only in two brief passages. In "Big Two-Hearted River," when Nick goes into the burned-over woods near Seney, Michigan, he leaves behind a number of complications inherent in his civilized life, including "the need to write,"[24] but Hemingway had cut a much longer reference to the actual problems that concerned Nick as a beginning writer,[25] deliberately deemphasizing Nick's vocation. Hemingway had apparently decided that Nick's problems with his craft belonged in the portion of the iceberg that remained beneath the surface, to use Hemingway's term for his technique of omission. Because his early work so frequently suppresses references to writing or authors or merely hints at them obliquely, as in "Big Two-Hearted River," Hemingway's interest in the theme is not always apparent.

A second, and more telling, reference to Nick as a writer is only a bit longer than the first, although its significance is much greater. In "Fathers and Sons," published eight years after "Big Two-Hearted River," Nick regards his writing as a means of purging troubling memories of his father: "If he wrote it he could get rid of it. He had gotten rid of many things by writing them."[26] Implicit in the reference to the "many things" that Nick must purge by his writing are his wartime experiences, a probable divorce, and his shaky relationship with his own young son. The small amount of space devoted to Nick's specific problems and concerns as a writer may seem surprising, but the author's reticence probably stems from the fact that, of all his characters, Nick is the closest to Hemingway himself. To reveal too much of Nick would be to confess too much about himself to his readers. In the 1920s and 1930s, Hemingway was not yet ready to bare his soul as completely as he would attempt to do after World War II.

Hemingway's protagonists in novels published during his lifetime are not writers, at least not primarily writers: Jake Barnes is a journalist (although in the original "Fiesta" manuscript Jake describes his account as his first attempt at writing a book);[27] Frederic Henry is a student of architecture; Harry Morgan is a charter fisherman turned rumrunner; Robert Jordan is a college professor (though he has written a book on Spain); Richard Cantwell is a career army officer; and Santiago is a fisherman. Only in the posthumous novels does one find artists in the foreground of the work: Thomas Hudson the painter and his double Roger Davis the writer in *Islands in the Stream* and David Bourne the writer in *The Garden of Eden*. Many have wondered why Hemingway chose not to publish these two works in his lifetime, and perhaps a partial answer is that they come uncomfortably close to being autobiographical disclosures. When Hemingway treats writers or artists in his published works, he usually employs them as secondary characters in novels or as the subjects of closely focused short stories.

To some extent, Hemingway is like Bill Gorton in *The Sun Also Rises*.

When confronted with Pedro Romero, a matador who daily faces a life-and-death struggle in the bullring, Bill asks Jake Barnes to translate how he feels: " 'Tell him I think writing is lousy,' " Bill says. " 'Go on, tell him. Tell him I'm ashamed of being a writer.' "[28] Similarly, Poor Old Papa in *Green Hills of Africa* is diffident about admitting that he is Hemingway the *dichter* when he meets Kandisky, an Austrian fan, in the African outback and apparently claims the distinction of having been published in *der Querschnitt* only because most of his output for that magazine has consisted of "some rather obscene poems" rather than serious literary efforts.[29] While Hemingway's act of distancing himself from writing might smack of false modesty, it seems sincere, the natural reaction of a man who wants to be seen as a rugged he-man and who is a bit embarrassed to admit that he works at an intellectual and aesthetic task rather than at hard or dangerous physical labor.

On the other hand, the writers that Hemingway does portray in fiction published during his lifetime make up a sort of rogues' gallery. Hemingway's Paris years and his exposure to the dilettantes of Montparnasse are reflected in his work of the 1920s. Hubert Elliot, of the short story "Mr. and Mrs. Elliot," writes long poems very rapidly and then uses his money and social prominence to get them published. Although he has simulated the behavior of a man of action by making the Princeton boxing team, Robert Cohn of *The Sun Also Rises* is a pretentious bore who has gotten into writing by the back door: devoid of any real artistic sensibilities, Cohn invests his inherited money in a literary magazine, likes the "authority" of editing, and then pulls strings to get his own books published. Cohn's "literary friend" Braddocks is a pompous British counterpart of the American writer, and their friend Robert Prentiss, a new writer who has arrived in Paris only recently, seems even more artificial than either Cohn or Braddocks. In Hemingway's first novel, Bill Gorton is the only writer treated sympathetically, perhaps because he alone does not take his writing too seriously.

In these works of the 1920s, Hemingway's analysis goes little deeper than the easy stereotypes of the would-be writers on whom he had reported in a *Toronto Star Weekly* story in 1922. Perhaps the chief reason for the lack of depth in these characters is that all are amateurs who attempt to fill their empty lives by playing at literature. They are not serious, dedicated artists who are willing to forsake physical comfort, money, fame, and even the happiness of spouses and families in order to pursue literature for its own sake.

In the 1930s, Hemingway began to go beyond the easy targets of the 1920s. Spurred by the negative reviews of leftist critics who wanted him to enlist in a war against the worldwide depression and the economic system that seemed to have produced it, he examined the involvement of the writer in social movements in "The Gambler, the Nun, and the Radio" and *To Have and Have Not*. The short story takes one side of the question by depicting a writer much like Hemingway himself who chooses not to become an activist. If art is an opium of the people, Frazer will employ it as an anesthetic to help the people bear the pain of the worldwide revolution postulated by the Marxists of the 1930s.

In *To Have and Have Not*, on the other hand, Hemingway satirizes Richard Gordon, a self-styled proletarian writer who writes about the hardships of the poor without having any personal experience or insight into those hardships. Gordon probably represents Hemingway's response to the Marxist critics of the 1930s who devalued his work because it lacked social engagement. Although Gordon fools the critics, who have more in common with him than with the proletariat, he is ineffectual as a writer because he is playing a role rather than writing from his heart. While "The Gambler, the Nun, and the Radio" and *To Have and Have Not* are more thoughtful treatments of the writer than the lampoons of the 1920s, each seems written to propound a position Hemingway already held rather than to explore, in the process of writing, how he felt about an issue.

The problems faced by a third important character of the 1930s, although also rooted in economics, mark Hemingway's attempt to look inward more than he had done in his works of the 1920s. In "The Snows of Kilimanjaro," Harry's failure is due to his slothful refusal to work at his writing. He can afford to be lazy because he has been "collected" by a wealthy woman and effectively placed on a shelf, but his retirement from writing would not have been possible without his own tacit connivance. Although Harry is not dismissed as simply as Richard Gordon is—his special problems interest Hemingway—he presents unadmirable aspects of the writer (as do most of Hemingway's fictional writers in his published work), since Harry allows his skill to atrophy from disuse and then blames others for his failure to write. On his deathbed, Harry remembers many painful experiences that he might have converted into fiction and realizes with regret that it is now too late to give them lasting significance as art. Among his memories are lost loves, broken marriages, and traumatic experiences as a soldier in World War I and as a correspondent in the Greco-Turkish war of the 1920s—the obvious parallels to Hemingway's own experiences indicate the extent to which he must have identified with at least some of Harry's conflicts, fears, and regrets. Having failed to meet his obligation to his art, Harry dies of a painless wasting illness that represents the gradual decay of his talent.

"The Snows of Kilimanjaro" joined two earlier stories of the 1930s in marking a turn to this deeper exploration of Hemingway's own psyche. Both "The Sea Change" and "Fathers and Sons" treat a problem of great personal significance to Hemingway: the balance which a writer must establish between the necessity to safeguard his own privacy and that of the people closest to him and the necessity to treat his inner life if he is to produce honest and meaningful fiction. Will Phil, the male protagonist of "The Sea Change," dehumanize himself if he encourages his lover in her sexual experiments so that he can write about her experiences? Similarly, would Nick Adams be culpable if he used the tragedy of his own father's suicide as material for his fiction? Nick feels uncomfortable sharing his feelings about his father with his own son, yet he knows that he will eventually share those feelings with his readers.

The Spanish civil war interrupted Hemingway's meditations on the struggle between the personal and artistic consciences of the artist. In "The Gambler, the Nun, and the Radio" and *To Have and Have Not* he had suggested that the writer should not become involved with political issues; art is timeless and should be divorced from even the most serious social issues of the day. But the war in Spain impressed Hemingway as so serious that it must be addressed, even if his serious work suffered. Not surprisingly, the creative writing that he produced between 1937 and 1939 reflects his involvement with the Spanish Republic. Although his play and stories written during the war years feature protagonists who are erstwhile writers, most have suspended their literary careers for the duration of the war.

Once the war was lost, Hemingway never really returned to his thoughtful portrayal of writers in his published fiction. When writers appear at all in the published postwar works, they are employed only in vignettes that depict writers in a bad light. During a battle Robert Jordan is approached by a famous British writer who offers him a cigarette for information that the correspondent intends to use to brighten up his writings about the war. The effect is to make the reader view the writer as a parasite on the participants in the war, who live life rather than merely observe it. Richard Cantwell looks across the room in a restaurant in Venice and sees a famous American novelist, obviously based on Sinclair Lewis, who visits foreign countries without ever going beyond the tourist stage. The writer is implicitly contrasted with the soldier, who left his blood in Italy's soil years before and bought an honorary citizenship.

But if Hemingway treats the problems of the writer less explicitly in the works published after 1940, he explores them in greater depth than ever before in the two major unfinished novels published posthumously.

As first conceived, *Islands in the Stream* would have treated many more autobiographical experiences than does the published version of the novel. More important, through the characterization of Roger Davis it would have addressed the specific moral dilemmas faced by the writer who is also a husband, father, and friend. Perhaps because he could not successfully distance himself from Roger's problems as an artist and as a man, Hemingway relegated the character to a supporting role, disguising his personal problems and trivializing his literary problems to avoid identification of Roger with himself. He then approached many of Roger's problems obliquely through his new protagonist, the painter Thomas Hudson. Yet even in the published novel, the relationship of Roger Davis and Thomas Hudson as doubles is readily apparent, and Hemingway's uneasiness concerning the problems of the aging artist shows through. Ironically, Roger's genuine talent has never achieved its potential because to write about his strongest feelings would require that he probe painfully into his own psyche, an action that Hemingway himself could not fully carry out in *Islands in the Stream*.

Finally, David Bourne of *The Garden of Eden* presents a thoughtful consideration of the writer's nature. While recent critical attention has been directed almost solely toward the sexual elements of Hemingway's latest posthumous book, perhaps to Hemingway the plight of the artist was the more important aspect of that novel. David must resist the pressures of his wife, Catherine, whose mental instability grows more serious as David increasingly shuts her out of his creative life. Jealous of his writing, Catherine first seeks to distract him from it, then tries to become his partner and direct him to the subject matter she chooses. When she is unsuccessful in these ploys, Catherine betrays her hostility toward David's artistic side by destroying David's manuscripts. Meanwhile David becomes increasingly withdrawn from the real world; the fictional world in which he spends his most important hours of the day becomes more real, more potent, and more significant than the external world. Like one of Hawthorne's inhumane protagonists—Ethan Brand, Roger Chillingworth, or Dr. Rappaccini—David is no longer bound to the rest of humanity, not even to the woman who is closest to him. He will pursue his art whatever the cost.

In *The Garden of Eden*, David seems to understand the price he is paying when he repeatedly looks into the mirror as if attempting to detect the signs of his corruption in the glass. But like Phil in "The Sea Change," who also looks into a mirror to see whether his outward image has altered, he sees no external transformation. Hemingway's repeated use of the face in the mirror as an objectification of the artist's ethical dilemma is a powerful recurring symbol. Often the subject of widely published photographs and paintings from the 1920s on, Hemingway had ample opportunities to examine his own image in pictures as well as mirrors. Did he find in these images signs of his past experiences and moral struggles as well as his physical trials? Whatever Hemingway saw in the reflections of his own face, his fictional artists bear witness to the inadequacy of the mirror as accurate reflector of the inner nature of its subject. Neither David nor Phil sees the horrible transformation his conscience has led him to expect.

Perhaps for any artist, the truest mirror is his art. At any rate, the most accurate reflection of Hemingway's own moral concerns about art and the artist lies in his works. Like a mirror image, which is not the real thing but its reflection, Hemingway's works are not the reality of his life or character; instead the works, like a mirror image, sometimes reveal heretofore unnoticed aspects of the author. A growing preoccupation with the writer emerges and leads to ominous implications, for no matter how Hemingway chose to approach the writer's problem in his final years, he reached the same conclusion: the writer cannot give complete allegiance to his art without surrendering some of his humanity. His uncertainty about who would be the protagonist of *Islands in the Stream* and his several drafts of *The Garden of Eden* may have been attempts to evade that inevitable conclusion to which his fiction kept returning.

From his earliest works to his posthumous fiction, Hemingway displays a keen sense of the writer's difference from his fellow human beings and an uncertainty about whether the writer's gift was a blessing or a curse. His work reflects the evolution of the writer's concerns, an evolution in his own shifting ideas and personal uncertainties, which were also reflected in his stormy relationships with other writers who sometimes served as mirrors for his own uncertainties and frustrations.

During his long literary career, Hemingway fought skirmishes of varying length and intensity with a staggering number of fellow writers—including Sherwood Anderson, John Dos Passos, T. S. Eliot, William Faulkner, F. Scott Fitzgerald, Ford Madox Ford, Henry James, Sinclair Lewis, Harold Loeb, Robert McAlmon, Chard Powers Smith, Gertrude Stein, Ernest Walsh, and Glenway Wescott. Some observers believed that Hemingway used other writers as stepping-stones, learning as much as possible or profiting in other ways from each relationship and then discarding the onetime friend when he or she was no longer useful. Referring to experiences with Hemingway and various other young writers, Ford Madox Ford felt that he "really exist[ed] as a sort of half-way house between nonpublishable youth and real money—a sort of green baize swing door that every one kicks both on entering and on leaving."[30] But another explanation of the numerous feuds Hemingway had with other writers, especially Sherwood Anderson, Gertrude Stein, F. Scott Fitzgerald, and John Dos Passos, is that he saw in other writers some of the problems, errors, and failings to which he himself had been subject at various stages of his career. By attacking the old friend, Hemingway attacked the heresy against his own true religion—the profession of writing—and by doing so tried to exorcise his own fault or rid himself of his own guilt.

Hemingway's complex responses to the roles the writer must fulfill in life are the subject of this book. Frequently the writer—who is also son, husband, father, friend—must choose between his commitment to other people and his commitment to art. As Hemingway told Morley Callaghan in the 1920s, the writer must stay detached with one part of his mind, even when he is going through the most harrowing human experiences, such as the death of a parent: the authorial side of him must be recording the perceptions and the emotional response of the human being whose body the writer's artistic identity inhabits.[31] Or, as he told Scott Fitzgerald, the secret of dominating the "hurt" that comes with life is to use it in one's art.[32]

But such advice was easier to formulate than to follow, easier to give than to take. Hemingway seems to have felt divided in his commitments through much of his life. Those who knew him during his early years in Paris in the 1920s have testified to his ruthless single-mindedness in pursuing his career; however, during later years he sometimes abandoned his career temporarily to assume family responsibilities, as when Patrick Hemingway was seriously ill in the late 1940s or when Mary Hemingway nearly died as a result of a tubal pregnancy shortly after World War II. There were also times when Hemingway must have felt guilty of being too deeply immersed in his career for his own good as a human being: perhaps if he had been less involved in writing *A Farewell to Arms* in the late 1920s and more cognizant of his father's problems, he could have done something to avert his father's suicide.

As the grain of sand in an oyster's shell causes the oyster to produce a pearl, the irritating problem of how the artist coexists with the man produced results in Hemingway's work. Despite the fact that Hemingway did not dwell on the problems of the artist as overtly and fully (or perhaps as self-indulgently) as many of his contemporaries, his work reveals his continuing consciousness and examination of those problems. Attempting to trace that figure in the carpet of Hemingway's oeuvre, I have examined his fiction to discover his treatment of questions such as these: How does a writer function as an artist whose work will outlive him while he maintains his role as a human being who pays proper respect to his contemporaries? How can one use the characters and lives of those about him without invading the privacy of wife, children, other family members, and friends? How does he prevent himself from becoming a detached, inhuman observer of the rest of mankind? Must the writer commit acts of such dubious morality that he fears to see himself indelibly marked by them when he looks at his own face in the mirror?

# 1

## A Gallery of Flawed Writers

How DOES A young man become a writer when he knows nothing about what the profession entails? Before Hemingway went off to Kansas City—and from there to the Italian front—he was a fairly typical boy of his era, living in a sheltered and rather provincial American town. As Michael Reynolds has noted, in the period immediately following the war Hemingway was handicapped in his efforts to become a writer by the almost complete absence of role models: "If he could sell a few stories to the *Saturday Evening Post* or *Red Book*, maybe he could go back [to Italy] as a writer. He was not sure how writers lived or how much money the *Post* paid. He did not know any writers."[1] While Oak Park did have some writers—authors of children's books, historical novels, and jungle thrillers—as Reynolds observes, these were hardly the best role models for the young Hemingway. Of the lot, probably only Edgar Rice Burroughs, creator of Tarzan, might have appealed to the young Red Cross veteran because of his popular success and the fact that he set his fantasies in far-off Africa. Still, the Hemingways were not on the same social footing as Burroughs.

As Charles Fenton has stated, Hemingway grew up with a certain resistance toward "artistic or semi-artistic endeavor," out of reaction to what he perceived as exaggerated honor paid to the arts in his home.[2] Judging from the surviving manuscripts written just after the war, Hemingway's early ambitions after returning to Oak Park were exceedingly modest.[3] Before graduating from high school, Hemingway had read Richard Harding Davis's *Stories for Boys* and had imitated Ring Lardner's Chicago *Tribune* column in writing for the Oak Park High School *Trapeze*.[4] Davis undoubtedly appealed because he wrote of the potential adventures awaiting boys—especially those who chose journalistic careers—while part of Lardner's appeal was his iconoclastic attitude toward society and his offhand refusal to take the writing profession too seriously. Now Hemingway advanced to other models, but they were still not the mentors a sophisticated student of literature might have chosen for him: they included O. Henry, Kipling, Stewart Edward White, and E. W. Howe, none

of them major influences on the mature Hemingway but all superior to
the young man who wanted to become a writer in 1919–1920.

That man was turning out formula fiction aimed at the popular magazines, trying to impress his skeptical parents and earn enough money to
buy his freedom from the restrictive establishment in Oak Park. For the
most part, the surviving manuscripts from Hemingway's first two years
of postwar effort are amateurish attempts at the same sort of "slick" fiction for which he would later condemn his friend F. Scott Fitzgerald.
Hemingway satisfied himself, if not the editors who rejected these stories,
rather easily in those years.[5] His first goal seems to have been mere publication of his work anywhere, so he was trying to turn out stories that
would get him into print. Hemingway's extreme devotion to writing as
an artistic discipline would not develop until he met some serious writers.
When he did so, their standards would become his standards, and as his
concept of writing grew with his increasing knowledge, he would discard
early role models in favor of more sophisticated ones.

The nearness of Oak Park to Chicago was a positive influence. Since
the 1890s Chicago had enjoyed a reputation as a literary center of sorts,
not comparable to New York, but producing enough writers of national
reputation so that one writer has referred to the city as "Montmartre in
the Midwest."[6] Henry Blake Fuller, Vachel Lindsay, Theodore Dreiser,
and Upton Sinclair became associated with the city early, and after 1912,
the year in which Harriet Monroe founded *Poetry—A Magazine of Verse*
and Margaret Anderson started the *Little Review*, Chicago authors included Carl Sandburg, Sherwood Anderson, Floyd Dell, Edgar Lee
Masters, Hamlin Garland, William Vaughn Moody, Robert Herrick, and
Ben Hecht. A young man from the rather tame town of Oak Park could
come into contact with writers who took art seriously as something other
than a way of making money by churning out entertainment.

In 1921 Hemingway met his first successful author, Sherwood Anderson. Anderson may seem an unlikely role model for a future winner of
the Nobel Prize, but in the 1920s his significance was greater than his
current critical reputation would suggest. For several years he had a local
reputation as Chicago's "great unpublished author."[7] In 1916 he remedied
that situation by publishing *Windy McPherson's Son*, followed by the relatively unsuccessful *Marching Men* (1917). By the time Hemingway met him
at Y. K. Smith's apartment, however, Anderson was gaining recognition
as one of the major literary forces of the 1920s, largely as a result of *Winesburg, Ohio* (1919).[8] Not a great popular success—according to Anderson it
took two years for the book to sell its first 5,000 copies[9]—*Winesburg*
nevertheless enjoyed considerable critical esteem. For Hemingway, groping

to find a literary identity, the model of Anderson's career suggested something that went beyond the tawdry models he had been trying to imitate with stories such as "The Ash Heel's Tendon."

Anderson had based his literary reputation on an elementary treatment of Freudian psychology (although he denied that he had read Freud until after the publication of *Winesburg*) and on a naive prose style often characterized as "primitive." He had recently returned from a trip to Paris, and he easily impressed the young Hemingway with his stories of the literary and artistic life there. Anderson passed on some advice to the beginner— he should plan to live in Paris rather than return to Italy to begin his life as an expatriate author—and he gave Hemingway a letter of introduction to Gertrude Stein. But he gave him something more important as well: a new and compelling concept of what the life and career of a creative writer might be.

Hemingway modified his earliest concept of the author as one who wrote solely for money: reputation now counted for something. Though money was important, that could come later. Anderson had written best when he wrote from experience; Hemingway too would begin to write from experience and would become contemptuous of those who did not. Clumsy as his psychology was, Anderson sought to look inside his characters; Hemingway too would become a more reflective, internal writer, less concerned with externals than he had been in his apprentice work. Finally, Anderson's success had not come overnight; Hemingway learned from him that a long period of hard work was necessary, often a long period when one was not published at all or was published only in small, fragile literary magazines. It was all right. Internalizing the values of self-examination, sacrifice, hard work, patience, and respect for art, Hemingway realized now that he could be a writer.

With his move to Paris, Hemingway's new awareness of himself as a writer led him to ask questions about the writer's role, questions he had never thought to ask when he envisioned writing as merely a glamorous kind of job. Now writing was a sort of sacred vocation, subject to rules that did not apply to mere jobs. He now saw that the really serious writer did not work merely to impress the audience of the moment. The best writers devoted themselves to the truth so that they might appeal to future generations as well as to the discerning contemporary reader. If one must live very simply, as his new friend Ezra Pound did, he must be willing to do so. The only question was whether one had the combination of talent and determination to make his mark as a writer. Young, enthusiastic, and even passionate about his vocation, Hemingway began to exalt writing and its purpose, seeing the apprentice writer as a postulant preparing for a literary priesthood. He also began to see other writers from a different perspective. Leaving behind his early uncritical admiration for any writer who was able to publish, he was now conscious of failings and weaknesses in more established writers. Indeed, with the zeal of the newly converted, he became impatient and even hypercritical of those failings. Artificially literary people whom he encountered in Paris revolted him, for Paris was not quite what it had seemed when Anderson described it to him.

A very early indication of his new negative attitude toward some writers was his 1922 *Toronto Star Weekly* story "American Bohemians in Paris," in which he ridiculed the American poseurs who sat all day in the Rotonde. These people were "nearly all loafers expending the energy that an artist puts into his creative work in talking about what they are going to do and condemning the work of all artists who have gained any degree of recognition. By talking about art they obtain the same satisfaction that the real artist does in his work."[10] These refugees from Greenwich Village, now transplanted to the Quarter, sought to simulate artistic activity by dressing and behaving in what they took to be an eccentrically creative manner, but they succeeded only in capturing some of the external marks of genuine creative artists. Hemingway doubted that there had been much serious poetry written in cafés such as the Rotonde since the days of Baudelaire.

This critical attitude would also find its way into Hemingway's fiction during the next few years. Youthfully confident and secure in his own integrity as a writer, he adopted a position of moral and artistic superiority and attacked those writers whom he judged to be less honest or dedicated (or perhaps even less struggling) than himself. The portraits of writers in his work of the 1920s are external studies dealing more with the personal faults of the writers as individuals than with the spiritual problems to which the vocation could lead. His personal satisfaction with the success of his own writing at first kept him from introspection while he investigated some of the simpler heresies to which a writer could fall prey.

## "Mr. and Mrs. Elliot"

In 1924 Hemingway published in the *Little Review* a slight but nasty satirical story, apparently intended to show up the literary poseurs of Montparnasse. Editor Margaret Anderson reportedly felt that "Mr. and Mrs. Elliot" was "a gem of a story," according to Nicholas Joost, who suggests that the story reflected Hemingway's hostility toward T. S. Eliot.[11] Writing in 1968, Joost was unaware that Hemingway had originally had a very different source for the poet in the story.

In 1969 Carlos Baker, in *Ernest Hemingway: A Life Story*, disclosed the fact that the original manuscript for the story had been entitled "Mr. and Mrs. Smith"[12] and that there had been an exchange of letters between Chard Powers Smith and Hemingway in 1927, when Smith belatedly read the story. Smith had published a book of poetry, *Along the Wind*, in 1925, but his chief claim to literary fame is his book of reminiscences on Edwin Arlington Robinson.[13] Smith is described by Jeffrey Meyers as "a contemporary of MacLeish at Yale and at Harvard Law School . . . [who] had a private income, never practiced law, hung about the Latin Quarter, [and] tried to write."[14] In 1969 Smith wrote to Carlos Baker, giving more details about the background of his tragic marriage and its connection with the story. According to Smith, in March 1924 his wife Olive had died while she was pregnant, an accidental bit of irony apparently not recognized by Hemingway. Smith added that the suggestions of a lesbian relationship between his wife and her best friend Janet Hurter were completely false.[15]

When Hemingway wrote the story he was a nearly penniless apprentice writer with little to lose in a lawsuit, but he might have felt that the use of the surname Smith, common as it was, would be too blatant, and he changed the name to Elliot, being careful to use a spelling that would not duplicate the name of another living—and better known—poet. Although T. S. Eliot had attended Harvard and had had his own marital difficulties, he had not gone to Harvard Law School, had not married an American southerner, and certainly did not write "very rapidly" or publish with vanity presses.

As he would do with *The Sun Also Rises*, Hemingway was drawing on people whom he knew to create fictional characters, even to the extent of using real names in his first draft, a practice that he acknowledged early in his career[16] but which he would deny as his career continued. In later years, he would use different terminology, saying of Margot Macomber, for example, that she was based on a woman whom he "knew very well in real life"; this woman, "the worst bitch I knew (then),"[17] was the *basis* for Macomber's wife, who was not simply a realistic portrait of the real woman Hemingway had in mind, elsewhere identified as Jane Mason. He claimed that he had simply developed the fictional Margot by putting a woman of this sort into the situation in which Margot finds herself and then letting the character develop from that point. In the 1920s Hemingway was not yet so sophisticated in his use of real people as models, and "Mr. and Mrs. Elliot" had repercussions.

Shortly after the first publication of the story, it was submitted to Boni and Liveright as part of *In Our Time*. The publishing house censor felt that the story was obscene because of its many Steinian repetitions on the Elliots' attempts to have a baby. Hemingway obligingly altered the story, although he told Horace Liveright that it had run in the *Little Review* without incident.[18] He also said that, to maintain the rhythm and humor of the story, he was adding some material that would replace the repetitions of "they tried very hard to have a baby." The additions contained details about the Elliots' Atlantic crossing and about the literary set to which they were introduced in Paris, naming two of Hemingway's own literary associates, Pound and Joyce, on whom Hubert Elliot makes no impression. The Boni and Liveright edition also changed the subject of Hubert's studies at Harvard from law to economics. It is not clear whether Hemingway or the publisher made this change, which was probably intended as an additional safeguard against a lawsuit by Smith.

Smith wrote to Hemingway on 1 January 1927. His return address indicates that he was living in Paris at the time, and he wrote Hemingway in care of the Guaranty Trust Company in Paris, perhaps thinking that Hemingway was also in town. Fortunately for both men, Hemingway answered the letter from Switzerland and not in person. Smith implied that Hemingway was lucky that Mrs. Elliot was not recognizable as having been based on his own dead wife, called Hemingway a "worm" and a "cad," and said that the attempt to satirize him was a failure because Hemingway had relied on reporters' tricks, which cannot produce "literary truth." He assured Hemingway that he had not been wounded by this "silly" attempt at satire because Hemingway had never earned more than his contempt.[19]

Hemingway replied with characteristic combativeness in a letter dated 21 January. He first professed surprise that Smith had identified himself as a model for "characters" in his book and sarcastically offered to inscribe copies in case Smith wanted to send them to his friends. After this witty beginning, he resorted to unalloyed nastiness. He wrote that it was obvious from the letter that Smith had known he was out of town; otherwise he would never have dared to use terms such as "contemptible worm" in addressing Hemingway. Regarding that term, he said that it took one contemptible person to recognize another, and that he felt "humble" in the shadow of one so much more contemptible than himself. Finally, he offered to "knock [Smith] down a few times" when he returned to Paris and suggested that Smith either be gone by March or be armed with a suitable number of pistols, sword canes, or other weapons.[20]

If Hemingway knew that Smith's wife had died shortly before he published his story, he gave no indication. Like his letter, the story itself seems a mean-spirited performance if it is read merely as an attack on two not very famous hangers-on in the literary Paris of the 1920s.[21] More significantly, however, the story is an attack on a then prevalent attitude regarding literature. This purpose was recognized as early as 1964 by Louis Broussard, who analyzed both *The Torrents of Spring* and "Mr. and Mrs. Elliot" primarily as literary criticism, and later by Sheldon Grebstein, who felt that Hemingway's dislike for the characters in the story and the values they stood for was "too strong and reckless to be constrained by technique."[22]

Hemingway linked Elliot's sexual life with his life as a writer, a connection that he would frequently make in his later fiction as well as in nonfiction and interviews. In an interview given in the late 1950s Hemingway equated the flow of literary power with that of semen when he wrote of having had enough "juice" to finish "Ten Indians," "The Killers," and "Today Is Friday" all in a single day.[23] However, writing was never to become a substitute for sexual activity. In *Death in the Afternoon*, he ridiculed the bloodless writers who sublimate their sexual drive exclusively into their work when he wrote about the "erectile" school of writing, saying that many of the people who have written on Spain have lacked "a few good pieces of that sovereign specific for making a man see clearly."[24] As a result, due to "congestion," all objects appear blurred and somewhat larger than after one has had sexual intercourse. Phallic images abound in the work of "erectile" writers, since their writing is the only place where they can express sexual desire.

Hubert Elliot may be an "erectile" writer. Mr. and Mrs. Elliot are first introduced with the information that they have "tried very hard to have a baby."[25] Hemingway uses Steinian repetitions to emphasize the difficulty and unpleasantness of this undertaking, repeating versions of the same clause five times in the first four lines of the story and linking the word "tried" with the word "sick," which he then applies to Mrs. Elliot five times in the next two lines. Charles Fenton called the repetitions at the beginning of the story "an ugly caricature of the [Stein] method" and believed that it was what Gertrude Stein had in mind when she accused Hemingway of employing her technique "without understanding it,"[26] but it is more probable that part of the humor Hemingway intended in the story stemmed from its parody of Stein's style as well as from its subject matter. At any rate, linking the verb "tried" to the adjective "sick" accomplishes Hemingway's objective: immediately to identify sex as hard work and as an unpleasant chore for the two title characters.

Hemingway follows this initial characterization with more information about Hubert Elliot's sexual nature. Now twenty-five, he had always kept himself "pure" for the girl he would marry someday and had often told the girls he met that he was a virgin. They quickly dropped him, suspecting correctly that he was a cold fish or worse, but when he tells Cornelia, she approves of his "clean life" and, in fact, seems to grow more ardent each time he tells the story. Cornelia, like Hubert, has a very low sex drive and seems happy to have found a kindred spirit. Both are delighted by the results of their experiments with kissing, a technique that the inexperienced Hubert has picked up by "hearing a fellow tell a story once" (162). These French kisses are the extent of their physical intimacy before they are married. Hubert was never sure when "it was decided" that he would marry Cornelia. The implication of the impersonal construction is that he did not decide: a man of few convictions, he has apparently been subtly pressured into marriage by Cornelia.

The honeymoon is disastrous. The Elliots spend the "night of the day they were married"—not their wedding night—in a hotel room in Boston.[27] Both are disappointed, suggesting that there was no "wedding night," no consummation of the marriage, probably because Hubert was impotent. After his failure in the bedroom, Hubert goes for a walk in the corridor and is stimulated by the sight of "small shoes and big shoes" (162) outside the doors of the other rooms. The thought of sex symbolized by the mixed pairs of shoes is more exciting to the cerebral Hubert than its reality. He is more used to responding to ideas in literature than to naked emotions in real life. Stimulated at last, he rushes back to Cornelia, who is asleep by this time. Hubert doesn't wake her; either he masturbates or, more likely, his feeble sexual appetite subsides, and he soon falls peacefully asleep. After all, he has finally stood ready to perform his duty as a bridegroom and has been saved by Cornelia's sleepiness. He remains in his artificial literary world of the intellect, blissfully insulated from the real world of the body.

In France the Elliots continue to try to have a baby whenever Cornelia feels well enough to "attempt it." They attempt their way across France, trying to achieve impregnation in Paris, in Dijon, and finally in Touraine, where they "tried very hard to have a baby in the big hot bedroom on the big hard bed" (164) in the château Hubert has rented. Physical discomfort has been added to the physical distaste associated with sex. Finally, in an ironic foreshadowing of the more sympathetic and mature view of the writer and his wife in *The Garden of Eden*, the Elliots settle down in a peculiar ménage à trois with Cornelia's girlfriend, who sleeps with Cornelia and has long cries with her while Hubert writes far into the night. Like Marita in *The Garden of Eden*, the friend is more supportive of Hubert's writing than Cornelia is. Some critics, such as Jeffrey Meyers, have inferred an overt as well as latent lesbian relationship between Cornelia and her friend, but even without that assumption, the sexual story in "Mr. and Mrs. Elliot" depicts a perversion of normal sexual relations.

Like the sexual theme of the story, the artistic theme is devastating. Hubert Elliot is characterized as a passionless poet, incapable of producing real poetry. Hubert's sole adventures before his marriage have been in literary and academic settings. His travels abroad since his marriage have not extended his horizons: in Paris and Dijon the Elliots associate mainly with Americans; they avoid the Rotonde in Paris because it "is always so full of foreigners" (163). When they settle in Touraine, they find it "a very flat hot country very much like Kansas" (164). Hemingway, who believed that the main wellspring for any writer was his own experience, again presents a writer who has no experience about which to write. Furthermore, Elliot's sexual abnormality places him in the "erectile" school, as a writer who has insufficient sexual intercourse and sees things from a warped perspective. Elliot grows more prolific as a poet as the sexual failure of his marriage intensifies.[28]

On the first page of "Mr. and Mrs. Elliot," the narrator establishes that Elliot has an income of "nearly ten thousand dollars a year" and that he writes "very long poems very rapidly" (161). The juxtaposition of these two statements taken together implies that Elliot is well paid for his writing. That implication is reinforced by Elliot's "severe" treatment of Cornelia when she types his poems: if she makes a single mistake on a page, Hubert forces her to type the whole page over, a considerable burden for Cornelia, who has difficulty typing as fast as Hubert can write. It is only on the last page of the story that the narrator separates Elliot's income from his poetry, stating that Elliot has almost enough poems for a book and has made arrangements for its publication, having "already sent his check to, and made a contract with, a publisher" in Boston (164). Elliot is finally revealed to be a wealthy dilettante who lives on inherited wealth and merely fosters the impression that writing is his profession.

By the end of the story, the Elliots arrive at a satisfactory though perverted living arrangement. Cornelia and her friend sleep in the big bridal bed together, whether in a lesbian relationship or not, and Hubert drinks white wine and stays up most of every night writing poetry. Cornelia's girlfriend has taken over most of the manuscript typing. In the evening they all enjoy sitting in their hot garden, Elliot drinking his wine and the women making conversation. The three are described as "very happy" (164), though their situation is clearly no Garden of Eden.

"Mr. and Mrs. Elliot" anticipates both *The Sun Also Rises*, written during the same period, and later thoughts Hemingway expressed on writing. Like Robert Cohn, Elliot uses his inherited wealth to publish his inferior work. Like Robert, his friend Braddocks, and their friend Robert Prentiss, Elliot has no real experience about which to write. All of these flawed writers commit the sin of "faking" their material, on which Hemingway would comment a decade later. Writing "straight honest prose on human beings"[29] was the true business of the writer, Hemingway wrote in 1934. Although it was "the hardest thing" to do, it was the task to which the writer must set himself.[30] Faking, as these writers do, is perhaps the most serious sin that can be committed by a writer. If he is sufficiently skilled, he may get away with it for a time, but "after he fakes a few times he cannot write honestly any more."[31] The perversion of writing lies eventually undermines the writer's talent and his very character. The concept of talent being irretrievably lost if it is abused is another harsh judgment of confident, idealistic youth—the sort of judgment that might haunt the aging Hemingway.

Hubert Elliot also anticipates another problem of the writer more fully treated in *A Moveable Feast*. Publication is so important to him that he will pay for it himself. In *A Moveable Feast*, in memories that are obviously distorted not only by nostalgia but by malice toward Gertrude Stein, Hemingway contrasts his early attitude toward publication with that of his mentor. He implicitly contradicts Stein's well-known condemnation of "Up in Michigan" as "inaccrochable" in a passage recalling his reaction to a rejection letter. As he prefers to remember the incident, Hemingway told himself that while there was now no demand for his stories because they were not understood by the editors, "they will understand the same way they always do in painting. It only takes time and it only needs confidence" (75). From Hemingway's point of view, the story was worth writing for the pleasure of writing it, whether or not it would ever be published. Assuming a purity of artistic character that he did not consistently possess, he strains to contrast his own high-minded virtue with Stein's baser desire for status: according to his interpretation, Stein, who said that his work was not fit for magazines such as *Atlantic* and the *Saturday Evening Post*, had not yet learned the lesson grasped by her youthful apprentice, for she aspired to have her work published in a magazine like *Atlantic*.[32]

During the 1920s, Hemingway had progressed from a merely utilitarian view of writing as a profession like journalism, by which one made a living, to an exalted view of writing as a holy vocation to which one devoted his life. The portrait of Hubert Elliot is thus analogous to the characterization of an apostate priest by a leader of the Inquisition. Hubert's heresies are that, in contrast to his creator, he writes without having experiences to draw upon or ideas to convey to his readers, even to the extent of deliberately ignoring experiences thrust upon him. Also in contrast to Hemingway, who had been working on very short sketches and stories, slowly and deliberately, Elliot writes long poems and writes them rapidly, the suggestion being that he never corrects a line nor throws one away. He pays a vanity publisher to distribute this false literature to an unsuspecting public, and he associates with other poetasters who feign admiration for his poetry, probably so that he will pretend admiration for theirs in return. Finally, he sacrifices the feelings of the person closest to him for the sake of his false "art," browbeating Cornelia when she fails to put the best possible face on his inferior work by typing it flawlessly. Elliot has lived close to academe, benefiting from its artificial shelter. Even in Europe he aligns himself with universities. His sterility in the marriage bed is symbolic of his sterility as a writer.[33] By the end of the story, Hubert's writing has become a full-fledged perversion. He has forsaken his marriage bed for the isolation of his writing room, from which he emerges each morning looking "exhausted." His writing has become a sort of literary masturbation, giving a limited pleasure to Hubert but to no one else and producing nothing that will live after him.

Read in these terms, "Mr. and Mrs. Elliot," while not one of Hemingway's best stories, is at least one of his most significant early attempts to articulate the writer's relationship to his art and to his fellow human beings. Coming near the end of a period of great productivity during which he had written the masterful stories of *In Our Time*, the story marks an introspective mood, a chance to reflect on the role of the writer as frequently manifested in the lives of some acquaintances and as it might someday be manifest in his own. The short story introduces themes that would be further developed in "The Sea Change" during the next decade of Hemingway's career and in *A Moveable Feast* and *The Garden of Eden* at the very end of his working life.

## "Banal Story"

Less fully developed than "Mr. and Mrs. Elliot" but nevertheless an important relic of Hemingway's effort to sort out his thoughts about writing and his own role as a writer is "Banal Story." This little piece was composed some nine months after "Mr. and Mrs. Elliot" and like the earlier story was published in the *Little Review*. The story juxtaposes two scenes: a solitary writer sits in his workroom attempting to find literary inspiration in the newspaper and in a promotional booklet distributed by the *Forum*; at the same time, one of the major toreros of the twentieth century dies of pneumonia. What unites the two scenes, as George

Monteiro has shown, is that both obliquely address the vocation of the artist.[34]

The *Forum* was a logical target for Hemingway's satire because of its entrepreneurial application of the business techniques of the 1920s to literature. The magazine was forty years old in 1925 when Hemingway wrote "Banal Story," but it had been struggling as recently as 1923, when its circulation was roughly 2,000. Under the editorship of Henry G. Leach, who took over in 1923, the magazine increased its sales to 102,000 by 1928.[35] Leach built up circulation by airing both sides of controversial subjects of the day—such as Prohibition—without taking a stand. Although its editorial policy thus appeared evenhanded, it was probably calculated to interest as many and offend as few readers as possible while appearing daring.

The *Forum* favored formula fiction, as represented by a story to which Hemingway alluded in "Banal Story": "And what of our daughters who must make their own Soundings? Nancy Hawthorne is obliged to make her own Soundings in the sea of life. Bravely and sensibly she faces the problems that come to every girl of eighteen" (361). As Phillip R. Yanella has observed, Arthur Hamilton Gibbs's romantic novel *Soundings*, which was run as a serial in the *Forum* in 1924–1925, seems "precisely the sort of thing made to offend a writer trying to produce serious fiction."[36] The novel's protagonist, Nancy Hawthorne, has been raised in England by her widower father. When she is eighteen, he inexplicably sends her to Paris to learn about life by making her own "soundings." As characterized by Paul Smith, the "soundings" are a "heady mix of deep thoughts and heavy petting,"[37] but Nancy's virtue triumphs. At the end of the serial, she is rewarded by marriage to a dashing American aviator. In short, Gibbs used the same sexual suggestiveness offset by showy moral purpose that had characterized Samuel Richardson's *Pamela* some two centuries earlier. In "Banal Story," Hemingway briefly tried his hand at a Fielding-like parody, although his major work in that genre still lay in the future. *The Torrents of Spring* was begun some nine months after the composition of "Banal Story."

Hemingway's protagonist, a young writer, seems to be looking for material and markets for his own writing. He turns from thoughts of a prize fight in Paris, heavy snows in Mesopotamia, and cricket matches in Australia to a promotional booklet for the *Forum*, apparently seeking clues about how to write "prize short-stories" and the "best-sellers of tomorrow" (360). According to the *Forum*, such stories should be aimed at the heart of the American reader. They should be "warm, homespun, American tales" whether set on ranches or in tenements. A "healthy undercurrent of humor" is a requisite ingredient of any successful *Forum* story. The writer vows to read some of these stories, but it is not certain whether his vow is serious or ironic.

He moves on to some of the intellectual topics to appear in forthcoming issues, ranging from social issues (the population increase and the possibility that it might be curbed by war if not by peaceful means) to artistic questions (are modern painting and writing really Art?). As pointed out by Wayne Kvam and George Monteiro, all of these topics were addressed in the *Forum* between late 1924 and September 1925. No promotional booklet has been discovered, but Hemingway obviously knew about forthcoming topics.[38] The litany ends with the assertion that Romance is everywhere for the mind that is open to its presence and with a reminder of the motto of the *Forum*: "Send your mind adventuring." To one who had read Sherwood Anderson's work, the motto must have recalled that author's frequent assertion that a character was about to "have an adventure."

The young writer who is reading the *Forum* is ambiguously characterized, perhaps one of the reasons for the relative unpopularity of the story among critics. The reader must wonder what constitutes the banality of the story. Is Hemingway viewing the would-be writer ironically because he is taking the *Forum* as a serious model, or is the writer reading the *Forum* ironically and implicitly ridiculing its precepts and suggestions? The various drafts of the story, from manuscript to *Little Review* text to *Men Without Women* text, prompt different conclusions.

In the original manuscript of the story as sent to the *Little Review*, Hemingway gave his would-be artist the habit of breaking wind from time to time as he read, perhaps with the sophomorically humorous intent of criticizing or providing a jeering, antagonistic chorus for the *Forum*'s profound pronouncements. The writer farts once as preface before he begins to read and again when he is in the middle of the magazine's highly intellectual issues. The references to flatulence were removed with Hemingway's permission before the first publication in the *Little Review* and were not restored when the story was reprinted in *Men Without Women*, even though Hemingway made some other small revisions in preparing his manuscript for the Scribner collection.[39] Hemingway's avowed reason for allowing these excisions was to avoid postal regulations against obscenity, but it is possible that his conception of the story was changing as well.

If one reads the story as written in manuscript, the writer seems aware of the tawdriness and intellectual pretentiousness of the *Forum*. His flatulent commentary on the magazine serves as a clue to the reader that the protagonist is reading the high aims of the magazine ironically and that he holds it in contempt. Once these clues are removed, the reader may be tempted to see the writer as a serious devotee of the *Forum* and to suppose that he is credulously accepting the insights it offers an aspiring author.

The story as printed in the *Little Review*, then, suggests a less cynical, more impressionable amateur author whose assumptions indicate that he is the sort of writer Hemingway had come to detest by early 1925—even though (or perhaps because) the aspiring writer bears some slight resemblance to Hemingway himself just a few years earlier, when he wrote such jejune stories as "The Ash Heel's Tendon" and "Portrait of the Idealist in Love." The young man in this version of the story seems to consider the *Forum* an ideal model and resolves to read it in order to emulate its contents. Hemingway moved further toward this interpretation of the story as he revised "Banal Story" for inclusion in *Men Without Women*. In the manuscript and *Little Review* versions, it could be assumed that the writer was reading copies of the *Forum* itself. Hemingway's revisions for the Scribner edition of stories added the fact that the protagonist is reading a promotional booklet.[40] In keeping with this change, references to the writer's thoughts in paragraphs 3 and 6 are changed to reflect his reading of the booklet rather than his thinking for himself. "He mused" became "he read," and "His thoughts raced on" became "He read on."[41]

The first section of the story (all but the final long paragraph) thus evolved so that it represents Hemingway's recognition and rejection of his early amateurism: it holds up a satirical mirror to a writer somewhat like Hemingway himself just a few years before, a struggling young author who had to learn how ridiculous it is to seek inspiration in banal current events or in "literary" magazines. Such banal material can only produce a banal story, since one who writes about life without having lived it can never write truly. However, Hemingway was not finished with the story: he offers a dramatic contrast to the first part of the story with a final paragraph about the death of Manuel Garcia Maera, whose vivid life and death provide an ironic commentary on the philosophical abstractions of the *Forum*.

The ironic juxtaposition of the second part of the story with the first is not the only clue to its major significance. In his home in Triana, near Seville, Maera lies "with a tube in each lung, drowning with the pneumonia" (361). The unlovely details of the tubes and the drowning, the specifics of a slow and difficult death (as opposed to a heroic death in the bullring), contrast sharply with the repeated references to idealized "Romance" in the first part of the story.

Further, the aftermath of Maera's death raises doubts about the legitimacy of all attempts to recreate the heroic in popular art forms. Maera's death is commemorated by several quasi-artistic tributes: all of the newspapers in the province have published "special supplements," and vendors are selling "full-length colored pictures . . . to remember him by" (361). These images, however, rather than reinforce the image of Maera in the minds of his admirers, cause them to lose the "picture they had of him in their memories" (361). After the funeral, the colored pictures are still being sold, but the men who buy them quickly roll them up and pocket them. Neither words nor pictures can recreate—or even accurately preserve—the reality of the living matador.

The fact that "Banal Story" was written by a man about to produce one of the major novels of the era makes the story an especially sobering one. Never viewed as one of Hemingway's better efforts, "Banal Story" must be taken seriously—if only because Hemingway thought it worth revising between its journal publication and its inclusion in *Men Without Women* in 1927. The first section of the story is the sort of parody that Hemingway had found easy and appealing since his high school journalism days, the undercutting of an incompetent would-be writer and of the sort of slick pseudointellectual "literary" magazine that his association with Pound and Stein had taught him to despise. The second part moves from that easy condemnation of the pretentious to a more difficult question: can written or pictorial representations ever succeed, or do they merely undermine reality as it has been experienced?

If the easy literary satire of "Banal Story" looks back to the theme of "Mr. and Mrs. Elliot," the parody anticipates *The Torrents of Spring*, which Hemingway would compose in November of the same year. The intellectual showiness of the *Forum* is not too far from that of Sherwood Anderson at his worst. More important, however, both "Mr. and Mrs. Elliot" and "Banal Story" anticipate *The Sun Also Rises*. The former short story's emphasis on sterility—both physical and literary—and the latter story's attack on fiction not based on firsthand experience are topics that would pervade Hemingway's first novel. The notion of writing as potential perversion would be tested not only in "Mr. and Mrs. Elliot" but in later work from the 1930s. Both Hubert Elliot and the unnamed writer in "Banal Story" might be found with Braddocks at his parties in the *bal musette*, rubbing elbows with Robert Cohn and making conversation with Robert Prentiss. Maera, the matador whose death brought relief to rivals because he "did always in the bull-ring the things they could only do sometimes" (361), clearly anticipates Pedro Romero. Finally, as George Monteiro has suggested, "Banal Story," at the same time that it satirizes other, less gifted writers, may be an attempt to leave behind its author's own "pseudo-Menckenian facility for rather easy sarcasm,"[42] which would not be part of his best literary efforts.

## The Torrents of Spring

One of the first literary acts which revealed Hemingway's new critical approach to the role of the writer was a rebellion against Sherwood Anderson—the author who had sent him to Paris in the first place. As he read some of Anderson's recent work, Hemingway reflected that Anderson was not the artist he had first taken him to be. He privately and cautiously suggested to Anderson that he saw faults in *Many Marriages* (1923), although he backed down when Anderson defended the book.[43] When *Dark Laughter* was published in 1925, Hemingway considered it a ridiculous book, influenced as it was by the exotic primitivism that accompanied the Harlem Renaissance. Perhaps he was embarrassed to have been so impressed by Anderson, or perhaps he felt that a faltering Anderson was a negative reflection on his own youthful judgment. The very excess of Hemingway's reaction to Anderson is a measure of the significance of the younger writer's unacknowledged debt to his erstwhile mentor. Hemingway's increasingly critical attitude suggests that he was spoiling for a fight, looking for some excuse to cut himself loose from an artist to whom he was indebted. Finally, his scorn for the decadent work of a man he had once admired combined with his more pragmatic desire to break his contract with Boni and Liveright, who regarded Anderson as their best-selling star, and he wrote his parody, *The Torrents of Spring*.

*Dark Laughter* is a confused novel in which Anderson blended strains from D. H. Lawrence's philosophy with the popular primitivism of the 1920s.[44] His protagonist has left both his modern marriage to a liberated woman and his job as a reporter for a Chicago newspaper. He travels to New Orleans, where he learns something about freedom from the "carefree" black people he observes. Assuming a false name, Bruce Dudley, he returns to the small Indiana town where he had spent part of his boyhood. He works for a time in a wheel factory, learning more about life from a fellow workman named Sponge Martin, who seems to have found true happiness by alternating hard manual labor with drunken fishing trips. Stirred by the coming of spring, Dudley leaves the factory, becomes the factory owner's gardener, and then runs off with his employer's wife. The novel is punctuated from time to time by a chorus of "dark laughter" from the Negro servants of the factory owner.

It was not a difficult novel to parody. Hemingway began with some improbable names, Scripps O'Neil and his daughter "Lousy" to match Anderson's Sponge Martin and daughter "Bugs." Signs are important in Bruce Dudley's life because he has taken his assumed name from two signs noted during his flight from middle-class respectability: "Bruce, Smart and Feeble—Hardware" and "Dudley Brothers—Grocery."[45] Scripps remembers a similar sign: "LET HARTMAN FEATHER YOUR NEST"[46]—but its purpose is simply humorous.

Hemingway satirizes not only *Dark Laughter* but Anderson's personal legend when, deciding that he doesn't know the meaning of life, Scripps leaves his job and home and walks down the railroad track to find himself. Anderson had wandered away from Elyria, Ohio, in 1912 under similar circumstances. Attributed to a breakdown at the time, the incident became part of the myth with which Anderson surrounded himself, and in his *Memoirs* (1942) he made the incident sound like a deliberate blow for artistic freedom and integrity:

> The thought occurred to me that if men thought me a little insane they would forgive me if I lit out, left the business in which they had invested their money. . . . I did it one day—walked into my office and called the stenographer—It was a bright warm day in summer. . . . A startled look came into her eyes. "My feet are cold and wet," I said. "I have been walking too long on the bed of a river." Saying these words I walked out the door. . . . I walked along a railroad track, toward the city of Cleveland.[47]

*The Torrents of Spring* is peppered with allusions to Anderson's works, not only to *Dark Laughter* itself (64), but to *Horses and Men* (52) and *Marching Men* (73). Throughout its pages the sound of Indian war whoops in the distance is a sort of chorus, just like Anderson's "dark laughter." Hemingway's Indians make fun of whites by pretending to be exotic, primitive people, speaking in pidgin English; when Yogi Johnson is mistaken for an Indian, he finds that the two Indians who have befriended him speak perfect English in private. Moreover, they lead him to an Indian speakeasy that resembles a posh country club. All of the members speak public-school British English when no whites are present.

Some of the funniest scenes in *Torrents* occur when the characters ask themselves vague questions about the meaning of life, as Anderson's characters often do. Scripps, for example, comes to a town as he wanders down the tracks in search of himself:

> He was standing knee-deep in snow in front of a railway station. On the railway station was written in big letters:
>
> PETOSKEY
>
> . . . Scripps read the sign again. Could this be Petoskey? [12]

Yogi Johnson wrestles with a more personal problem. It is spring, and he doesn't want a woman. What does it mean?

In *Dark Laughter*, living with an emancipated woman who writes fiction and follows literary fashions becomes boring to Bruce Dudley. Hemingway reverses that formula: Scripps marries Diana, an elderly waitress from Brown's Beanery, and their life together becomes a parody of Bohemian literary sophistication in the 1920s. Mandy, the waitress who replaces Diana O'Neil, begins to lure Scripps away, not because she is younger or more desirable, but because she engages Scripps in a higher level of literary small talk. Desperately, Diana O'Neil studies the *Literary Digest*, the *Bookman*, and the *Saturday Review of Literature* but to no avail.

Yogi takes on some of Bruce Dudley's characteristics when he solves his problem as Dudley solved his, by rediscovering his sexuality: Yogi finds that he once more wants a woman when an Indian woman, clad only in moccasins and a papoose carrier, enters the beanery. At the end of the novella, Yogi and the Indian are walking happily down the railroad tracks, a scene that recalls not only Dudley's elopement with his employer's wife but also his earlier desertion of his wife and Anderson's own flight from his business and family responsibilities.

*The Torrents of Spring* is a funny book at times, especially when Hemingway is content to parody Anderson's stylistic tics and thematic preoccupations. Too often, however, its humor is sophomoric or heavy-handed, as when he frequently characterizes Scripps as a writer and refers familiarly to "that old writing fellow Shakespeare" (9), "that critic fellow Henry Mencken" (10), or Anderson himself (53) or when he engages in personal asides to the reader. Anderson was not far off the mark when he wrote that "the satire . . . didn't come off. Heavy and dull."[48] Yet as an index to Hemingway's thinking in the middle of the 1920s, *Torrents* reflects a growing uneasiness about the integrity of the literary profession. In its attack on the artificiality of some writers, it has much in common with *The Sun Also Rises*, the novel written in rough draft before *Torrents* and revised just after its completion. Hemingway's exposure to bona fide literary figures such as Anderson himself, Gertrude Stein, and Ezra Pound had raised his level of sophistication far beyond the level of five years before, when all he wanted was to be a publishing author. In his first real novel, he would explore the failings of minor or insincere writers more fully and skillfully than in *The Torrents of Spring*.

## The Sun Also Rises

In writing his first novel, Hemingway was torn by his ambivalent attitude about writers and writing. In spite of his own desire to become a successful author, his exposure to the literati of the Left Bank strongly suggested that writers were often self-centered, self-important, and artificial to the point of stifling their own humanity. Such writers were interested only in the impression they would make on others, not on the honesty of their work. A few years later, Hemingway would emphasize the idea of the paramount importance of a writer's honesty and his quest for the truth in nonfiction in his "Monologue to the Maestro," a column written for *Esquire*, where his persona tells an aspiring writer "Good writing is true writing,"[49] and at the beginning of *Death in the Afternoon*, where he describes his earliest effort to know "what you really felt, rather than what you were supposed to feel, and had been taught to feel" and to "put down what really happened in action."[50]

In warming up for the writing of *The Sun Also Rises*, therefore, Hemingway created a narrator much like himself at the time. Jake Barnes is and is not a writer, since he is a reporter rather than a writer of literature and thus corresponds to the reporter facet of Hemingway's own identity in the middle of the 1920s. He can see the literary world from the privileged position of a quasi insider, yet he possesses the perspective to allow him to judge the Paris literary scene and its inhabitants accurately, if sometimes harshly. Unlike the self-conscious literary people who inhabit the Left Bank world, Jake is a journalist who daily goes to his office and files his cables, although for outsiders he maintains a pose: "in the newspaper business . . . it is such an important part of the ethics that you should never seem to be working" (11). Jake's deliberate understatement is an ironic reversal of the expatriate writers' overstatement of their accomplishments: they identify themselves as writers, but they spend their time talking about their work rather than doing it.

In chapter 2 of the original opening of the typescript Hemingway sent to Scribner's, later cut from the galleys of the novel after a suggestion by Scott Fitzgerald, Jake Barnes introduces himself as a newspaper man with certain literary ambitions. After reporting for the New York *Mail* immediately after the war, he went to work, and now works as European director of a news service he helped to found, the Continental Press Association, writing daily dispatches as well as managing the Paris office of the company. He observes the would-be artists of the Quarter with a great deal of scorn, noting that in the Quarter, the "state of mind is principally contempt. Those who work have the greatest contempt for those who don't. The loafers are leading their own lives and it is bad form to mention work. . . . There are contemptuous critics and contemptuous writers. Everybody seems to dislike everybody else."[51] Before he got involved with Brett, Mike, and Robert Cohn, Jake says, he had seldom been in the Quarter except for occasional visits to view the curiosities there.

Jake's explicit meditations on his own feelings about writers and their milieu, wisely excised from the novel at the proofreading stage, may have been a necessary part of Hemingway's own preparation not only for the writing of a novel and the creation of Jake's character but also as an exercise in defining himself as a writer. After several years of working as a journalist and publishing an occasional short story, Hemingway had recently published a real hardcover book with a major American publisher. Now he was beginning a novel that would consolidate his reputation as a serious author. He needed the self-reflective pages at the beginning of the manuscript to help him to understand and construct his own persona as a writer, even though the book was better without them. (He would, incidentally, also write a similar exercise after completion of the novel. Item 530 in the Hemingway collection is a sketch in which Jake Barnes encounters Brett and Mike in the Dingo Bar and attempts to reassure himself that he has done no lasting harm to Brett by publishing his novel.)

Jake's reflections in the first three galleys mirror the quandary in which Hemingway found himself. In spite of his distrust for the literary set and his feeling that he has nothing in common with them, Jake has begun a novel, perhaps because "like all newspaper men I have always wanted to write a novel," even though he realizes that the book may "have that awful taking-the-pen-in-hand quality that afflicts newspaper men when they start to write on their own hook."[52] Jake's fears are, in fact, borne out in the early galleys. He refers to himself quite self-consciously when he explains to the reader that he had planned to write a book in the more objective third person (which would be more consistent with the reporting instincts of a veteran journalist) but that he was forced into the use of the first person by his closeness to Brett Ashley. Because he is so close to the principals, he might have chosen not to write about incidents that will reflect badly on most of them. Why does Jake choose to share his text with an audience? He assures the reader that his motivation is not moral but literary: he is writing his novel solely because he thinks that "it is a good story."[53] Frequently his comments on the Quarter seem self-consciously witty in an artificial literary manner, as Fitzgerald observed when he criticized this version of the opening of the novel.[54] Hemingway, who had already learned the secret of constructing powerful short stories, was working to develop a voice that would sustain interest and sympathy throughout a longer work.

He was also attempting to clarify for himself how he felt about the people who lay behind the characters of the roman à clef that he was creating. Jake attempts to distance himself from Cohn's writer friends such as Braddocks and Robert Prentiss. In the early manuscript Hemingway did not achieve the crisp succinctness of the published novel, but (while he was sometimes clumsy during the first few pages) by the time he completed the novel, he was in full control of a devastating satire, which he directed effectively against most of the writers in *The Sun Also Rises*. A minor vignette shows him at his best when Jake meets Robert Prentiss, "a rising young novelist," according to Mrs. Braddocks. Prentiss was based on Glenway Wescott, a young friend of Ford Maddox Ford and, like Hemingway, from the Midwest (Wisconsin). Wescott had irritated Hemingway with his adopted British accent, his publication in the *Dial* (which had recently rejected Hemingway's "The Undefeated"), and his publication of a novel, *The Apple of the Eye* (1924), which had struck Hemingway as precious and false.[55] Robert Prentiss has recently arrived from New York but originally came from Chicago. Jake immediately notices that the writer speaks with "some sort of an English accent" and offers him a drink. Predictably, Prentiss answers that he has just had a drink, showing by his temperance that he is no Hemingway hero. Prentiss soon angers Jake by asking if he finds Paris "amusing," then simpering at him when Jake gets angry. Mrs. Braddocks rescues Prentiss, excusing him to Jake by saying that "he's still only a child" (21). But Hemingway's satire is aimed not at youth and inexperience or even at Prentiss's probable homosexuality but at his artificiality, a key part of the persona that Prentiss believes an author must assume. As Hemingway knew well, people from Chicago don't speak like English earls unless they are posing as something they are not, and Prentiss's masquerade as an Englishman suggests that he is also masquerading as a serious artist.

Cohn's "literary friend" Braddocks is—as the similarity of the names Braddocks and Madox suggests—closely modeled on the worst features of Ford Madox Ford, a man to whom Hemingway had been beholden in his first years in Paris. Ford had made a name for himself as a British novelist with *The Good Soldier* (1915) and as an editor with the *English Review*. In the 1920s he had begun to publish his ambitious four-part series *Parade's End* and had founded *transatlantic review* in Paris. Ford had published several of Hemingway's stories in *transatlantic review* and had flattered the young man by taking him on as an unpaid assistant editor. But now it was time for Hemingway to declare his independence of Ford.

Braddocks is supposedly a writer but is never depicted in the process of writing. Unlike Ford, who was busy during the 1920s—*Some Do Not* was published in 1924, *No More Parades* in 1925, *A Man Could Stand Up* in 1926, and *The Last Post* in 1928—Braddocks seems to spend most of his time dining and hosting parties. In the manuscript novel, Hemingway demolished Ford in a two-page satirical vignette—later used in *A Moveable Feast*—showing Braddocks's self-centered obtuseness, but he was a long time achieving the crisp succinctness of the published novel, in which Jake says, "Braddocks was [Cohn's] literary friend. I was his tennis friend" (5). Braddocks plays the stage Englishman, formal and wooden, hailing Jake with a British "I say," then properly standing up when Jake brings Georgette, an obvious *poule*, to his table (17–18). Braddocks enjoys slumming at a bal musette he has discovered in a working-class section of Paris and is in the process of changing the whole character of the place so that the workers of the Pantheon quarter will no longer be comfortable there. He is more delicately satirized in the published form of the novel than in the chapters cut from Hemingway's false start. In manuscript he is described as completely wrapped up in himself to the extent that he "found it increasingly difficult to read the works of writers other than himself."[56] When Cohn gives him the manuscript of his novel to read and criticize, Braddocks neither reads it nor admits that he has not read it. He stalls Cohn with vague comments and finally asks Jake to read the manuscript and tell him if it has any merit. Both Jake and Hemingway believe that, although the writer should take himself seriously, he should never exaggerate his own importance by posturing before others.

As *A Moveable Feast* makes clear, much of the portrait of Braddocks reflects Hemingway's hostile reaction to Ford, a reaction which Hemingway was forced to conceal in the 1920s when he was a nobody and Ford an established author. In *A Moveable Feast* he allowed his anger free rein, telling how physically repellent he had found Ford and recounting how Ford had told him about the wonderful little bal musette he had found on the rue Cardinal Lemoine. When Hemingway tried to tell Ford that he had lived in a third-floor apartment over the place, Ford acknowledged the information but then persisted in explaining carefully how to find the address. Braddocks exudes a similar air of obtuseness, but the satire in the 1926 novel is less cutting than it would be in the 1964 portrait.

Although Hemingway's fictionalized version of Ford as Braddocks did not display the full depth of his hostility, he was less restrained when he drew the portrait of Mrs. Braddocks, whom he modeled on Stella Bowen, Ford's Australian wife. Although Bowen was herself a creative person, a sculptor, Mrs. Braddocks is transformed into a mere tasteless patron of the literary and artistic poseurs of the Left Bank. She apologizes for Robert Prentiss's artificiality, but he is her sort of writer, probably short on talent but a social asset at a tea or a party. Jake characterizes Mrs. Braddocks as a Canadian, with "all their easy social graces" (17), who speaks French in a manner that indicates her pride and astonishment that she is able to do so. When Jake tests her wit by introducing Georgette as the well-known singer Georgette LeBlanc, Mrs. Braddocks takes the name at face value and pursues Georgette's identity relentlessly; then, when she finally understands the joke, she explicates it for Braddocks with equal tirelessness.

The Braddockses and their friends enjoy their forays into lower-class Paris for much the same reason that their counterparts in the United States relished visits to Harlem during the 1920s. Bloodless people themselves, they need the stimulation of "real" people who live closer to the facts of life than they do.[57] By confronting the French working class, they hope to get back in touch with a primitive facet of their own characters. But even more important, Braddocks and friends such as Prentiss are seeking material for their writing. Perhaps the very rational, cold-blooded nature of their pursuit of French life dooms their attempts at intimate knowledge. Mrs. Braddocks and her friend Frances Clyne will never know Paris the way Georgette knows it, nor would they really want to. Hemingway is anticipating his attack in *Green Hills of Africa* on writers who spend too much time with other writers. In the later book, he would insist that writers should work alone and should see each other infrequently and only when their work was done. Writers who work closely together lose their individuality; they become "angleworms in a bottle," derivative of each other and their environment; they may be influenced into conforming to various artistic and social movements that enjoy temporary vogues but will threaten the writer's integrity and uniqueness.[58]

The portraits of Robert Prentiss, Braddocks, and his wife are merely preludes to the major attack in *The Sun Also Rises* on Robert Cohn, an American writer who embodies all that is wrong with the writer who is not true to his vocation. If Hemingway began his literary career attempting to know "truly what you really felt, rather than what you were supposed to feel, and had been taught to feel,"[59] Cohn spends his time parroting the lessons he has been taught about how he should feel. Unlike Hemingway, who had dedicated himself to his writing since 1919, Cohn has drifted into authorship by accident after his graduation from Princeton. After helping him to squander most of his inheritance, his wife had left him for an artist, so it was only logical that Cohn should try to become an artist of sorts himself. He got his chance on the West Coast, where he "fell among literary people" (4) in Carmel, California. Members of the literary community there persuaded Cohn to use some of the remainder of his inherited money to finance a review of the arts, first as a silent partner and later, when Cohn began to assert himself, as editor. The review later moves to Provincetown, Massachusetts. At odds with the American literary establishment, Hemingway includes a brief slur on the two coastal centers of what he might have regarded as precious literary movements, although the western site produced at least one major poet, Robinson Jeffers, and the eastern location America's major dramatist, Eugene O'Neill.

Cohn's rise from a mere name on the masthead to sole editor of the magazine is explained in purely monetary terms: "It was his money and he discovered he liked the authority of editing" (5). Hemingway's jaundiced view of editors in 1925, gained from a series of what he considered capricious rejections and reinforced by his observations of Ford's editing of the *transatlantic review*, emerges clearly in this part of Cohn's biography. Cohn's review, like many of the little magazines of the 1920s, died after its move to the East Coast, but it died simply because Cohn decided that it had become too expensive. Editors might maintain that they operated their publications for the good of Literature, but decisions were made on the basis of crass financial considerations in the end.

Like a Jamesian character, Cohn continues his eastward pilgrimage—at the prodding of his mistress, Frances Clyne—and eventually settles in Paris. Having dabbled in the arts long enough to become acclimated, Cohn "discovered writing" (5). Hemingway worked hard to convey early in this first chapter just what sort of writer Cohn was. In the galleys cut from the beginning of *The Sun Also Rises*, Jake says that Cohn's book was a "first and last novel," that Cohn was the hero, and that it contained a good deal of fantasy. He then damns it with faint praise, saying that "it was not too badly done" and had been published by a New York firm.[60] In the first chapter of the novel as published, the praise is fainter yet: "He wrote a novel, and it was not really such a bad novel as the critics later called it, although it was a very poor novel" (5–6). In the latter version, Hemingway manages a statement that cuts both ways, against the critics and against the novelist whose work they condemn—probably for all the wrong reasons.

Already, Cohn had been deftly created as the sort of author for whom Hemingway could have no respect. For Cohn, writing is one of a rich boy's toys, along with women, travel, and tennis. Like Hubert Elliot, he has bought into the game with his inherited capital and has no fund of experience on which to draw. Robert O. Stephens has observed that, in his prefaces to the books of other writers, Hemingway almost always stresses the personal experience that underlies the work itself, whether it is the drawings of John Groth in *Studio: Europe* or the Spanish civil war novel of Gustave Regler, *The Great Crusade*.[61] Whether writing on war, big-game hunting, or deep-sea fishing, the writer should have lived the experiences before attempting to chronicle them. Hemingway applies this rule to fiction as well as to nonfiction.

If Cohn has no experiences to write about, he also has no compelling reasons to write about them, at least no reasons that Hemingway would consider valid. His motivation is external rather than internal. He writes partly because Frances has decided that he should and partly because it seemed the thing to do after living in the company of literary people in Carmel, Provincetown, and Paris. But Cohn lacks any view of the world to impose on his writing and thus lacks an artistic voice of his own with which to express that view. His ideas must be copies of the ideas of others, his voice an echo of other literary voices. Such imitation, as Emerson had warned his generation, is deadly.

This is not to say that Hemingway believed a writer should ignore the work of other writers. While some types of reading were good only to distract one from his own work, Hemingway told the "maestro" that reading was good for a writer because it showed him what he had to beat in the work of the great writers of the past.[62] More significantly, Hemingway believed—almost like T. S. Eliot—that a special bond connects living writers to those of the past and that reading grounds the writer in the literary tradition of which he will become a part. But once the writer knows that tradition, it is time to break new ground. As Hemingway said in his Nobel Prize acceptance speech, the writing of literature would be easy "if it were only necessary to write in another way what has been well written. It is because we have had such great writers in the past that a writer is driven far out past where he can go, out to where no one can help him."[63] Cohn is familiar with the masterpieces of the past but is unable to add to them because of his own lack of experience with real life. In Emersonian terms, he has studied only books, not nature.

If Cohn had been a somewhat pleasant nonentity as an aspiring author, publication brings out the worst facets of his character. When he delivered his manuscript in person, "publishers had praised his novel pretty highly and it rather went to his head" (8). At the same time, lion-hunting women in New York took him up, and Cohn began to see himself as a heroic writer in a Byronic vein. Never self-assured with women, he had previously allowed himself to be manipulated by his wife and by Frances; now he is ripe for sexual adventures befitting a published author who lives in an exotic city.

There is only one thing wrong with Cohn's plan. He has no idea how to become the sort of literary hero he aspires to be. Consequently, he looks for the answer in books: in literary biography and in imaginative fiction, specifically in the novels of W. H. Hudson. Hemingway had nothing against Hudson and in fact greatly admired the Englishman's nature writing.[64] Jake, on the other hand, is more cynical. Describing *The Purple Land* and Cohn's reaction to it, Jake suggests that Cohn is celebrating his male menopause by reliving adolescent schoolboy fantasies. Jake sees the book as "sinister" when it is read by a man of a certain age who will accept uncritically the "amorous adventures" of an Englishman in South America. Cohn accepts the novel as a "guide-book," which he assumes to be as accurate and literal as "an R. G. Dun report" (9). The reference to the Dun report once again links Cohn, literature, and money: Cohn knows something about money and should stick to what he knows. Instead, he obstinately insists on pursuing a dream engendered by the reading of fiction.

In an extended conversation soon after the passage on W. H. Hudson, Hemingway plays off Cohn's artificial attitudes against Jake's sensible nature, which is made up of hard-boiled journalistic cynicism tempered with Emersonian insights. Cohn asks Jake to go with him to South America so that Cohn can begin to live his life. Cohn laments that his life is passing him by without his ever having the experiences a writer should have. By his calculations, half of his life has passed, and he has yet to feel really alive. His solution is to seek a storybook land where he can live a storybook life—recreating the adventures he has read in the Hudson novel. Experiences for Cohn can come only through books, not directly from life.

Although ironically Jake too has done his share of running away from problems and will do more in the course of *The Sun Also Rises*, he answers, echoing Emerson, that " 'going to another country doesn't make any difference. . . . You can't get away from yourself by moving from one place to another' " (11) and observes that Cohn is already living in one of the most glamorous cities in the world. He suggests that Cohn begin to live his life in Paris. He should relax, "cruise around," and simply let life come to him. Experience is necessary for a writer, but Jake has found that experience need not be sought out if one is active enough. Jake enunciates the same philosophy of experience that Hemingway would explain in his introduction to *The First 49*:

> In going where you have to go, and doing what you have to do, and seeing what you have to see, you dull and blunt the instrument you write with. But I would rather have it bent and dull and know I had to put it on the grindstone again and hammer it into shape and put a whetstone to it, and know that I had something to write about, than to have it bright and shining and nothing to say, or smooth and well-oiled in the closet, but unused.[65]

Cohn's "instrument" has remained unused throughout his life. He has unsuccessfully tried to gain experience, but his effort ended prosaically: he was stopped by a bicycle policeman. Jake gives up the argument, underscoring the problem with Cohn by remarking that, since Cohn has gotten the idea that he wants to go to South America from a book, probably his disillusionment with Paris also comes from a book.

Throughout chapter 2, the main theme is Cohn's bookishness. Rather than live life and then translate his experiences into literature, Cohn tries to make his life conform to literature. His writing then will be twice removed from reality as he attempts to emulate the descriptions of life that he finds in the literature of the past. Moreover, even his sources are suspect. Like Howells's Editha Balcomb, Cohn is addicted to romantic literature, and he has to strain to see life in the terms in which his literary models have presented it. This characterization is important, for Cohn's predilection to model his life on literary ideas becomes more pronounced in later chapters of *The Sun Also Rises*.

In chapter 5, for example, Cohn publicly overreacts when Jake jokingly tells him to go to hell. More angry than is justifiable, given the situation, Cohn stands up at their table, his face white (in comic contrast to the plates of hors d'oeuvres), while Jake admonishes him to " 'cut out the prep-school stuff' " (39). Cohn refuses to sit down again until Jake has taken back his remark. If this episode smacks of prep school, so does the incident that sparks the argument, for Cohn has been romantically defending the honor of Brett Ashley: he had asked Jake to tell him what he knows of Brett but is then offended by Jake's frank cynicism.

In chapter 6 Cohn's immaturity is underscored when Harvey Stone sums up his character. Harvey pays him the mock compliment of telling Cohn that he is not a moron but then says, " 'You're only a case of arrested development' " (44). Cohn is a case of arrested development in a literary sense as well as in the personal sense of having the emotional development of an adolescent: while in the midst of a hotbed of avant-garde literary movements, he imitates century-old literary attitudes. When his lady fair is attacked, he prepares to invoke the code duello more appropriate to the 1820s than to the 1920s.

Frances Clyne, Cohn's cast-off mistress, shows great insight into his faults as a man and a writer when she stages her memorable scene with Cohn in the Select. She first accuses him of dropping her in his search for new literary materials and says that " 'he was so busy all the time we were living together, writing on this book, that he doesn't remember anything about us' " (50). Her accusation speaks to Cohn's lack of involvement with real life and his tendency to live in a purely literary world that is subject to none of the rules of the real world. To be able to write so artificially, he must distance himself from reality, not draw closer and observe it. She is wrong, however, when she implies that Cohn is capable of experiencing a new love affair and then transmuting it into meaningful fiction.

Her next observation is even more perceptive than the first. She tells Jake that she has suddenly received a vision revealing why Cohn is sending her away, but the truth is that the knowledge has been building during her years with Cohn. Robert, she says, has always wanted a mistress, " 'and if he doesn't marry me, why, then he's had one. She was his mistress for over two years. See how it is?' " (51). Frances is suggesting that Cohn sees himself always as some future biographer might see him. His life has no essential reality because he fails to live it in the present but always looks back on it from the perspective of a literary biographer. Hemingway would later point out in interviews and essays that the act of writing itself was far more important than anything that came as a result of it—publication, fame, money, or critical acclaim—although in 1926 all of these things were important to him. Cohn lives for the reaction to his writing and seems to find the process of writing more painful than satisfying.

Frances has accused Cohn of faults that are far worse than mere infidelity and self-importance. She says that he uses people for material, cultivating them only for their value to his worthless writing, an accusation that will be made by other writers' wives and mistresses in Hemingway's later work as the theme of the moral bankruptcy of the writer becomes more prominent. In Cohn's case, however, the sacrifice of those who are close to him is pointless, since Cohn is both unwilling and unable to learn anything from gritty real life. When he does encounter it, late in the novel, it destroys him rather than helping him as a writer.

Nowhere is Cohn's bookishness more apparent than in his dealings with Brett Ashley. After they have lived together at San Sebastian, Cohn refuses to call off his trip to Spain with Jake, Brett, and Brett's fiancé, Mike Campbell. Jake is puzzled about Cohn's willingness to put himself in such an embarrassing position, but when an argument breaks out in a Pamplona café, something about Cohn's look gives Jake the insight to explain Cohn's behavior. He realizes that Robert has put up with the agony of seeing Brett with another man and has suffered the insults that Mike and others have heaped on him because "it was his affair with a lady of title" (178). Once again Cohn's attention is less on the pain of the current situation than on how the events might look to a hypothetical literary biographer. A painful affair with "a lady of title" is enriched when things do not go smoothly. If Cohn cannot bring himself to use the Pamplona incidents in a future novel, at least they will linger in his memory as actions appropriate to the life of a literary gentleman. When Mike threatens Robert physically, he stands proudly and happily, "ready to do battle for his lady love" (178).

Although no battle materializes on this occasion, Cohn has an opportunity to act out yet another romantic cliché later, when Brett falls in love with Pedro Romero, the young matador. Cohn attempts to save Brett from the bullfighter by going to the matador's room while Brett is there, planning to "make an honest woman of her" (201). Instead, he gets into a fight with Romero, whom he repeatedly knocks to the floor. In spite of his superior boxing skills, Cohn is unable to defeat Romero, however, for Romero refuses to acknowledge that he has been beaten. Cohn's romantic attitudes have at last encountered a reality that they cannot overcome. Brett refuses to leave Romero's room with Cohn, Romero remains spiritually undefeated, and both refuse to reconcile with Robert Cohn on his schoolboy terms—by shaking hands with him as if they were all characters in a juvenile novel. Cohn leaves Pamplona the next day, completely "ruined," as Mike says. He can no longer maintain the role of swashbuckling writer that he has conceived for himself.

Of course, not every writer appearing in *The Sun Also Rises* is satirized. Jake's close friend Bill Gorton, for example, is treated sympathetically and furnishes some of the most amusing lines in the novel, often making jokes at his own expense, as Robert would never do. In clear contrast to Cohn, Gorton embraces life's experiences and recognizes the primacy of life over art. Juxtaposed with a matador who faces death every time he enters the ring, Bill admittedly feels inferior to the man of action.

While Hemingway's treatment of writers and writing is not the main theme of his first novel, it nevertheless supports that theme and continues to develop Hemingway's evolving philosophy. During the 1920s Hemingway had been modifying and enlarging his notion of what a writer could and should be, and the book documents his formation of strong opinions on the subject, primarily by negative definition. Most of the writers who appear in the novel—Prentiss, Braddocks, and Cohn—are treated as artificial, lacking in sincere, deep emotions, and less perceptive than the average person rather than more so. All of the full-time writers except Bill Gorton also lack joy in their lives; they seem unable to laugh, especially at themselves. In keeping with the second epigraph of the novel, Cohn, at least, is obsessed with the vanity of his own literary ambitions, often to such a degree that he cannot correctly interpret what is happening in the real world. The vanity of the writer, then, is set in the larger context of mankind's vanity, which Hemingway (like the preacher of Ecclesiastes) has been attacking. Against the permanence of sun and wind, rivers and sea, humankind seems small and insignificant.

*The Sun Also Rises* serves as Hemingway's first major evaluation of the role of the writer. While the novel only hints at a more sinister side of the writer that would be exposed in the stories and novels of the 1930s, it significantly betrays the fact that even the young Hemingway harbored deep misgivings about whether a writer could balance his personal life and his professional life, whether it was morally proper to use one's own life and the lives of one's friends and family as literary material, and whether a writer could withstand the notoriety that comes with success. The novel foreshadows psychological conflicts of which Hemingway himself might not yet have been conscious.

Hemingway had begun his exploration of the less pleasant aspects of the literary life, an exploration that would take him into a dark place far from the dreams of the Oak Park boy who aspired to authorship. Reverses in his career during the 1930s would lead him deeper into that darkness.

# 2

## *A Closer Look at the Face in the Mirror*

IN THE 1930s Hemingway's career went sour. During the 1920s he had become accustomed to one success after another with the publication of the American edition of *In Our Time* (1925), *The Sun Also Rises* (1926), *A Farewell to Arms* (1929), and even a second collection of short stories, *Men Without Women* (1927), to round out the decade. Small wonder that Hemingway's friend Archibald MacLeish would later sum up those years by writing, "Famous at twenty-five: thirty a master."[1] During such a successful period, Hemingway had felt great self-satisfaction and had had no great need to question his own integrity as a writer while he directed satirical barbs at less secure authors by creating characters such as Robert Cohn and Hubert Elliot. In the early 1930s, however, even though he produced some of his finest short stories, his total output suggested that the young master had lost his way. His two book-length products up to mid-decade, *Death in the Afternoon* (1932) and *Green Hills of Africa* (1935), disappointed many readers and critics. Meanwhile, he had stepped down from the ivory tower that he had built for himself during his first decade as an author and had begun to publish in a popular men's magazine, *Esquire*, and to exploit his celebrity status at the expense of his artistic side, which had flourished during the period before he was widely recognized.[2] Not surprisingly, several authors that Hemingway created in his fiction during the 1930s suggest that problems in his own life and career were causing him to re-evaluate the role of the writer—his methods, subjects, and sources of inspiration—and that he was not always happy with his conclusions.

Thus in the 1930s, and even into the published works of the 1940s, Hemingway's stories and books display a shift of emphasis. In the satirical portraits of writers he had created in the 1920s, Hemingway had been most critical of writers who allowed themselves to be influenced by past literary works and by their notions about how literary people should lead their lives and conduct their careers. In the years following his first divorce in 1927, and his father's suicide and the beginning of the Great Depression in 1929, he shifted his emphasis to areas that might best be defined by rhetorical questions: First, what right does the author have to recreate incidents from his own personal life and the lives of those closest to him? Second, what should be the relationship of the individual writer to society? And third, are the negative effects of a writer's fame inescapable?

The use of material from his personal life became an especially serious problem in the late 1920s, following two serious crises in the author's life. Hemingway had implied in his fiction of the 1920s and had directly stated in conversation that a writer must write from experience, using even the most painful experiences as material for his art. The pain that accompanied the breakup of his marriage to Hadley and the suicide of his father gave Hemingway powerful emotional experiences that could be translated into his fiction. The disadvantage was that such profound personal losses as that of Hadley or his father were sacred in a sense, and to make literary capital of them profaned the experience. In addition, individuals close to the author could be hurt by revelations in his fiction if the stories he wrote could be too easily identified with autobiography. In "The Sea Change" and "Fathers and Sons," especially in the early manuscripts of those works, Hemingway struggled with a deeply felt conflict about the use of such sensitive material in his fiction.

The early 1930s raised the problem of the writer's responsibilities to society for Hemingway in spite of the fact that the economic depression that followed the crash of 1929 had little personal effect on him. Married to a wealthy woman and reaping considerable financial benefits from the products of his early lean years, Hemingway not only lived as well as he had during the boom of the latter 1920s but also took an extended African safari and constructed a custom-designed deep-sea fishing boat. However, the depression did affect him in more subtle ways as critics began to demand that the arts become involved with the social issues of the day and began to denigrate authors like Hemingway whose values seemed to reflect nothing of the economic and social chaos that was engulfing the entire world economy. In "The Gambler, the Nun, and the Radio," Hemingway shows an author grappling with the problem of the writer as potential social activist and coming to the tentative conclusion that the artist should instead produce certain essential "opiates" to offer relief to mankind. By the time he wrote *To Have and Have Not* (1937), he was ready to launch a concerted attack on the type of writer who profited from human misery by employing it as the raw material for his fiction while holding himself aloof from experiencing it firsthand.

Hemingway's concerns regarding the burdens of artistic fame appear in a major short story that documents his real growth during the 1930s—

"The Snows of Kilimanjaro," first published in 1936. In that pivotal work, he again considered both the question of whether the artist should use his emotional capital as the basis for stories and the question of whether the writer should respond to the social and political climate of his times. The latter he would dispose of fairly easily, while the former would continue to occupy his mind as he attempted to reconstruct his literary career after World War II. But his own increasing reputation brought with it new concerns: the effects of success on a writer—how sloth can curtail a writer's career and leave him with regrets at the end of his life—and the nature of literary fame—is it worth having after all, and if so, is it truly attainable in the form the writer might wish it to be? "The Snows of Kilimanjaro" illustrates better than any other work of the 1930s just how seriously Hemingway was examining his art during that decade; it also serves to predict better than any other work the direction that his unfinished postwar novels would take.

Psychologically, these key works of the decade delineate the profile of an author who was beginning to think of his writing in new terms. Although Hemingway occasionally wrote remarks to himself in the manuscript of *The Sun Also Rises*, almost certainly intending all along to cut them before publication,[3] such private notes were designed to help him to work out artistic problems concerning point of view and to clarify his own thoughts about the abstract themes that he was introducing into the fiction. In these 1930s works, on the other hand, Hemingway is beginning to use his writing as a therapeutic psychological tool, to heal some of the wounds that had been dealt him since his first confident years as a writer. The 1930s, then, were a decade of stocktaking, rebuilding, and seeking new artistic directions after the productive years that had come before.

In attempting to treat his own malaise through his writing, Hemingway often concealed more than he revealed. The author might be compared to a patient who seeks help in therapy but who cannot articulate or directly confront his underlying problem. The psyche censors even material that the patient consciously wishes to convey. The stories leading up to "The Snows of Kilimanjaro" frequently have more meaning beneath their surfaces than is apparent to most critics who analyze the words on the page. But just as the patient in analysis, who on one level wants his therapist to decipher the riddles which he is posing, drops clues—sometimes by accident—to help the therapist solve the mysteries, Hemingway left internal and external clues to the subtexts of the stories.

The fact that Hemingway felt increased pressure to confront and analyze the problems of the writer is apparent in the progression notable throughout the decade: from early stories that conceal deeply embedded secrets not apparent even in the manuscripts, through works in which the manuscript offers material that was deleted during the process of revising for publication, to stories in which Hemingway allows the full force of his meditations to come to the surface.

## "The Sea Change"

With "The Sea Change," first published in December 1931, Hemingway embarked on this decade of greater introspection into the literary and personal problems of the writer. Perhaps because the story seems to depend on what Hemingway himself called a "wow" climax,[4] the revelation that the lover for whom the young woman is leaving Phil is a woman, not a man, the story has not been valued highly by the critics, most of whom have paid it little attention. Carlos Baker, for example, accorded only half a paragraph to the story in *The Writer as Artist* and referred to it in *Ernest Hemingway: A Life Story* as a "curious story, a lesser twin to 'Hills Like White Elephants.' "[5]

More recently, critics who have considered the rather obvious implications of Phil's reactions to his lover's conversion to lesbianism have reached various conclusions: that Phil and the young woman have had a relationship based on a "vice" as serious as the lesbianism she intends to embrace; that Phil is left contemplating a homosexual adventure of his own; that the story unmasks Phil's degradation, hinting that he is more guilty for permitting the woman's adventure than she is for carrying it out; and, most recently, that the significant theme of the story is Phil's "relinquishment of masculine power."[6]

But while critics focus on the restrained treatment of sexuality in "The Sea Change," the story is, in fact, more significant in the Hemingway canon than most critics have acknowledged because it treats the culpability of the writer who uses the lives of others in his work. In effect, the story reverses the writer's situation in "Mr. and Mrs. Elliot" and *The Sun Also Rises*: Hubert Elliot and Robert Cohn are false artists because they fail to translate their own lives into their work; in "The Sea Change," Phil may become a damned soul because he intends, by the end of the story, to invade the sacred privacy of another human being in order to use her life as the basis for his work.

Hemingway gave two hints about an underlying meaning of the story—one in an essay intended for publication but published only posthumously and the other in a private note to himself. In an essay written in 1959 he referred to the "iceberg principle" that he employed in some of his stories and cited "The Sea Change" as an extreme example: "In a story called 'A Sea Change,' [*sic*] everything is left out. . . . I knew the story too too well. . . . So I left the story out. But it is all there. It is not visible but it is there."[7] One omission that provides a logical connection between the title of the story and its ending—and that also explains several puzzling details—is the identification of Phil as a writer. Despite the fact that many elements fall into place when one views Phil as a writer, this hypothesis might be difficult to accept if it were not for indirect evidence that Hemingway thought of Phil as a writer, evidence provided by the manuscript of *The Garden of Eden*. In the earliest version of the novel, David Bourne was apparently named Phil, for on the first page of the rough draft as it now exists in mixed typescript and holograph, Hemingway had written a note to himself to change the name of the main character from Philip to David throughout the manuscript.[8] Furthermore, the term "sea change" is used in the fourth chapter of the manuscript.[9] It seems quite likely that the story that Hemingway knew "too well" and omitted from "The Sea Change" formed the basis for his later novel.

A coherent reading of the story requires the correct interpretation of two literary allusions, both identified by Philip Young in footnotes in his book-length study of Hemingway's work.[10] An understanding of the interaction—even tension—between the allusions makes it clear that Phil, the male protagonist of "The Sea Change," is a writer and that his perversion is more degrading than the lesbian tendencies of his former lover. Phil wants the woman to come back and tell him "all about" her sexual experiences, not just to satisfy his own morbid curiosity, but to furnish the raw material that he needs for his writing. Hemingway uses meanings of the word "perversion" in a way that recalls a key idea of Nathaniel Hawthorne, as summarized in a notebook entry:

> The Unpardonable Sin might consist in a want of love and reverence for the Human Soul; in consequence of which, the investigator pried into its dark depths, not with a hope or purpose of making it better, but from a cold philosophical curiosity,—content that it should be wicked in what ever kind or degree, and only desiring to study it out. Would not this, in other words, be the separation of the intellect from the heart?[11]

Hemingway would reflect his own concerns about the alienation of the writer from the rest of humanity later in the 1930s in *Green Hills of Africa*. There he dwells on the necessity of the writer's self-imposed solitude (21), which affects both him and those who are closest to him. Poor Old Mama talks about the difficulty of living with a writer (195); for his part, Hemingway admits "To work was the only thing" that is important to a writer

(72). Much later, during his interview with George Plimpton in the 1950s, Hemingway would return to that theme, remarking that a writer could write at any time, as long as he was "ruthless enough" to demand that he be left alone.[12]

Several prevalent misreadings of "The Sea Change" have arisen from critics' emphasis of a passage that Phil attempts to quote from Alexander Pope's *An Essay on Man*. It reads:

> Vice is a monster of so frightful mien,
> As, to be hated, needs but to be seen;
> Yet seen too oft, familiar with her face,
> We first endure, then pity, then embrace.
> But where th' Extreme of Vice, was ne'er agreed. . . . [13]

One critic, following Philip Young's lead, focuses on this passage and on the young woman's remarks to Phil—" 'We're made up of all sorts of things. You've known that. You've used it well enough' "[14]—to conclude that Phil too has his own unnamed perversion.[15] Two other critics have gone even further, asserting that Phil has reached the point at the end of the story where he is willing to capitulate to homosexual tendencies in his own nature.[16] However, if Phil is a writer, as suggested by other elements in the story and by the two pieces of primary evidence cited above, her comment makes much better sense: he has used "all sorts of things" in human nature to enrich his writing.

That homosexuality should be viewed not as Phil's true "perversion" or "vice" but as an effective metaphor for the writer's perverse willingness to use others for the sake of his art is suggested by an alternate ending for the story that Hemingway discarded in favor of the existing conclusion. Among the manuscript versions of the story is a fragment in which Phil moves to the bar after his female companion has left the café; joining two other customers—who may be male homosexuals[17]—Phil orders a drink in words that might suggest his own conversion to homosexuality. He asks James the bartender what drinks "punks" usually order and then tells James to look at him closely and mix him a drink—perhaps the sort of drink a "punk" would order. James, oblivious to Phil's inner turmoil, compliments him on his appearance, but Phil replies that he can see himself—all too clearly—in the mirror behind the bar.[18]

Phil's reference to himself and the revelation of the mirror into which he is looking does suggest contempt for himself, but it is not contempt for his sexual nature, as might be suggested by his use of the term "punks" for homosexuals. The Hemingway persona of *Death in the Afternoon* told the Old Lady that stories about homosexuals "lack drama as do all tales of abnormality since no one can predict what will happen in the normal while all tales of the abnormal end much the same" (180). Perhaps it was to avoid the implication that Phil had changed his sexual preference that Hemingway cut the above ending for the story: an explicit link between Phil and homosexuality might have misled the reader into taking literally an allusion intended to be a metaphor for what Phil has discovered himself to be—an exemplar of the "Extreme of Vice." Thus, Hemingway does not so much condone the lesbian affair of the woman—although in his own personal life he had had friendly relationships with a number of lesbians—as imply that the man's vice constitutes a great moral wrong. The ending he chose emphasizes Phil's feelings of guilt rather than his sin. The specific nature of that sin is most clearly suggested by the title of the story and the literary allusion that it provides, perhaps the most important clue to the hidden meaning of the story.

The "sea change" of the title, as Philip Young pointed out years ago, alludes to "Ariel's Song" in Shakespeare's *The Tempest*:

> Full fathom five thy father lies;
>    Of his bones are coral made;
> Those are pearls that were his eyes:
>    Nothing of him that doth fade
> But doth suffer a sea-change
> Into something rich and strange.[19]

The sea change of "Ariel's Song," macabre as its images are, is a transformation of decaying human materials into bright coral and rich pearls. Surely if Phil had undergone a change from heterosexual to homosexual, Hemingway could have used such a title only to underscore an ironic point.

But if the story is interpreted differently, Hemingway could be hinting that something "rich and strange," something of great value, might grow from the "perversion" of Phil's former lover as well as from the greater sin of which Phil himself is guilty. The explanation of how this transformation is possible is not readily apparent in the text of the story; rather, the key to the connection between the title and Phil's ultimate recognition of his own perversion is, in fact, the "thing left out" of the story or the part of the iceberg that lies beneath the surface. The textual key that points to the underlying meaning is contained in Phil's last speech to his departing mistress. After he offers her his approval of her sexual adventure, he tells her, " 'And when you come back tell me all about it' " (400). This request marks the abrupt change that comes over Phil, for after he says these words, he is aware that "his voice sounded very strange"

(400) to him so that he does not recognize it, and soon afterward, look-ing into the mirror behind the bar, he sees himself as "quite a different man" (401).

Identifying Phil as a writer of fiction causes the details of the story to fall into place. First of all, if Phil is a writer, "Ariel's Song" reads perfectly as a description of the creative process of transforming life (or reality) into something more enduring, more beautiful—into art. An au-thor takes the materials of life, which he may obtain through a sort of heartless observation of his fellow human beings, and transmutes them, if he is lucky, into something that is indeed "rich and strange."

Appearing as it did at the beginning of the 1930s, "The Sea Change," like *To Have and Have Not* later in the decade, forms a bridge between the satirical portraits of unsympathetic writers, such as Robert Cohn and Hubert Elliot, and the more fully realized portrait of the ruined writer Harry, of "The Snows of Kilimanjaro," who has made a living by prosti-tuting his own vitality, first for readers and then for a wealthy wife. Phil is more sympathetic than the early characters but less sympathetic than Harry. Or is it that Hemingway allows the reader to see less of Phil's internal torment than of Harry's? Unlike some stories of the period, "The Sea Change" offers few glimpses into the evolution of Hemingway's thought during composition even in its manuscript versions.

Sheldon Grebstein is correct when he asserts that Phil is "more culp-able" than the woman in "The Sea Change" because Phil is motivated not by an emotional attachment or a sexual urge that he cannot resist, but by a cool and detached intellectual certainty that he has more to gain if he lets his mistress go than if he persuades her to give up her lover and stay with him. Phil is overcome by the Faustian desire to barter his personal and human relationship with the woman in exchange for the chance to use her potentially tragic experience as material for his fiction. Small won-der that his voice changes to such a degree that he can't recognize it and that he sees a "different man" staring back at him from the mirror in the bar after he has sent his lover away. He is aware of the depth to which he has fallen, the temptation to which he has succumbed, by sacrificing the relationship they have shared in favor of his art.

Hemingway underscored Phil's self-realization and the internal change that has taken place in his character when he wrote that Phil "was not the same-looking man as he had been before he had told her to go" (400–401), and Phil says to the barman, " 'I'm a different man, James. . . . You see in me quite a different man' " (401). Phil feels that, like Hawthorne's Roger Chillingworth, his external appearance should reflect his inner cor-ruption. But the modern age differs from the romantic era. Chillingworth's exterior appearance really does reflect his moral ugliness; however, while Phil feels perverted and dirty and comments that " 'Vice . . . is a very strange thing,' " the barman, in a characteristic touch of Hemingway irony, sees only externals and assures him that he looks " 'very well' " (401).

Both literary allusions thus have a logical organic relationship to the story when the reader accepts the assumption that Phil is a writer. In fact, the allusions work together, producing a tension that reflects the writer's dilemma. Phil's desire to embalm his mistress as a character in a literary work of art becomes so strong that his roles as man and lover are secondary to his role as an artist; although he realizes what he is doing, he nevertheless embraces the "monster of Vice," perhaps even the "Extreme of Vice" at the end of the story. He has been seduced by the possibility that the product of the writer's unprincipled violation of another's privacy can be something as "rich and strange" as the pearls and coral of Shakespeare's own somewhat grisly sea change. The negative overtones of Pope's words and the positive connotations of Shakespeare's provide symbolic poles for the conflict over the nature of the artist. Both allusions are implicit in the words of Phil's mistress: " 'We're made up of all sorts of things. You've known that. You've used it well enough' " (400).

Like Hawthorne characters such as Ethan Brand and Dr. Rappaccini, Phil is risking his human integrity and perhaps even his soul to achieve something in which he believes totally. The story is open-ended: the reader cannot know whether the created work of art will justify Phil's sacrifice, whether Phil the human being will survive the ruthlessness of Phil the artist. But the implication of the title, with its suggestion of the miraculous transformation of corrupt materials into jewels, may indicate Hemingway's own positive point of view on the nature of art and the function of the artist. Aside from possible autobiographical implications, "The Sea Change," read as a writer's moment of self-recognition, at the very least offers a new aspect of Hemingway's exploration of the writer and the demands of his art. He would continue this exploration through much of the decade. But his next portrait of a writer, a response to economic and social events, marked a turning away from the writer's spiritual struggle within himself. Instead, it tentatively examined the question of the writer's public responsibility during times of social upheaval.

## "The Gambler, the Nun, and the Radio"

"The Gambler, the Nun, and the Radio" was published at a difficult point in Hemingway's career and has autobiographical origins in a period fraught with frustration and physical pain. It is not surprising, therefore, that the writer in the story, Mr. Frazer (phraser), suffers from self-doubt and insomnia as he finds himself in a no-man's-land between conflicting philosophies, exemplified by the three units in the title Hemingway ultimately chose and by one of the visitors who come to see the Mexican gambler.

The story is based on Hemingway's stay in St. Vincent's Hospital in Billings, Montana, in November and December of 1930. Leaving the L——T ranch in north Wyoming with John Dos Passos, Hemingway drove through Yellowstone on his way to Billings. At dusk on the evening of November 1, twenty-two miles west of Billings, Hemingway was blinded by the lights of an oncoming car, lost control of his vehicle, and went off the road. A passing motorist took him to St. Vincent's, where he spent the next seven weeks after his badly fractured right arm had been repaired by unusual surgical techniques. Hemingway described his accident and the ensuing surgery in a letter dictated to his friend Guy Hickok: "Coming into Billings with Dos en route to Piggott, had spill brought on by loose gravel and Saturday night drivers and six days later when the doctor operated on my upper arm to fasten the bone together by boring a hole through it and then lashing the ends with kangaroo tendon, the inside of the arm looked like the part of an elk you have to throw away."[20] To Archibald MacLeish he complained that his right hand was numb, and he worried about finishing _Death in the Afternoon_ without the use of his writing hand.[21] Because of the severity of the break and the experimental nature of the surgery, Hemingway's doctor refused to let him out of bed for the first month after the surgery. Pauline noted that he suffered almost constant pain as well as insomnia during that first month.[22] All through the spring of 1931 he would continue to have difficulty with the arm, and his writing was confined to letters written or typed left-handed.[23]

But the experience in the hospital was far from wasted. Through the haze of his own pain, Hemingway observed his surroundings carefully. To MacLeish he mentioned the Russian across the hall—he was brought into the hospital with a gunshot wound and "groaned a good deal at first"[24]—and contrasted him with a more seriously wounded Mexican who took his pain stoically. He also mentioned the contrasting tranquility of the artificial world on the radio that was his chief distraction during the hospitalization and observed Sister Florence, who helped to cheer him up with talk of sports. This setting and cast, considerably enlarged by Hemingway's imagination—and by his brooding over the economic depression into which the world was falling—allowed Hemingway to test values in a story that he was to publish some eighteen months later.

The period during which Hemingway actually wrote the story was an uneasy time even though Hemingway's economic situation was more than comfortable. Pauline's uncle, Gus Pfeiffer, bought the house on Whitehead Street in Key West for $8,000 and offered his favorite niece and her husband up to $25,000 for an African safari. On his own, Hemingway was able to earn a healthy income from his writing: *Scribner's* paid him $600 for serial publication of "Wine of Wyoming," his share of the movie rights for *A Farewell to Arms* came to $24,000, and by 1933 he was being offered $250 per column by *Esquire*. On the national scene, however, the number of unemployed had risen from 4 million to 15 million—one-third of the work force—between 1930 and 1933. Wages of those still employed in 1932 had dropped to 40 percent of total 1929 wages, while farm income went from $7 billion to $2 billion and construction dropped from $10 billion to $1 billion during the same years. By 1933 an estimated one million homeless Americans were on the road. Those citizens fortunate enough to qualify for relief had to feed whole families on less than three dollars per week.

The political climate in 1932 and 1933 was disturbing. As Carlos Baker has noted, Hemingway was dismayed by the choice between Hoover and Roosevelt in 1932;[25] in spite of the gravity of the economic crisis, he made it clear in a letter written that summer that he had no intention of falling into line with the "Leftward Swing" then becoming popular with some authors and critics.[26] He could not know that Wyndham Lewis was preparing an essay that would inspire a number of other critics during the 1930s with its assertion that Hemingway's work was seriously flawed by his ignorance of politics. Hemingway could see that this "leftward swing" was hurting his reputation, which had risen so rapidly during the 1920s but now seemed to be declining in the early 1930s. He must have wondered which direction his career would take in the decade ahead.

Although economic and political affairs might be critical, Hemingway may have been more concerned about his artistic career during the period immediately preceding the writing of "The Gambler, the Nun, and the Radio," for he was in a fallow period only partially induced by the injury to his right arm. *Death in the Afternoon* had taken longer to complete than he had planned, and he had lost momentum with his fiction. In spite of the time it had taken to write *Death in the Afternoon*, he found the early reviews of the book disappointing (although the most scathing reaction, Max Eastman's "Bull in the Afternoon," was not published until after the story had been written). He had no new novel in the works, perhaps because he felt unable to write one appropriate for an era that would welcome Dos Passos, James T. Farrell, and John Steinbeck; and while he was to produce some brilliant short stories in the 1930s, he would be forced to pad his 1933 collection *Winner Take Nothing* with inferior stories ("The Mother of a Queen" and "One Reader Writes") and with previously published material ("A Natural History of the Dead") to bring it up to book size.

The story about the hospital offered Hemingway an opportunity to probe his own values, to take stock, and to find a way out of his current impasse. Other stories in *Winner Take Nothing*—stories such as "After the Storm," "A Clean, Well-Lighted Place," "The Light of the World," and "God Rest You Merry, Gentlemen"—present a bleak existential picture of life, but only "The Gambler, the Nun, and the Radio" proposes and tests tentative answers as well as posing questions. In the story's first title, "Give Us a Prescription, Doctor," Hemingway admonished himself to produce a cure for the existential dilemma posed by the twentieth century and most particularly by the depression of the 1930s.

Given the genesis of the story, it is not surprising that the earliest draft is written in the first person. Hemingway initially concluded the story in a logical place, right after Cayetano Ruiz tells the narrator about his gambling philosophy. But if parts of "The Gambler, the Nun, and the Radio" were found art, Hemingway was not content simply to report the gambler's story. On the contrary, the material needed artistic shaping. After the initial conclusion, Hemingway added a philosophical passage in which he free-associated about some of his recent concerns. His own bad luck and that of his father no doubt underlie the assertion that everyone is damned twice although many people fail to realize that they are damned or deny it. At any rate, he concludes, this universal problem cannot be solved through "economics."[27] These remarks could apply in a general way to some of the characters in the story, but Hemingway was not satisfied. In a second version of the conclusion, he added "many listen to the radio," to the list of those who escape the knowledge that they are damned; he also tinkered with the wording of the statement about economics.[28]

Still not satisfied, Hemingway incorporated a new point of view. Item 420 in the Hemingway Collection at the Kennedy Library is a typescript of the early version of the story but incorporates Mr. Frazer (or Fraser—both variants exist on page 2 of this manuscript), and the holograph conclusion proceeds from the former ending. Cayetano Ruiz is set among some of the other accident victims in the hospital—a rodeo rider with a broken back, a carpenter who has fallen with his scaffold, and a boy who must have his badly set leg rebroken—to illustrate the proposition, stated so baldly in the earlier manuscript, that all are damned at birth. Even when the story was published in *Scribner's Magazine* in May 1933, it had not yet reached its final form. In addition to the different title, the magazine version of the story ends with the sentence "The opiums are for before and for after."[29] Before its appearance in *Winner Take Nothing* in October 1933, Hemingway not only changed the title and corrected a geographical error but added fifty-three words to the conclusion. Hemingway's careful reworking of the story suggests that he did not take it lightly, that he thought of it as an important piece of work.

The story as finally published, like the more masterful "Snows of Kilimanjaro," which would appear three years later, questions a writer's values at a time when his physical infirmity mirrors his psychic unhealthiness. Mr. Frazer is immobilized in Hailey, Montana, by a badly broken leg, an injury sustained in a fall from a horse. Although, unlike Hemingway, he is physically capable of writing, Frazer is experiencing a period of impotence in his work and can produce nothing while he lies in his hospital bed. Or is Frazer simply going through a period of gestation in preparation for a new stage of his work? His artistic impotence is dramatized by his role as a spectator rather than as an active participant in the life of the hospital: he spends his time reading the newspaper, looking out the windows, listening to the sounds of the ward, and, above all, listening to the radio. His isolation from other patients and, by inference, from the rest of the world is symbolized by his private room and by the fact that Frazer normally receives no visitors from the outside world.

Frazer is flanked by two figures who share his pain and immobility because their injuries are similar to his own. The gambler of the title, Cayetano Ruiz, has been shot in the abdomen and has a paralyzed leg, and a Russian was shot in the thigh. Each man copes with his pain differently. The Russian, whose wound is painful but not serious, cries out so loudly that everyone in the area hears him. On the other hand, Cayetano Ruiz, whose abdominal wound develops peritonitis and who may never walk again without a crutch, behaves stoically, refusing to make a sound. Frazer chooses to emulate the quiet acceptance of pain demonstrated by Ruiz—although he does cry quietly when he is by himself, saying that he finds crying "restful." Frazer's choice of mentors prepares the reader for the second, more important, lesson that Frazer will learn from the gambler.

Frazer lacks strong spiritual and moral values. That he has no religion is evident in his discussions of prayer with Sister Cecilia. Nor does he have any remaining illusions about the myth of America: the West he lives in, its sugar beet workers replacing the mountain men and the cowboys of an earlier era, has little to do with the West of popular myth.[30] For Frazer, the westward migration has become a mere parody in which he participates nightly as he moves westward through the radio stations from Minneapolis to Seattle, in an electronic retracing of the approximate route of the Oregon Trail. The new myths created by Hollywood hold little appeal. As the detective who questions the gambler notes, Hailey, Montana, is not like the movies. In other words, during a time when it is the fashion for writers to enlist their talents in the service of a cause, Frazer can bring himself to make no commitments.

Immobilized, Frazer is passive while several alternative myths vie for his support, from the religion of Sister Cecilia to the communism of the thin Mexican activist who comes to visit. "Give Us a Prescription, Doctor," Hemingway's title when he published the story in *Scribner's Magazine*, refers to the advice given by Sister Cecilia, the thin Mexican, and Cayetano Ruiz, each of whom has a cure for the narrator's malaise.

These three influential figures move into Frazer's moral void, alternating with the mindless relief offered by the radio, an inexpensive, ubiquitous, and relatively harmless "opium of the people" that Frazer uses, along with the "giant killer" alcohol, to make his pain and confinement bearable. Sister Cecilia attempts to win Frazer back to the comforts of organized religion and even to recruit him as a religious propagandist, but she talks unconvincingly of the joys of sainthood, and her religion becomes suspect when she treats prayer as Huck Finn might—she uses it to assure a win for Notre Dame on the football field or to pray for her favorite baseball team, the Athletics, during the World Series.[31] Although the satire of Sister Cecilia is gentle, the author's rejection of the panacea she offers is unmistakable.

At the other end of the spectrum is the thin Mexican shopkeeper, a visitor who denigrates religion as the "opium of the poor" but who preaches his own religion—communism. Hemingway added this invented character to a cast based on real people at St. Vincent's, for when he wrote Archibald MacLeish about the people he had encountered there, he mentioned only two Mexican visitors, both of whom drank scotch with him.[32] Unlike his more affable companions, the thin Mexican repeatedly refuses to succumb to the alcohol that is their "opium of the people" because liquor "mounts to my head" (476). He is also tied to the Left by his remarks about revolution, by his love for "La Cucaracha," the song of the Mexican revolution, and by the echoes of Marx in his speech. Frazer rejects what the thin revolutionist advocates, thinking of him as "that dyspeptic little joint-keeper" (485) and calling him into his room to tell him off.

In rejecting politics, Frazer echoes a choice Hemingway also articulates in his nonfiction of the 1930s. The writer should beware of getting caught up in political arguments about the areas of life he depicts, he said in *Death in the Afternoon*: "Let those who want to save the world if you can get to see it clear and as a whole" (278). Later in the 1930s, under attack by the leftist critics who expected him to take a political stand in his work, he spelled out his principles more explicitly in one of his *Esquire* columns:

> Now a writer can make himself a nice career . . . by espousing a political cause, working for it, making a profession of believing in it, and if it wins he will be very well placed. . . . and if his outfit gets in he can get to be an ambassador or have a million copies of his books printed by the Government. . . . But none of this will help the writer as a writer unless he finds something new to add to human knowledge while he is writing.[33]

It is true that Hemingway's statements in the 1930s were responses to attacks from the Left and might be considered overly defensive, but years later, in his interview with George Plimpton, Hemingway would assert the same idea: while reserving for writers the right to hold any political opinions they wished, he nevertheless remarked, "All you can be sure about in a political-minded writer is that if his work should last you will have to skip the politics when you read it."[34] Truth, he felt, would always win out over expeditious political statements.

It is Cayetano Ruiz who has the most to teach Frazer. The closeness between the two men goes beyond their physical conditions. Ruiz has soft hands that have never done hard physical work; like the writer, though, he works with his hands as well as his head. One of the first scenes makes it clear that Frazer and Ruiz speak the same language—both literally and figuratively—as they joke in Spanish about the questions of the detective who is investigating the shooting that sent Ruiz to the hospital. Gradually, they discover they have more in common than they might have guessed. A gambler, like a writer, needs luck to succeed. Although Ruiz has had little luck recently, he is devoted to his gambling; as a dedicated man, he presents an unexpected parallel to the writer who must dedicate himself to his craft as he waits for the luck to turn his way. Ruiz's motto, "Continue, slowly, and wait for luck to change" (484), conveys much the same sentiment as Hemingway's motto "il faut (d'abord) durer." Just as the gambler who would succeed must wait for his luck, the writer who wishes to endure must agree with Hemingway that "the great thing is to last and get your work done . . . and write when there is something that you know; and not before; and not too damned much after" (*Death in the Afternoon* 278).

Although his game is not normally as dangerous as boxing, bull-fighting, or big-game hunting, Cayetano Ruiz has been associated with Hemingway's "code heroes" and with good reason. He is quietly stoical through pain and tragedy. He knows and accepts who he is, not a philosopher but "a gambler of the small towns" (484), yet he has the philosopher's trait of examining the life he leads. What, then, can this man who knows himself teach Frazer, the writer struggling to sort out his ideas and know himself? Ruiz says that he is a "poor idealist," or "the victim of illusions" (483). The professional gambler must create illusions for others while remaining aloof from them. Ruiz, however, comes to believe in the illusion that gambling can bring glory. He plays for months, using his tricks to amass a stake in small towns, then gambles away his winnings in a short time. Nor are his losses merely monetary: when he says about gamblers, "No gambler has luck with women. He is too concentrated" (484), he echoes what Hemingway experienced and wrote about writers and women. Both writers and gamblers may drive their loved ones away by too great an absorption in their work. Both may come to have such commitment to their work that they lose sight of everything else and become victims of their own illusions—the illusions they have been creating for others.

What Cayetano Ruiz says contradicts the myths set forth by Sister Cecilia and the thin Mexican. That night, as Frazer listens to the music from the gambler's room, he comes very close to self-awareness, and the reader perceives for the first time that the reasons for Frazer's insomnia go beyond the pain in his injured leg. As he lies alone in his room, Frazer remembers the thin Mexican's remark about the "opium of the poor" and thinks of all the other things that are also "opiums of the people": music, economics, patriotism, sexual intercourse, drink, the radio, gambling, ambition, belief in new forms of government, and finally bread. One significant omission is literature.

For real literature is an opium of the people also. It serves no utilitarian purpose but simply exists for the sake of humanity, not just in the present age, but in all ages. Presenting its own set of illusions to a public willing to suspend its disbelief in illusions, it makes the burdens of mankind a little lighter. Frazer, like his mentor Ruiz, does not put these ideas into words but merely asks the little Mexican radical, "Why should the people be operated on without an anaesthetic?" (486). The reader can now read, between the lines, the reason for Frazer's impotence as a writer and the possible solution of his dilemma.

But Frazer is not in the desperate condition of Harry in "The Snows of Kilimanjaro," and unlike Harry, he retreats from a complete act of self-analysis. Telling himself that he is "thinking well, a little too well" (487), Frazer resolves to use the "giant killer" and the radio to avoid confronting himself. Frazer's shrinking from final self-knowledge makes this story less than completely satisfying and has caused some critics to ignore it. However, considered as a step in Hemingway's growing awareness of the writer's peculiar problems and the possible heresies to which he can fall victim, "The Gambler, the Nun, and the Radio" takes on a new significance. The story opens a line of inquiry to which Hemingway would return in later works.

## "Fathers and Sons"

In "Fathers and Sons," Hemingway again attempted to confront the divided responsibilities of the human being versus the writer, the conflict that he had approached so obliquely in "The Sea Change." This time, however, he employed his autobiographical character Nick Adams, and his manuscripts show evidence of the emotional turmoil that he suffered while he was writing the story. Although a few years earlier he had pontificated to Morley Callaghan that it was important to store up impressions even when one's father is dying,[35] Hemingway obviously found it difficult to deal with his own father's final illness and death and especially with his own feelings about the suicide.[36] He therefore treated the problem by employing his now famous "iceberg principle."

Hemingway enunciated the iceberg principle a number of times, from the early 1930s to the early 1960s. The earliest definition of the principle came in *Death in the Afternoon*:

> If a writer of prose knows enough about what he is writing about he may omit things that he knows and the reader, if the writer is writing truly enough, will have a feeling of those things as strongly as though the writer had stated them. The dignity of movement of an ice-berg is due to only one-eighth of it being above water. A writer who omits things because he does not know them only makes hollow places in his writing. [192]

Years later, in his interview with George Plimpton, he saw no reason to change his mind and echoed his earlier statement so closely that it is tempting to believe that he had just reread it: "I always try to write on the principle of the iceberg. There is seven eighths of it under water for every part that shows. Anything you know you can eliminate and it only strengthens your iceberg. It is the part that doesn't show. If a writer omits something because he does not know it then there is a hole in the story."[37]

His final definition, in *A Moveable Feast*, applies the theory to one of the first stories in which it was employed. Hemingway recalled that in writing "Out of Season," he had "omitted the real end of it which was that the old man hanged himself. This was omitted on my new theory that you could omit anything if you knew that you omitted and the omitted part would strengthen the story and make people feel something more than they understood" (75). In his posthumous essay "The Art of the Short Story," written in 1959 but not published until 1981, he went so far as to say that the "test of any story is how very good the stuff is that you . . . omit."[38] Although the theory did not always work—for example in "Out of Season" itself—when it did work, it produced some of Hemingway's greatest successes.

One such success is "Fathers and Sons," where Hemingway reacts to Clarence Hemingway's suicide, an event that troubled him deeply, without bringing the suicide of Dr. Henry Adams to the surface level of the story, where it might attract the attention of biographically inclined critics. His difficulty in treating this sensitive subject is evident in the number and the nature of the manuscripts that document the genesis and growth of "Fathers and Sons," first called "The Tomb of My Grandfather." Item 382 in the Hemingway collection consists largely of notes toward a story with only a few trial passages. A pencil manuscript in first person, it says nothing about the problems of a writer who might attempt to write about the painful death of his father, but later manuscripts would. Item 383, which follows the first attempt, is another first-person pencil manuscript that advances the story somewhat.

Hemingway's third attempt at the story makes explicit some of the problems he had experienced in getting the story started. In a statement that, in modified form, would eventually be included in the final draft of the story, he apologized that there were still too many living people who would be hurt if he wrote frankly about his father, who had been "betrayed" not only by his own bad luck but by his family. While he waited for the deaths of two family members, Hemingway concluded that he would at least praise his father's marvelous eyes.[39] The garbled syntax of the interpolation suggests Hemingway's emotional involvement as well as the trouble he was having with the story, perhaps because he was attempting to narrate it in the first person at this stage of the composition.

By changing to the third-person point of view and attaching "Fathers and Sons" to Nick Adams, Hemingway distanced the events of the story not only mechanically but psychologically. Although Hemingway had earlier merely hinted that Nick was a writer in a single published line in "Big Two-Hearted River,"[40] he had thought of him as a writer, as evidenced by material he had cut from that story, published posthumously in *The Nick Adams Stories* as "On Writing." There Nick asserts that "the only writing that was any good was what you made up, what you imagined," and insists that writing about real memories was bad: "It always killed [them]."[41] However, Nick, like Hemingway, was to discover the other side of that proposition when he thought about writing Dr. Adams's story. Some memories are better lost than retained, and writing about them can provide catharsis for the writer.

Because Hemingway's fourth version of the story is a typescript with pencil corrections, the composition seems to have been moving faster than it had in its earlier stages even though the pencil insertions suggest that he was relinquishing his privacy only gradually and painfully. For example, after the statement "Nick could not write about him yet" in the typescript, Hemingway inserted a clause promising to do so, and to tell the whole truth, eventually.[42] The rationalization of the story as an attempt at psychoanalysis, alternating with periods of repression, is apparent at this stage as well. Nick reflects that thinking about his father always makes him sad; the typescript follows that statement with the flat sentence, "So he decided to think of something else." Between the two sentences Hemingway inserted in pencil the observation that writing about his pain would purge it. Ultimately, he would have to write the full story.[43]

Even when the story was typed in its fifth version, Hemingway was still adding some of its most telling lines in pencil. After the assertion that thinking about his father always made Nick sad, Hemingway again attempted to capture the bittersweet nature of his own memories of his father with a penciled insertion about his happy family memories from before things went wrong.[44] Again, after "But it was still too early for that," he inserted another comment about people being hurt if he wrote the story now and the conviction that he would know it better as time passed. Finally, at the end of the meditation on his father's face, so skillfully reconstructed by the undertaker, another penciled addition has Nick telling himself that he should forget these bitter memories until he needs them for his writing.[45]

The phrase about "needing" the material helps to explain the struggle to tell this story that is documented by the multiple manuscripts. Hemingway had personal reasons—his own painful memories of the suicide of his father—for being unable to tell the story without a great deal of effort. But he also had painful professional scruples about writing such a story. The writer's capital is his experience, and Hemingway had already accepted the fact that unhappy love affairs, broken marriages, and psychological breakdowns must all be considered fair game for the writer. But it seems unlikely that any of these subjects had disturbed him as deeply as his father's death by suicide and his guilty feeling that he might have prevented his father's death if he had been more perceptive. The recognition of his artist's urge to profit by that death, the knowledge that on one level he had been coldly observing while the rest of the family mourned, storing up details to exploit later in his fiction—these were not truths that Hemingway could accept easily. Thus, two levels of justification run through the story. First, it is a story that deserves to be told, both to commemorate the father and to document the failures of those closest to him, thus affixing the blame for his death. Second, the writing will be a form of therapy for Nick Adams—and implicitly for his creator as well— who needs to "get rid of" an unhealthy obsession with the suicide.

"Fathers and Sons" is, of course, many things besides the story of how a writer comes to grips with a personal problem. In fact, because of Hemingway's technique of omission, many readers who come to the story for the first time miss the fact that Nick is a writer. Nick's identity as a writer is established in just six sentences in "Fathers and Sons" as it was finally published:

> Nick could not write about him yet, although he would, later. [*Short Stories* 490]

> If he wrote it he could get rid of it. He had gotten rid of many things by writing them. But it was still too early for that. There were still too many people. [491]

> It was a good story but there were still too many people alive for him to write it. [491]

Virtually all of these sentences were originally pencil emendations to Hemingway's earlier drafts of the story. The apparent reluctance with which Hemingway analyzes his thoughts explains their slow genesis and reflects his own painful, gradual realization of Nick Adams's true thoughts and feelings about his father.

Like the process Hemingway followed, Nick's approach to the writing he must do about his father, both to tell the story and to cleanse his memory of the experience, is tentative and piecemeal, like the revelations of a deeply disturbed patient on a psychiatrist's couch. The sentences, like those of "Big Two-Hearted River," in which Nick is also under an emotional strain, are mostly terse and choppy, carefully holding Nick's emotions under control. Like his creator, who has worked through so many drafts before telling only a part of his own father's story, Nick has a hard time dealing with his father's death, personally and artistically.

Nick's difficulties with his father's death and his tendency to take refuge in his art are emphasized by his inability to talk to his son about so many of the things that are important to him—things about which he can write for his impersonal readers. When the boy asks about the Indians, Nick reflects that it is impossible to "say that [Trudy] did first what no one has ever done better," so he merely says that Trudy and her brother Billy "were very nice" (497). When he tries to talk about his father, Nick is even less revealing. Dr. Adams was "a great hunter and fisherman" and "a much better shot" than Nick (498). The story ends with the suggestion that, just as Nick and his son will have to visit the tomb of the boy's grandfather, Nick will have to come to terms with his father's death, perhaps through his writing. In telling Nick's story, Hemingway had himself done what Nick was not yet able to do: he had sorted out many of his feelings about his own father and, through his technique of omission, had implied much more.

Although he revealed less than he left beneath the surface, perhaps Hemingway was able to "get rid of" some of the guilt and bitterness surrounding Clarence Hemingway's death through his veiled references to what had happened to Nick Adams's father. The "handsome job" of the undertaker hints not only at the sort of physical reconstruction necessary to the deceased after a death by a gunshot to the head but also at the psychological reconstruction necessary for the survivors of the violent death of a loved one. In effect, Hemingway's story is itself a "handsome job." The suggestion that people who were still alive could have helped Nick's father proclaims both Hemingway's perceived guilt about not helping his father and his anger toward Grace Hall Hemingway and George Hemingway, who might have helped in their various ways to avert the suicide.[46] If "Fathers and Sons" is not as explicit as some of Hemingway's other writing about the problems of the writer, it nevertheless carries considerable emotional freight.

As he purged some of the bitterness and sorrow surrounding the death of his father, Hemingway ironically exploited both his early Oedipal conflict with him—foreshadowing his actual death—and his father's suicide. He was thus able to ease his own pain even while he was marketing his emotional capital to his readers. This act must have taken a certain toll on Hemingway's own psyche. But as Hemingway was often to observe, for the true writer, nothing else is possible. As he would demonstrate with his portrait of Richard Gordon in *To Have and Have Not*, Hemingway had no sympathy for the writer who simply observes others from a distance and attempts to write about them without a true understanding of their inner nature. The best writing must come from within—exposing pain and all.

### *To Have and Have Not*: Portrait of the Artist as a Bad Man

Like "Fathers and Sons," Hemingway's only novel of the 1930s was difficult to write although for different reasons. He faced a number of distractions as he worked—the war in Spain, his declining critical reputation, and perhaps the beginning of his dissatisfaction with his marriage to Pauline. Nevertheless, as a part of his mechanism for defending the type of writing he did, he needed to return to a theme that he had considered but not fully worked out in "The Gambler, the Nun, and the Radio." Accordingly, he set to work to turn two stories from the early 1930s into the nucleus of a novel that would treat the problems of the depression in conjunction with the writer's relationship to social issues. Although these two stories about Harry Morgan had a certain power by themselves, it was not easy to graft a writer's story onto them, and Hemingway himself wondered where the novel was going even after he had completed the first twenty chapters.

Item 617 in the Hemingway collection is a batch of working notes found with the manuscript of *To Have and Have Not*. In his notes to himself, Hemingway was brutally frank about the mounting pile of manuscript his sessions had so far produced: "Question—what the hell is going to happen in this novel?" he asked himself at one point.[47] He went on to remind himself that a novel "has to move and have some story. That was true of Sun—went from here to there. Reason for my dispairs [*sic*] has been that they was fundamentally unsound due to depending entirely on invention every day—fine if you are full of juice but impossible [illegible] unless there is a framework."[48] The self-accusation is borne out by Item 645, a set of three fugitive pages found with the manuscript. Numbered from 172 through 174, these pages seem to be a local color insert to the novel describing the observations and impressions of winter visitors to Key West. The segment goes nowhere and reflects Hemingway's frustration: there are two drafts of page 173, but unlike most passages that Hemingway revised laboriously, these pages contain no profound thematic or artistic possibilities.

One difficulty may have been that Hemingway was out of training to write a novel—his last had been *A Farewell to Arms* (1929)—but another was undoubtedly the nature of the character he was creating, Richard Gordon, the writer. This acidulous portrait of Gordon would examine new facets of the writer's psyche and expose new heresies or pitfalls to which the writer was subject, some of which Hemingway now knew at first hand.

Viewed from this perspective, Richard Gordon, the self-styled proletarian writer of *To Have and Have Not*, is one of Hemingway's more significant characters, although Gordon has evoked little interest among critics. In *The Writer as Artist* Carlos Baker summed up Gordon's functions: the "crack-up of Richard Gordon, proletarian novelist, playboy, and sojourner in the Key West artist's colony" serves as counterpoint to the failure of Harry Morgan; Gordon is a "representative figure" whom Hemingway played off against his virile but doomed hero. Gordon is a "have" economically, while Harry is a "have not," but in keeping with the double meaning of the novel's title, Gordon is a "have not," while Harry is a "have" in human terms. Baker sums up the differences between the two:

> Harry's marriage is a success, Gordon's a miserable failure. Harry is tough, bitter, honest with himself; Gordon is a self-deceiver, a self-apologist, a self-pitier. One is an expert strategist in all that concerns his means of livelihood and his life as a man, while the other is a false practitioner who manages to conceal his limitations even from himself. Morgan can handle his own affairs; Gordon is a kept man in a morally unkempt society.[49]

Baker barely mentions that Gordon, unlike the group of wealthy parasites treated panoramically in chapter 24 of the novel, is a writer. But for Hemingway, Gordon's profession is the central fact about him.

In *To Have and Have Not*, Hemingway combines two themes concerning the role of the writer, only one of which has generally been recognized. In this novel he not only attacks the type of writer who cashes in on timely trends but also assesses the primary responsibilities of any writer. For Hemingway, the 1930s, more than any other period except the last few years of his life, were years of painful self-examination that centered on his identity as a writer; not only in "The Sea Change," "The Gambler, the Nun, and the Radio," and "Fathers and Sons" but also in *Green Hills of Africa* and "The Snows of Kilimanjaro" and in *To Have and Have Not*, Hemingway seems both concerned and troubled about the possible failures of a writer, potential heresies against the faith that had informed his whole life. These concerns are central to his 1937 novel, in which he became so intrigued with the question of the writer's role that it developed into an important secondary theme, perhaps to the detriment of the novel, since it distracted attention from the more powerful story of Harry Morgan.

The first dimension of Richard Gordon has long been recognized. Gordon specializes in the sort of fiction that Hemingway has avoided, in spite of the taunts of the leftist critics of the 1930s. By the time his career was well launched, Hemingway, who had not been too proud to woo Edmund Wilson in the 1920s so that Wilson would review his early work, had become wary of the critics and mistrusted their opinions. For him, the best guide for the writer would always be his own integrity and artistic judgment. In *Green Hills of Africa*, written during approximately the same period as *To Have and Have Not*, he had attacked the critics directly by reflecting that it was disgusting to write "well and truly" about a topic one knew very well and then to have "those who are paid to read it and report on it" call it a "fake" because of their own failure to understand or appreciate the subject (148–149).

In *To Have and Have Not*, he dramatizes what happens when literary critics corrupt the public taste. When Herbert Spellman, a fan whom Gordon encounters in a Key West bar, learns that Gordon's new novel will deal with a "strike in a textile plant," he can scarcely wait to read it. " 'That's marvellous,' " he says. " 'You know I'm a sucker for anything on the social conflict.' "[50] During the ensuing conversation, it becomes obvious that Gordon uses stock characters: Spellman is able to predict that the new novel will feature "a beautiful Jewish agitator" (197). Both Gordon and Spellman have been trained by the critical establishment to accept stock characters and hackneyed plots as long as the novelist is writing on a social theme from a leftist perspective. Spellman's own credibility as a literary critic is damaged, however, when he announces that he is a stork, begins to babble incoherently, and has to be removed from the bar by his keeper. Like Don Quixote, Spellman has been addled by reading books— in this case books of criticism rather than romances but, like Don Quixote's romances, far removed from reality.

Gordon's method of working is evident from the short chapter (chapter 17) in which he sees Marie Morgan crying as she hurries down the road on the morning after the Cuban revolutionaries have robbed the bank and commandeered Harry's borrowed fishing boat:

> In today's chapter he was going to use the big woman with the tear-red-dened eyes he had just seen on the way home. Her husband when he came home at night hated her, hated the way she had coarsened and grown heavy, was repelled by her bleached hair, her too big breasts, her lack of sympathy with his work as an organizer. He would compare her to the young, firm-breasted full-lipped little Jewess that had spoken at the meeting that evening. It was good. It was, it could be easily, terrific,

and it was true. He had seen, in a flash of perception, the whole inner life of that type of woman. [177]

In spite of his egotistical faith in his perception, Gordon has demonstrated nearly total insensitivity: Harry still loves Marie, likes her bleached hair and big breasts, and is anything but a labor organizer.

The manuscript of *To Have and Have Not* shows additional ways in which Gordon is a bad writer according to Hemingway's own standards. Hemingway believed that the writer should turn his mind aside from the work he was doing and not dwell on it lest he impede the sensitive subconscious process of creation. In *A Moveable Feast* he recalled that he had learned early in his Paris years to stop "when I knew what was going to happen next. That way I could be sure of going on the next day" (12). He had told George Plimpton much the same thing a few years before when he said that one should write "until you come to a place where you still have your juice and know what will happen next and you stop and try to live through until the next day when you hit it again." [51] The well should never be pumped dry by working to the point of exhaustion, as Hemingway claimed Fitzgerald had often done.

To stop one's work for the day meant to leave it completely behind and to refuse to think about it. He told Plimpton that although when a writer is engrossed in a book, "nothing means anything until the next day" [52] when he returns to his writing, the writer must "get through" the intervening time without consciously thinking about the book. It took deliberate discipline to force one's mind off one's work, but if the writer was to be successful, Hemingway believed that his creative faculties needed a rest. He wrote in *A Moveable Feast* that he had learned to follow this regimen because he realized that if he spent his nonworking hours worrying about his work, he might find himself impotent when he tried to work again, whereas if his conscious mind stopped working on a literary problem, "my subconscious would be working on it" (13).

Some critics have suggested that the Hemingway of the 1950s and 1960s revised his early opinions to fit later events, meaning that *A Moveable Feast*, which Hemingway invited readers to read as fiction, represented the way his career should have been rather than the way it was and that this book presented recently pontificated "truths" as discoveries made early in his career. However, Richard Gordon's experience as a writer shows that Hemingway held his opinions about the importance of giving the subconscious its freedom as early as the 1930s.

Unlike Hemingway, Gordon thinks about his work all the time, to the point where he is unable to sleep at night and awakens in the morning feeling drained rather than ready for a day of work on his novel. In Item 204, part 6, he wakes up after a largely sleepless night and appeals to his wife, who has brought him breakfast in bed, for sympathy. He tells her that he cannot sleep because passages from his work in progress race through his mind all night. But in the morning he cannot recall the scenes that have seemed so vivid in the night. Moreover, his sleepless night and the futile use of his creative energy have left him too exhausted to work.[53] Helen tells Gordon that every writer has probably gone through the same ordeal. Her remark might suggest that Hemingway, who had sometimes had to substitute sheer will for inspiration while working on *To Have and Have Not*, might have experienced the same problems. Gordon replies that knowing others have faced the same problem does not help him.[54] When he does get started, however, Gordon writes at almost unbelievable speed, in contrast to Hemingway, for whom 500 words was a good day's work. On the same day that Harry Morgan is dying on his boat, Gordon, who has finally gotten his story moving, is exhilarated after producing 3,500 words.[55]

Although Gordon has apparently fared well both with the reading public and with reviewers, he has not done so well with intelligent members of the working class. In another bar he encounters Nelson Jacks, a communist veteran who is part of the Works Progress Administration force that has been put to work on the Florida keys and the Tortugas. Jacks talks intelligently about social issues, winning Gordon's admiration and leading him to admit that he is a writer. Instead of displaying enthusiasm, Jacks falls silent when Gordon tells him his name. When Gordon presses for an evaluation of his labor novels, Jacks reluctantly admits, " 'I thought they were shit' " (210).

Such criticism of Gordon is emphasized in a manuscript segment that does not appear in the published novel: Tommy Bradley analyzes Gordon's showy variety of Marxism and implies that he has heard Gordon's excuses for the failure of his fiction. Gordon maintains that the critics dislike him because he is a Trotskyite. Bradley defines a Trotskyite empirically as a renegade Marxist who can't sell his books and jokingly vows that if he ever becomes a genuine revolutionist, he will sign on as a Trotskyite.[56]

Unlike Richard Gordon, Hemingway had been attacked by the critics of the 1930s for failing to address the social and economic problems created by the depression. Perhaps the carping of the critics was nearly as influential as his involvement with the Spanish civil war in forming his next novel, *For Whom the Bell Tolls*. In the middle of the decade Hemingway found himself paradoxically doing two things: complaining about the shallowness of political standards for works of art and yet attempting to regain his former popularity by adapting his work to the new standards of the 1930s. In *To Have and Have Not* his unconvincing capitulation to the same critics that he condemns was unsuccessful as he revised the effective story of Harry Morgan, turning it into an economic exemplum that would fit the depression era. Harry dies only after uttering a statement about the solidarity of mankind: " 'No matter how a man alone ain't got no bloody fucking chance' " (225). Even while giving the leftist critics what they wanted, however, Hemingway struck back at those who had criticized him while praising socially orthodox writers—such as his erstwhile friend John Dos Passos—writers whom he believed to be his artistic inferiors. Gordon embodies Hemingway's negative image of the committed social writer of the 1930s, one who grinds out orthodox proletarian fiction but who is inwardly hollow. Furthermore, Hemingway uses Gordon to make the point that even the writer who plays the game can fall victim to some faction of critics if he does not fit their narrow political biases.

Although the critics are not uniformly pleased with Gordon, he is adopted by literary lion hunter Helène Bradley, who has made the seduction of writers her specialty. Through his depiction of Mrs. Bradley, Hemingway unsuccessfully attempted to undermine the taste of those readers who pursued fashionably "red" authors of the 1930s. Helène Bradley is not committed to the cause of international socialism; she just wants some exciting times in bed. Like the Left-leaning critics, she is no better than a prostitute. Hemingway wrote two manuscript versions of the scene in the published novel in which Gordon is caught in Helène Bradley's bedroom by her husband Tommy. In the first and shorter version, he merely depicts Mrs. Bradley as the sort of woman who sleeps with writers in a sexual parody of a literary salon.[57] Hemingway canceled this passage with two large X-shaped marks and replaced it with a more full treatment in which Gordon goes to the Bradleys' house looking for his wife but instead encounters Helène, who has prepared to meet him by buying copies of his three novels, *The Ruling Classes*, *Brief Mastery*, and *The Cult of Violence*. She archly displays them for the proud author,[58] but the omniscient narrator explains that Mrs. Bradley routinely orders the books of any author who appears in Key West so that she can have them on hand. Part of her seduction ritual is getting the writer to autograph copies of his books. The episode suggests that Hemingway saw pitfalls in the transition he himself had made—from an unknown newcomer on the literary scene who had no choice but to devote himself to his writing to the "public writer" who was sought out as a celebrity more than as a man of letters.

In this dimension Gordon represents an extension of the writer's dilemma faced by Harry, the dying writer of "The Snows of Kilimanjaro," published only a little more than a year before *To Have and Have Not*. Harry had succumbed to the seduction of the easy life, forsaking meaningful work to accept a life of pleasant idleness; Gordon succumbs to the blandishments of a critical establishment and a public that reward the production of party-line formula fiction—"suckers for the social conflict," represented by Herbert Spellman and by Helène Bradley and her sexual blandishments. But more notable than this treatment of a very bad writer is the analysis of how any writer works—a more complex question and one which had concerned Hemingway for some time.

In spite of his bold statements to Morley Callaghan and Scott Fitzgerald about the priestly nature of the writer and the necessity of using painful personal experiences in one's fiction, Hemingway had long harbored certain reservations about the role of the writer vis-à-vis his role as a human being. The difficulty with being a writer is that one must risk violating the privacy of human relationships with the people to whom one is most closely bound. This side of Richard Gordon surfaces soon after he is introduced in Freddy's bar. Discussing Helène Bradley with his wife, Gordon says, " 'I like her, you know. . . . She interests me both as a woman and as a social phenomenon.' " His wife, Helen, who is hurt by the remark and by what it conceals, counters with the questions, " 'Do people go to bed with a social phenomenon?' " and " 'is it part of the homework of a writer?' " Gordon answers ambiguously: " 'A writer has to know about everything. . . . He can't restrict his experience to conform to Bourgeois standards' " (140).

Within the two pages in which Gordon first appears, Hemingway has introduced the irony that beneath Gordon's handsome and "well-built" appearance lies something as rotten as Harry's gangrenous leg in "The Snows of Kilimanjaro." Gordon will go to bed with Helène Bradley (188–190) and he will do so at least partly to explore the "social phenomenon" as his writer's "homework." In manuscript this point is emphasized by two additional remarks, one made by a former lover of Helène Bradley and the other by Helen Gordon. While he watches Helène taking Gordon upstairs, her rejected lover muses that the writer will gain new and, he implies, unwanted material for his future work.[59] Helen has earlier told Gordon that writers are intrinsically "selfish." She stresses that she is not criticizing her husband but is making an observation about his "trade."[60] Such passages in the manuscript were undoubtedly intended to prepare the reader for further disclosures by Helen Gordon concerning the plight of those closest to the writer, but this area of the plot is de-emphasized. Hemingway does not follow it up fully in the manuscript, and his revision downplays the theme. The bar scene ends with Gordon claiming that he intends to remain downtown for a while as Helen fights back her tears, knowing that he really plans to meet Helène Bradley.

It is not just Gordon's infidelity that bothers his wife but his reason for pursuing his affairs. When Gordon returns from his liaison with Helène Bradley, the Gordons have a fight, and the notion of the "homework of a writer" again comes to the fore. When Gordon suggests that all men are unfaithful, that even Helen's father has committed his adulteries, she replies that if he did sleep with other women, it was because " 'he couldn't help it. . . . He didn't do it out of curiosity, or from barnyard pride' " (187). She is suggesting that, like Phil in "The Sea Change," Gordon exploits sexual relationships to satisfy his writer's curiosity. But Gordon goes a step further in his "barnyard pride" because his writing is partly a form of boasting about his sexual exploits. Like Harry in "The Snows of Kilimanjaro," Gordon could identify himself as a rooster who crows over the "dunghill" of love.

The Gordons also echo the sterility of the Elliots' marriage. Gordon's emotional sterility is symbolized by Helen's references during this quarrel to their childless marriage, childless because, according to Gordon, they cannot afford children, though Helen points out that there was money enough " 'to go to the Cap d'Antibes to swim and to Switzerland to ski' " (183). Instead of filling her with children, Gordon has filled her with " 'ergoapiol pills to make [her] come around,' " with quinine, and with " 'catheters and . . . whirling douches' " (185–186). The ugly medical images contrast violently with the concept of creative generation. Gordon's real children have been his books, Helen implies, but evidence elsewhere in the novel demonstrates that the books were not worth the destruction of the marriage nor the harm that he has done to Helen. In fact, Helen, a lively and life-affirming character among the effete literary set of Key West, is willing to condemn books and writing in general. Her finest speech in the novel affirms the ascendancy of life over literature when she reviles the " 'dirty little tricks you taught me that you probably got out of some book,' " and ends with the greatest insult she can think of: " 'You writer' " (186).

After the fight, Gordon realizes that he has lost his wife; in his last function in the novel, he encounters the roughest element of Key West in waterfront bars, attempts to take revenge on Professor MacWalsey (the man for whom Helen is leaving him), and finally staggers drunkenly down the street on his way home. Marie Morgan, seeing him go, sympathetically pronounces him " 'some poor goddamned rummy' " (255) in a judgment that ironically mirrors Gordon's earlier misunderstanding of her life. For it is not alcohol as much as his writing career that has doomed Richard Gordon. He has allowed his writing to become a perversion that supersedes his regard for human life.

Hemingway's interest in the problems of a writer in general and of Gordon in particular is further evident in the large section of the manuscript novel that he scrapped before publication. That portion of the book would have dealt with Tommy Bradley, Helène's husband, who has only a cameo role in *To Have and Have Not* as it was published. In the manuscript, a lengthy subplot involves Tommy and Richard Gordon in a plan to deliver dynamite and small arms ammunition to a rebel group off the coast of Cuba. In this plot, Gordon, the man of inaction, would have attempted to do something rather than merely write about the actions of others, although he does have his own writer's reasons for participating in the plot. The irony is that, when Gordon finally does become involved in action, it leads to nothing. The two would-be filibusters fail to find the boat with which they are to rendezvous, and Gordon adds only the experience of extreme seasickness to his materials for future literary work.

There were good reasons for eliminating the long uneventful passage, but Bradley's observations are useful in interpreting Gordon's character. They fill in the underwater part of the iceberg. Bradley is an extreme cynic, but he is also a keen judge of character. When he first talks to Gordon, he notices that the writer is observing and classifying him for future use in his writing.[61] Gordon shows this same trait when he is involved in the smuggling plan. He tells Tommy that he has been disappointed by the "prosaic" nature of a venture that he had hoped would yield rich raw material for his writing.[62]

At times on the trip to Cuba, Gordon shows an appealing side to his character. He apologizes for some of his writer's traits, such as his tendency to ask too many direct questions, a habit he acknowledges is a "heel's trick" to which a writer falls prey.[63] He is surprised that Tommy finds life so enjoyable while he, Gordon, finds his so empty when he is not able to write. He admits to Tommy that writing is the only thing that has given his life meaning and that he has been devastated to learn how great his ignorance of real life is. He had hoped that the smuggling trip with Tommy would ground him in actuality by exposing him to real adventure, but the trip has been as uneventful as the rest of his life.[64] Although such passages do not redeem Gordon, they make some of his actions in the published novel more explicable. Not satisfied with being just a hack, Gordon is too limited to bear up under the intense emotional pressure of the writer's life, a pressure that has caused even greater men to crack. Consequently he becomes a grotesque parody of all that the writer should be.

Hemingway considered pursuing the theme of the writer's role in life by using several real writers as prototypes for characters in the novel. It has been a critical commonplace to assume that Gordon is based on Hemingway's old friend John Dos Passos, an assumption that the manuscript contradicts.[65] Dos Passos appears in a very brief role in the manuscript novel at one of Helène Bradley's parties, where he is characterized as a supposedly incorruptible social novelist who trades on his reputation by borrowing money from his friends.[66] Tommy Bradley also knows a good deal about Harry Crosby, Hart Crane, Scott Fitzgerald, and James Joyce and discourses on them: Crosby was "crazy," Crane a "buggar" [*sic*]; Fitzgerald began writing too young and lacked the brains to go with his talent; and Joyce was an excellent writer who was stopped only by his blindness.[67]

Finally Hemingway even brings himself into his modern "Fable for Critics." Although he has never met Hemingway, Gordon despises the "big slob" and says so to a crowd of local drinkers in a bar. They reply that Gordon can tell Hemingway that to his face. To the conches of Key West, Hemingway is a hero because he makes a great deal of money yet is never seen working. Gordon's resentment of Hemingway stems from the fact that his reputation is inflated—according to Gordon, Hemingway has written just one good novel and is now content to write mere "tripe" for *Esquire*. He feels that Hemingway, softened by an easy life with a rich wife, has betrayed his profession.[68] None of these observations on writers adds a great deal to the picture of Gordon, and Hemingway wisely removed them: such elements would have distracted attention from Gordon and caused an already poorly focused novel to become even less coherent.

The treatment of writers and writing in *To Have and Have Not*, however detrimental it may have been to the novel, was significant to Hemingway's later work. Along with the meditations on writers and writing in his earlier short stories of the decade and in "The Snows of Kilimanjaro," the analysis of a writer's career and its dangers seemed to serve as a catharsis in the middle of a decade that had seen Hemingway growing unsure of his direction, as evidenced by his own shift from fiction to nonfiction. One question that he had to answer for himself concerned the writer's responsibility to the mass of his fellow men, and in *To Have and Have Not* he dismisses the notion that mankind can be served by the mechanical grinding out of thesis novels. (Unkind critics might say that the novel ironically illustrates the same point by its own failure.)

Although none of the works of the 1930s definitively settles all of the questions Hemingway had raised about the problems of the writer, *To Have and Have Not* comes to a specific conclusion about writing in order to conform to social trends. The example of Richard Gordon shows that the writer must be true to himself, not to the critics, if he is to maintain his integrity. The more important question that Hemingway had to settle in his own mind before he could progress in his career was whether he had been right in baring his soul to his reading public. As his second marriage deteriorated, it must have seemed impossible for a writer to have both a distinguished career and a happy personal life.

## "The Snows of Kilimanjaro"

Perhaps Hemingway's most ambitious single work published during the 1930s, "The Snows of Kilimanjaro" grew out of a serious illness that marred the author's African safari with Pauline in 1933–1934. Reminiscent of François Villon's "Mais où sont les neiges d'antan?" "The Snows of Kilimanjaro," as has been widely recognized, strongly appeals to the nostalgic feelings most readers share, feelings of regret for lost opportunities and of nostalgia for what was best in the past. More importantly, however, it grew out of Hemingway's increasing awareness of the perils writers face. "Snows" is Hemingway's successful attempt to convey this awareness almost "as though it telescoped so that you might put it all into one paragraph if you could get it right" (*Short Stories* 68) or, if not into a paragraph, at least into one powerfully compressed short story that examines the nature of literary fame and the possible heresies of which a writer may be guilty.

Hemingway had had occasion to reflect on his own mortality in late 1933 and early 1934 when he contracted amoebic dysentery while hunting in Africa. Although he attempted to endure the disease and continue his safari, he eventually gave in to Phillip Percival's insistence that he be hospitalized after his lower intestine prolapsed. He was flown out of the hunting camp on the Serengeti Plain and received treatment in Nairobi.[69] While he was probably not in danger of death, the experience was severe enough to cause Hemingway to imagine a writer who was about to die and to examine through his character some of the failings to which writers are subject. Another powerful stimulus was Hemingway's growing awareness that as his fame increased and he associated with new friends from his second wife's social class, he was moving away from the identity that had nurtured his early success.[70] Like Harry Walden, Hemingway was no longer the hungry young writer who lived simply in a Left Bank apartment, forsaking creature comforts for single-minded artistic commitment.

Even though the manuscript that Hemingway sent to Arnold Gingrich for publication in *Esquire* shows signs of hasty, last-minute corrections, with pencil additions to the typescript and a cut-and-paste interpolation made near the end of the story,[71] "The Snows of Kilimanjaro" was the result of considerable reworking before it got to the stage represented by that typescript. Item 702 in Kennedy Library, for example, is an earlier version of the story entitled "The Happy Ending." Although it follows the general outline of the finished story, this version is less sophisticated, beginning with the heavy irony of its title, in obvious contrast with the subtlety of Hemingway's final title.

Hemingway's concern with the epigraphs he chose for the story is also a sign of his determination to make "Snows" one of his major works. Even in the manuscript he sent to Gingrich, he included not only the epigraph that appears in the story as printed in *The Short Stories of Ernest Hemingway* but a second epigraph that pointedly suggests the main theme of the story. A quotation from Vivienne de Watteville, this second epigraph obviously applies to literary fame as well as to its ostensible subject, the climbing of Kilimanjaro: "The difficulties, he said, were not in the actual climbing. It was a long grind, and success depended not on skill, but on one's ability to withstand the high altitude. His parting words were that I must make the attempt soon, before there was any risk of the rains setting in. V. De Watteville [*sic*]."[72] Hemingway must have been pleased with the passage as a powerful found symbol for the writer's career. Not only does it parallel the writer's climb to literary acclaim—through the ability to withstand the "long grind" rather than through mere innate skill—and suggest the burdens of fame (the "ability to withstand . . . the altitude") but it contains two symbols that were personally important to Hemingway, the mountain, representing purity and detachment, and the rain, suggesting death and defeat.

Nevertheless, Hemingway had reservations about the use of the second epigraph. The margin of the *Esquire* manuscript contains a holograph note that reads, "Maybe better out. EH."[73] One can only speculate about why the second epigraph was better left out. Did Hemingway think that it rendered his message too explicit and removed the mystery inherent in the epigraph he did use? Did he think that it overlapped or clashed with the epigraph about the desiccated carcass of the leopard lying forever at the top of the mountain—the House of God? Whatever his reason, Hemingway chose to omit the second epigraph and let the first stand alone to prepare readers for the story.

Hemingway worked hard on the first epigraph, revising it until it delivered its oracular message in just the right wording, as Item 704 attests. He moved the reference to the Masai term for the summit (*Ngàje Ngài*) from the end of the passage to its current position in the second sentence, and he pruned a first prosaic attempt to describe the carcass of the leopard.[74] Representing the dying writer who had dared to make the Promethean gesture of climbing into the realm of the gods, the leopard is present, but the wording in the original passage lacks the crispness Hemingway's editing achieved in the final version.

The story introduced by this guidebooklike description of Kilimanjaro depicts the heightened awareness of a writer, Harry Walden in the manuscript, as he nears death and suddenly faces the reality of what his artistic life has become, as if the approach of death were a "wind that makes a candle flicker and the flame go tall" (*Short Stories* 67). As his writer's conscience flares up into a last bright flame before his death, Harry sees illuminated all the mistakes he has made and the sins he has committed against his literary talent. The corruption of the progressive disease from which Harry is dying symbolizes the progressive moral decay resulting from his series of transgressions. The "painless" nature of the comfortable life of sloth into which he has allowed himself to sink, like the painless gangrene from which Harry suffers, can mean the end of hope for the literary distinction that he has sought. On its most important level, the story is about the achievement of literary immortality and the nature of that honor.

Harry's regret about the work he has left undone is first introduced on the third page of the story. "Now it was all over," Harry reflects. "So now he would never have a chance to finish it." He has saved up certain experiences, not writing about them "until he knew enough to write them well" (54). But now as he nears death, he begins to realize that this notion might have been merely a fiction to excuse his fear that he might attempt the stories and fail: "[H]e would not have to fail at trying to write them either. Maybe you could never write them, and that was why you put them off and delayed the starting" (54). It is a realization that Harry, anesthetized by alcohol and by the comforting remarks of the wealthy people with whom he has been associating, has fended off for many years.

The lost opportunities appear in the italicized passages throughout the story and span twenty years of an eventful life. Even more powerfully compressed than the "miniatures" that made up *in our time* (1924), these passages contain what Hemingway claimed was the raw material for four novels, a statement that is not as great an exaggeration as a skeptic might assume.[75] The fact that he was willing to squander so much of his artistic capital—for these vignettes represent Hemingway's capital as surely as they do Harry's—strongly underscores the importance of his conscious decision that a writer should not hold back his stories for any reason. He must not allow his own privacy or that of loved ones to keep him from using the truth, nor should he fall victim to Harry's greatest artistic sin and allow himself to put off their use until he believes his skill is great enough to create masterpieces of his material. Hemingway had commented on this masterpiece complex in *Green Hills of Africa*, published the previous year, that he knew two "good writers who cannot write because they have lost confidence through reading critics" (23). One of these two was certainly Fitzgerald, then struggling to finish *Tender Is the Night*, who had been hurt not by negative reviews but by too much praise. Now the two writers feel that to live up to their reviews, "they must write masterpieces. . . . The critics have made them impotent" (24). He adds that if these writers had simply written, some of their work would have been good and some bad, but the important thing was that the good work would have been published.[76] The way to the summit depends more on a determined application to the "long grind" and a disdain for distractions along the way than it does on skill.

As Harry mentally "writes" the stories that he had saved, each segment suggests a substantial, fully realized story lying beneath it—the best exemplification extant of Hemingway's principle of the iceberg. And if Harry could have completed the stories, his canon would have had an impressive historical, geographical, and thematic range, from tragedies witnessed in World War I and the Greco-Turkish war that followed to the pleasures of postwar skiing in the Austrian Alps and hunting in the American West. The exactness with which Hemingway evokes the rich texture of Harry's experience gives credibility to Harry's internal lament that he has forsaken a great career.

Many of the experiences are so obviously significant that nonwriters would naturally remember them, but as an artist Harry differs from ordinary people. He recalls the many loves he has had and the quarrels that could themselves have furnished the subject matter for stories—just as Hemingway had written "Hills Like White Elephants," "Out of Season," and "A Canary for One" out of his own remembered domestic unhappiness. Harry realizes that he had not only a great ability but a duty to employ that ability: "He had never written any of that because, at first, he never wanted to hurt any one and then it seemed as though there was enough to write without it. But he had always thought that he would

write it finally. There was so much to write. He had seen the world change
. . . and it was his duty to write of it; but now he never would" (66; italics
omitted).

In short, Harry has lost what Robert W. Lewis, Jr., and Max Westbrook call "his sense of selfless dedication" to his art, the dedication that
would have allowed him to write, even about the most painful subjects,
with the necessary objectivity of the artist.[77] Harry's greatest sin against
his talent, then, has been sloth, while a lesser sin has been the opposite
of that committed by Phil in "The Sea Change." While Phil will violate
the privacy of a former lover to use her story in his writing, Harry has
gone to the other extreme—neglecting certain important areas of his experience from a sense of delicacy. Hemingway's treatment of both courses
as dangerous failings suggests the ambivalence he felt about the use of his
private life and the lives of those closest to him. He recognized both sides
of the question, but "The Snows of Kilimanjaro" suggests that he had
personally arrived at the conclusion to which Harry comes too late—that
using private materials is not only justifiable but absolutely necessary if the
artist is to live up to his potential.

Harry recognizes that his art—and all art—is a form of exhibitionism.
At its worst, art is the "crowing" of the artist. Harry tells Helen, " 'Love
is a dunghill. . . . And I'm the cock that gets on it to crow' " (57). In *To
Have and Have Not* Helen Gordon accuses her husband of using his writing to "crow" about extramarital sexual exploits; in "Snows" Harry suggests that his own writing has been partly a chronicle of his personal
sexual experience. However, since his marriage to Helen, he has employed
his sexual powers directly—by pleasing his wealthy wife—rather than sub-
limating them in literature, as he acknowledges with his overtly Freudian
reflection that he has "chosen to make his living with something else instead of a pen or a pencil" (60). But Harry's attraction for Helen is more
than sexual: she soaks up the writer's vitality as a feeding vampire might.

Similarly, the rich people who surround Harry and Helen are pleased
to associate with a well-known writer, partaking of his strength and vitality even though they "were all much more comfortable when he did not
work" (59). Being outsiders, they cannot know that a writer is a writer
only when he is actively writing, and they assume that the empty shell of
a writer reflects fame on those who surround it. Harry salves his conscience by pretending that he is "a spy in their country," studying the rich
in order to write about them someday. Ironically he falls into the same
trap as his friend Julian, whose "romantic awe" in the presence of the
wealthy has "wrecked him just as much as any other thing that wrecked
him" (72). Instead of heeding the warning posed by Julian's experience,

Harry allows himself to be seduced by the same comforts—physical and psychological—that have "wrecked" Julian. Unlike Julian, Harry attempts to protect his self-esteem with harsh ironic judgments of the rich.

Harry's most profound analysis of his ruin is a single passage in the first third of the story, a passage that contains echoes of the seven deadly sins as well as the biblical parable of the talents entrusted to the three servants:[78] "He had destroyed his talent by not using it, by betrayals of himself and what he believed in, by drinking so much that he blunted the edge of his perceptions, by laziness, by sloth, and by snobbery, by pride and by prejudice. . . . What was his talent anyway? It was a talent all right but instead of using it, he had traded on it. It was never what he had done, but always what he could do" (60). The rest of Harry's regrets play variations on this summary of his faults as an author. Perhaps Hemingway had Fitzgerald partially in mind when he created Harry (although it is Julian who is most closely identified with Fitzgerald), for he felt that Fitzgerald had betrayed his talent by using his manuscript of *The Last Tycoon* the way "a mineing [*sic*] prospector" uses "a salted mine," never intending to complete the book but continuing to draw advances from Scribner's.[79] But Hemingway also had to be aware that his own career had taken a wrong turn since those days in Paris when he was considered the most promising writer of his generation. "The Snows of Kilimanjaro" should be read not as an indictment of a specific writer, however, but as an examination of what can go wrong with the creative life of *any* writer. As Hemingway had noted in *Green Hills of Africa*, something does go wrong with most American writers, and often, like Harry, and perhaps like Hemingway himself (as he might have feared), they fail to fulfill their early promise.

In *Green Hills of Africa* Hemingway had suggested that the ruin of American writers was caused by economic problems: after the financial success of their early works, they developed expensive tastes and were forced "to write to keep up their establishments, their wives, and so on, and they write slop" (23). Harry's predicament, however, shows another aspect of the successful writer's financial dilemma. The money that Helen has brought to their marriage has made Harry so comfortable that he no longer exerts himself. Although other sins are mentioned—drinking excessively and prostituting his sexual and creative vitality—Harry's primary sin against his talent is the same one attacked in the biblical parable. Like the unwise servant who fails to increase the yield of his talent, Harry has "destroyed his talent by not using it" (60). Once he had traveled around the world seeking material for his fiction; now, like Helen's rich friends, whom he despises, he seeks sensations for their own sake.

But traces of Harry's former virtues and his identity as a writer persist in spite of neglect. A writer is an illusionist, creating images for his audience. Lying on his deathbed, Harry incorporates both artist and audience in his own person: he creates the illusion that recalling the stories he has never told is, in fact, the act of writing them. After his internal monologues, he tells Helen that he has been writing, and he seems to believe that he has been. Lacking a stenographer to transcribe his last attempts at fiction, Harry internalizes them, and the effort of recalling them and structuring them—in his mind if not on paper—leaves him exhausted. He is in this state, emptied as if from a prolific writing session, on the last night that he lives.

Harry's vision at the hour of his death is the last creation of his artistic consciousness. With no time left to tell the stories and explore the themes that his reverie has engendered, Harry's mind focuses on the problem that most concerns the artist—his own chances for literary immortality. During his last moments, his artistic consciousness creates an elaborate metaphor for the career of the artist.

With his conductor Compton, a surrealistic figure comparable not only to Charon[80] but to Vergil, Harry leaves behind his earthbound camp and, to a large extent, the reminders of mortality represented by the decaying leg, the vultures, and the hyena. Moving away from earth, he views it with the detachment of the artist—the hills flattening, the plain spreading, the animal life diminishing in size and importance as his removal from the day-to-day events intensifies. He makes discoveries—"new water that he had never known of" during his life on earth—and flies through an airborne storm high above the earth. As Compton smiles and beckons, Harry sees ahead the "unbelievably white" top of Kilimanjaro and realizes that it is his destination (76). Removed from earth and its constraints, Harry's soul is preserved, like the work from his early productive period, in the snows of the mountaintop, far above the mundane concerns of nonartistic men and women.

But the story does not end at the top of Kilimanjaro. Instead, the third-person narrator returns to the camp and Helen's discovery of Harry's dead body, its gangrenous leg divested of its dressings, displaying its gruesome testimony to Harry's mortal corruption. This ending serves as a reminder that the writer is two beings. While the artistic self soars, like Daedalus, the mortal self may fall back to earth like Icarus. The earthbound part of the artist may fester on earth, causing misery and pain to those closest to him. Thus the final depiction of Harry is not as a triumphant Faustian figure, suggested by Wirt Williams,[81] but as both artist and frail mortal, a bittersweet duality encompassing both triumph and tragedy, depending on whether the perspective is short term or long term.

In works published during Hemingway's lifetime, Harry is the most successful characterization of a writer, a multifaceted portrait that reveals different aspects of the artist's problems, and "The Snows of Kilimanjaro" is the most penetrating exploration. Although its open-ended conclusion suggests that the conflicts within the artist would continue to trouble him, Hemingway, like his character Nick Adams, had temporarily purged a serious problem by writing about it, incorporating many of his own doubts in Harry. The catharsis would clear the air sufficiently so that, after a brief interlude during which he considered various aspects of the writer's role in time of war, he could progress to the writing of his best book of the decade, *For Whom the Bell Tolls*, which is relatively free of artistic questions. But *The Fifth Column* and the civil war stories suggest that his artistic preoccupations remained to be dealt with, and Hemingway would also return to them in his two posthumous novels, in which writers are important figures.

# 3

## *The Writer at War: An Interlude*

IN THE INTRODUCTION to *Men at War* (1942), Hemingway said of his goal in compiling the book that the writer must always tell the truth: "His standard of fidelity to the truth should be so high that his invention, out of his experience, should produce a truer account than anything factual can be."[1] In the same introduction, however, he noted that the best writing about World War I had been completed and published only after the war had been over for several years, when the writers had gained a necessary distance from the events about which they were finally able to write. He admitted that he was not impartial about the current war—that he wanted the Allies to win World War II and that he had three sons who might well participate in battle if the war were not won quickly. Finally, and perhaps most important, he stated that in time of war it was necessary "to suspend your imagination and live completely in the very second of the present minute"(xxvii). That faculty, he said, is the "greatest gift a soldier can acquire" (xxvii), but he added that the soldier's temperament is the direct opposite of the writer's. The writer's imagination, in other words, must never shut down, and he can never afford to ignore the tragedies and suffering to which the ideal soldier must be oblivious.

Although he was writing about another war, the conflict between man of action and man of letters that Hemingway attempted to analyze in these remarks is the very one that had plagued him during the Spanish civil war just a few years before. His play *The Fifth Column* and a cluster of related short stories are dominated by the intellectual and emotional crises of a series of writer figures who can be rather closely identified with Hemingway himself. The protagonists of several of these short stories bear Hemingway's initials, and Philip Rawlings, the main character of *The Fifth Column*, bears the same first name as several of Hemingway's other writer figures.

In effect, the Spanish civil war and World War II caused Hemingway to interrupt the meditation on the role of the writer and his responsibilities to his talent and to his fellow human beings that was evident in works such as *To Have and Have Not* and "The Snows of Kilimanjaro." Yet, from time to time in *The Fifth Column*, in the civil war short stories, and in one story of World War II, the writer's problem underlies the main theme. In several of the stories, for example, the protagonist is either a journalist who reports on what he sees, ideally without making the kinds of subjective interpolations that give fiction its distinctive voice, or a filmmaker who directs the filming of war scenes in the service not of art but of propaganda for the Spanish Republic. These filmmakers anticipate Thomas Hudson in Hemingway's unfinished postwar novel, *Islands in the Stream*, both because they are visual artists for whom meaning is captured not in words but in images and because they have had to give up their art for the duration of the war, and they have lost greatly in doing so.

## The Fifth Column

Hemingway's play about the Spanish civil war, *The Fifth Column* (1938), was the first literary fruit of his participation in that conflict. Composed rapidly between August and late October of 1937, it offers convincing proof of Hemingway's later contention that good war literature could only be written some years after the experience. As Hemingway intended, the play gives an authentic sense of life in Madrid under the constant threat of death from insurgent artillery. As he did not intend, it also offers some negative perspectives on the Loyalist forces and their foreign supporters. Finally, as Carlos Baker has accurately pointed out, the play has a number of autobiographical aspects:

> [Hemingway] amused himself by giving his protagonist, Philip Rawlings, certain habits and qualities of his own. Rawlings had "big shoulders and a walk like a gorilla," commonly skipped breakfast, read all the morning papers, liked sandwiches made of bully beef and raw onion, drank regularly at Chicote's. . . . In short, the figure of Philip Rawlings, a correspondent secretly engaged as a counterspy in besieged Madrid, was a projection of Ernest himself, based on his imagination of how it might feel to be an actual insider.[2]

Unfortunately, these ingredients have lost their freshness with the passage of years, and without the topical relevance that the play had for its 1930s audience, it remains one of Hemingway's weakest works. Still, it has some interest beyond its autobiographical elements. It is thematically tied to the works just before it, *To Have and Have Not* and "The Snows of Kilimanjaro," and to postwar works such as *Islands in the Stream* and *The Garden of Eden*. In spite of his preoccupation with the war, in *The Fifth Column* Hemingway continued to explore some of his complex feelings about the role of the writer, even if that theme was relegated to the margins of the play. He explores these ideas through his delineation of the characters of Robert Preston, Dorothy Bridges, and Philip Rawlings—all writers or journalists of one sort or another.

Preston's role—like that of Hubert Elliot in "Mr. and Mrs. Elliot" or Robert Prentiss, Braddocks, or Cohn in *The Sun Also Rises*—offers a negative prototype of the writer. Preston ridicules Dorothy Bridges for not understanding anything that is happening in Spain, but his own understanding seems purely cerebral: it is based more on reading maps and listening to conversations at Chicote's than on personal observation of actual battles at the front. In his conversation with Anita the Moorish tart and the hotel electrician (act 1, scene 2), he proves that he understands the language—he translates several conversations for the less proficient Dorothy—but demonstrates that he does not understand the thinking of the Spanish defenders of the city. This scene is most revealing, for the writer is by definition a man of words, not a man of action.

Preston is first depicted looking at a map, an indication that his grasp of the war comes to him secondhand, through interpretive media. He reinforces this impression and also proves that he is a coward when he goes to the basement as soon as the nightly shelling starts, even though he is the only one in the room to feel endangered by the artillery. Dorothy Bridges pronounces the final summary of Preston's method of writing about the war when she says, "He never goes to the front. He just writes about it."[3] Preston is the sort of author whom Hemingway despised, the "quick study" who writes about a profound subject without the necessary experience to offer a true picture of the events he chronicles. Preston, like the people "you meet . . . [,] like Michael Arlen at Saint Moritz" (82), has no relevance during wartime.

Rawlings overlooks Dorothy Bridges's faults for a time because he is sexually attracted to her and because she sincerely tries to comprehend the war even though her privileged Vassar education has left her ill prepared to do so. When Dorothy is introduced, she promises to "finish that *Cosmopolitan* article just as soon as I understand things the *least* bit better" (10), but she never reaches an understanding of the conflict. Rawlings pays Dorothy a carefully limited compliment when he tells Max that she writes "quite well too, when she's not too lazy" (66). At one point, he reminds Dorothy of her alleged business in Madrid when he asks her if it's true that she's a "lady war correspondent" and commands her to "get out of here and . . . write an article" (33). Hemingway obviously used his own subjective—and curiously unsympathetic—view of Martha Gellhorn as a model for his portrait of Dorothy Bridges as well as for the correspondent Elizabeth in "Landscape with Figures": Martha had gone to Bryn Mawr, a similarly prestigious school, and her physical description matched that of Bridges. Martha, however, was anything but the dilettante depicted in *The Fifth Column*.

One major difference between Dorothy Bridges and her source is their relative ambition. Unlike Martha, Dorothy channels her ambition mostly through Rawlings. Her assumptions about Philip's future writing suggest an undisclosed literary career in Philip's background. She tells him that when the war is over, the two of them will escape to a "lovely" environment where he can write whatever he wants to write—although she has some very specific ideas about what he *should* want to write: novels, articles, and a nonfiction book about the civil war. She also proposes that he do a book about politics, since "books on politics sell *forever*" (24). Dorothy's agenda is more practical than idealistic, but she tries to acknowledge Philip's current political interests as she perceives them by suggesting a book of dialectics, which would appeal to Philip's conscience and would also be instantly marketable in the 1930s. Dorothy anticipates Catherine in *The Garden of Eden*, the would-be helpful feminine partner who effectively paralyzes the writer with her help. Similarly, the imagined "lovely" background anticipates the "Eden" in the south of France, where David Bourne will experience both his greatest triumphs and his worst tragedy.

In spite of the flaws in her vision, Dorothy Bridges represents Philip's literary potential, which he must hold in abeyance, like his love for her, during the course of the war. Dorothy's surname, Bridges, suggests her unsuccessful role in recalling Philip to his true career: her effort to draw him back across the gap that separates life and literature, war and peace, fails—as it must because she considers the ends or goals of writing while she ignores the writer's own compulsion to express an inner vision, to create his own fictions. Catherine Bourne will make a very similar mistake with David.

Although the raw material for great fiction—or at least competent reporting—is all around Dorothy, she fails to perceive it. She summarizes the very incident that Hemingway would use as the basis for "The Butterfly and the Tank" less than one year after completing his play, but she fails to see its potential. She remarks that the whole affair was "*very* depressing," not because an innocent prankster was killed but because of the victim's dirty and shabby clothes and her personal inconvenience: like the other patrons of Chicote's, she was sequestered for two hours while the police investigated the shooting, and no drinks were served during the investigation (22). Herself unable to turn such material into literature, she can only serve as flawed muse to Rawlings, the true artist.

Philip Rawlings's complex characterization is achieved through an ironic contrast between Dorothy's perception of him and the audience's superior perception. Early in the play, Dorothy tells the Spanish chambermaid, who knows more about Philip than she does, that Rawlings is wasting his time in Madrid: although he is accredited by a London newspaper, someone at the censorship office has told her that he seldom sends any dispatches. She fails to see that, as Philip will later describe himself, he is really a "second-rate cop," or a counterspy, masquerading as a "third-rate newspaperman" (36).

Dorothy cannot understand why a nonwriting journalist who never sends dispatches—and who disappears for long periods and comes back covered with mud—should confess to her that he cannot sleep because he gets "the horrors" (57). Her grasp of reality, like that of Robert Cohn and Richard Gordon, has been blunted by the reading she has done in college and continues to do in the war zone, as Rawlings suggests when he accuses her of reading *Esquire* while waiting for him in a bar. Although he himself wrote extensively for *Esquire* and probably intended the allusion to be an insider joke, Hemingway was also aware that the leftists of the 1930s thought the magazine pandered to capitalists, and he attributes to Rawlings that same disdain that left-leaning critics had expressed about a serious author writing for such a publication.

In the third scene of the first act, the set for *The Fifth Column* depicts Philip's and Dorothy's rooms as having a connecting door with a large wall poster tacked over the doorway. The two lovers' lives are graphically separated by the poster, and metaphorically by the war, even when the door is open. A similar barrier separates Philip from his writing. He never writes fiction or even news dispatches on stage, but he does work with the communists as a commissar. He regretfully says goodbye to his mistress and, by extension, to his writing in two speeches near the end of *The Fifth Column*. He tells Dorothy that the world is about to enter a series of undeclared wars that may last fifty years; he has enlisted "for the duration" (80). For now, she is unable to "bridge" the way back to his peacetime identity or his writing career. Philip declares his solidarity with the workers and fighters who will oppose fascism in terms that anticipate the words of Robert Jordan: "where I go now I go alone, or with others who go there for the same reason I go" (83). If Hemingway's theme in *A Farewell to Arms* is that war kills love, in *The Fifth Column* he asserts that it also kills art, or at least that it makes the production of art impossible for the duration of the conflict.

It is extremely ironic that, some six months after composing *The Fifth Column*, Hemingway disproved its contention that art could not be created in the midst of war by writing a very short story that encapsulated the tragedy of war in a mere three pages. William Braasch Watson has traced the writing of "Old Man at the Bridge" from the field notes Hemingway wrote on 17 April 1938 to the final draft, sent to *Ken* by cable later that same day, as proved by the date accompanying the military censor's stamp. Watson concludes that Hemingway "probably had no more than four or five hours . . . in which to write it."[4] The story was then published by *Ken* on 19 May 1938, just over a month after it was first conceived, yet Hemingway thought enough of this rapidly composed story to include it in *The Fifth Column and the First 49*. However, most of the civil war stories written after *The Fifth Column* and "Old Man at the Bridge" continue the play's theme of the writer who must forgo his serious artistic work while he participates in the active life required in wartime.

## The Writer and the Civil War

Soon after completing "Old Man at the Bridge" in mid-April 1938, Hemingway returned to a writer protagonist somewhat like Philip Rawlings in a series of stories. Most of the protagonists in these stories bear Hemingway's initials, either in correct order or inverted to H. E., as first noted by Kenneth G. Johnston.[5] Paul Smith has remarked on the cohesion of the three stories set in Chicote's, a Madrid bar, pointing out that all three concern "the issue of the writer's engagement and responsibility in the political controversies surrounding a war he observed as a foreigner" and suggesting that the stories have in common "a writer-narrator contemplating both his aesthetic and moral involvement in his material."[6] To these three stories, "Landscape with Figures" should probably be added, because even though Hemingway never published that story in his lifetime, he thought of collecting it with the other civil war stories in the late 1930s. More important, Edwin Henry, the narrator of two of the Chicote stories, is also the narrator of "Landscape with Figures."

Sometime between May and September 1938, Hemingway completed "The Denunciation," a story narrated by a writer named Henry Emmunds, who also plays a principal part in the plot. The title of the story seems to refer to a waiter's call to the security police, who arrest Luis Delgado, a Franco follower who appears at the bar, but the denunciation is also that of Emmunds because he supplies the waiter with the telephone number of Seguridad headquarters, and at the end of the story, he tries to take the blame for the denunciation, supposedly so that the fascist will die without ever knowing that a waiter at his favorite bar has turned him in.

If Emmunds feels culpable for a wrong that he has not directly committed, it may be because he feels guilty for what Kenneth Johnston calls his "moral aloofness" or refusal to commit himself completely to the Loyalist cause he claims to support.[7] The waiter who denounces Delgado approaches Emmunds six times, asking what he should do. Emmunds answers that it is not his business, that it is the waiter's own problem, or that it is not his war, since he is a foreigner. Yet something else is also at stake in the story. Emmunds manipulates the waiter into calling by giving him the telephone number, and he does so partly because he is a writer.

As he examines his conscience after supplying the number, Emmunds has to admit to himself that one reason for having done so is "the always-dirty desire to see how people act under an emotional conflict, that makes writers such attractive friends" (97). The writer is like a scientist who performs an experiment: not only does he dehumanize himself by inhumanely observing others while they are under stress, but he may also set up stressful situations so that he may observe them. In this case, Emmunds's experiment will yield three possible reactions for the writer to treat in some later fiction. First, he sees how the waiter reacts as he is torn between his conflicting emotions. Second, he can see how Delgado reacts when the Seguridad forces arrest him (a reaction that he finally chooses *not* to observe, leaving the bar before the police arrive). Third, he can analyze his own reaction to his betrayal of a former acquaintance.

While the reader may understand and perhaps even sympathize with Emmunds's experiment and the motive that lies behind it, Emmunds's own view of himself as revealed so starkly in the first-person narration colors the reader's response. Both "always-dirty" and the bitterly ironic statement that writers make "attractive friends" emphasize Emmunds's recognition of the dubious morality of his part in the denunciation. The allusion to Pilate in the same paragraph carries a host of similarly judgmental connotations. But perhaps even more damning is Emmunds's admission just a few lines later: "My curiosity as to how people would act in this case had been long ago, and shamefully, satisfied" (97). That the denunciation was superfluous is underscored by the fact that Emmunds leaves the bar before the arrest, which he refuses to witness. In Emmunds's final exchange with the waiter, the writer's moral dilemma is emphasized as the waiter refuses to tell Delgado that Emmunds denounced him because " 'Each man must take his responsibility' " (98). Emmunds now fully understands his own responsibility, and his attempt to expiate it, by taking the blame, fails. Hemingway's lengthy and explicit examination of the writer's culpability in "The Denunciation" sharply contrasts with his more subtle treatment of the same issue in "The Sea Change."

The reader's unfavorable impression of Emmunds deepens with frequent references to the ten pounds of fresh meat he has picked up at the American Embassy. His willingness to take advantage of such a privilege when most Spaniards are denied meat strikes the reader as somehow wrong. It becomes clear that the meat is a scarce and valuable commodity, a thing of value to be traded, like Delgado himself, whom Emmunds "trades" for a moment of insight that he may later use in his writing. In "The Butterfly and the Tank" Hemingway uses the Spanish term *fiambre*, meaning "cold meat," and explains that in slang the term connotes a corpse—a connection that ties Emmunds's package of raw beef to Delgado's body when the reader realizes how quickly the fascist will be executed. With obvious Freudian "forgetfulness," Emmunds leaves the meat behind when he leaves Chicote's; he must be reminded to take it with him, just as he must take up the burden of responsibility for his role in the denunciation.

Emmunds judges himself severely for his part in the affair, even calling Seguridad headquarters and directing his friend Pepe to tell Delgado that he, Emmunds, betrayed him—a futile gesture because, as Pepe points out, Delgado's end will be the same. By trying to take the blame, Emmunds seems to be seeking absolution for his part in the incident. But in a larger sense, Emmunds may feel the need to atone not just for his present transgression but for an ongoing crime against humanity that a writer may commit repeatedly. In a sense, any writer "denounces" humanity for its failures. This minor theme surfaces briefly in each of the other three stories that are tied by their protagonists to Hemingway's own identity as a writer.

"The Butterfly and the Tank," the second of the three stories set in Chicote's, is narrated by a nameless writer. The story focuses on the social role of the writer: does he have an obligation, in time of war, to refrain from treating material or employing incidents that may be harmful to a cause with which he sympathizes? Does the literary value of a story that cries out to be written outweigh the political harm that writing it may do?

The narrator encounters an oddly matched couple in Chicote's, an extremely forceful-looking woman whom he describes as "terrible" and her notably weaker consort. Sitting at the same table with the couple, the narrator finds them the sort of uninteresting people who test the assumption that a writer is "supposed to have an insatiable curiosity about all sorts of people" (102). Like the narrator, the forceful woman has strong Loyalist sympathies, but her humorless observations make him dislike her. This static scene recedes into insignificance when a man is shot for spraying three soldiers with a flit gun. Absurdly, when the police arrive, the killer and his friends break through their lines, while all other patrons of the bar are detained for a lengthy "investigation."

After the shooting, the writer offers the opinion that "the whole thing was a pretty good story" (106) that he would write sometime. The woman rebukes him, telling him that writing such a story would be "prejudicial" to the Republic, presumably because it would suggest that law had broken down in communist Spain. The writer counters with the argument that he had seen numerous shootings in Spain under the monarchy as well as in New York, Chicago, and Key West. Why should he not write about a tragic event that evolves out of comic circumstances—a drunk spraying other drinkers with a flit gun?

From the detached point of view of an uninvolved observer or reporter, the writer has seen the "comic" killing as the basis for an amusing story. However, the next day, the waiters and manager of Chicote's influence him to react more humanely when they tell him more about the victim, an invalided soldier whose flit gun was filled with cologne, and about his distraught wife. Like the narrator, the manager sees the incident as the germ of a story that must be written, but he emphasizes the pathos of the event—an example of gaiety colliding with the tragedy of war, much as if a butterfly should collide with a tank. The narrator rejects the "Spanish metaphysics" of the manager's interpretation, but he also rejects his own early impulse to tell a comic story. In the end, his recollection of the appearance of the dead man, so small, insignificant, and gray, and his final reflection on the wife's grief leave him pondering the futility of war. The metaphysical title, now used ironically, helps to underscore that futility.[8]

In "The Butterfly and the Tank" Hemingway returned, if only briefly, to the theme of the writer's social responsibility that he had treated at some length in *To Have and Have Not*. In the novel he had shown how an author who panders to social causes proves to be artistically bankrupt. In "The Butterfly and the Tank," he sketches the opposite proposition. The free writer, who becomes interested only in material in which he perceives genuine literary possibilities, may be censored by hostile politically motivated censors (the forceful woman) or by well-meaning friends lobbying for what they take to be "literary" interpretations (Chicote's manager). The writer's own artistic conscience, however, will lead him to make the right decision, to remind himself that the story he tells has nothing to do with politics or metaphysics. Finally, only the writer can shape his own story, for every story may be viewed from quite different points of view and told for quite different purposes.

The thinking represented in stories such as "The Butterfly and the Tank" was a necessary step if Hemingway was to write honestly about the Spanish civil war, for in any honest fiction he would have to admit—as he later would in both "Under the Ridge" and *For Whom the Bell Tolls*—that the Republic was not a workers' paradise and that its military and political forces were capable of the same sort of corrupt practices and atrocities that had been committed by Franco's insurgents. Like "The Denunciation," "The Butterfly and the Tank" can be viewed as an exercise in perspective: in both stories, artistic and moral quandaries hinge on the attitude of the narrator toward his story. In both, the writer can choose or adopt a point of view that will justify his actions, exculpate him from blame, or force him to accept responsibility with its attendant guilt. The other three civil war stories also explore perspectives.

One pair of the civil war stories is united by three common features: each employs writer Edwin Henry as the protagonist, each has Henry involved in filming the war (like Hemingway during the making of *The Spanish Earth*), and each criticizes a flawed would-be writer. Although the various protagonists of most of the civil war stories—Henry Emmunds, Edwin Henry, and the unnamed narrator of "The Butterfly and the Tank"—all seem to be writers by profession, like Philip Rawlings in *The Fifth Column*, none spends his time writing. On the contrary, Hemingway depicts writers who *do* write while the war is going on, like Robert Preston in *The Fifth Column*, as unworthy writers, whose actions range from ridiculous to despicable. Together, "Night Before Battle" and "Landscape with Figures" suggest that Hemingway was ambivalent about the noncombatant role he had been playing in the war and about the role of a writer who uses war as an opportunity to eavesdrop on the rest of mankind during a life-and-death struggle.

The fact that Edwin Henry is engaged in filming the war is undeniably autobiographical but is also appropriately significant. Hemingway must have realized that an artist standing by passively, filming the anguished conflicts of people with whom he is intimately acquainted, functions as a powerful symbol for the writer's method of gathering his material. His erstwhile literary friend John Dos Passos, who was also involved with the Contemporary Historians' film project, had used "The Camera Eye" as a recurring segment treating the most autobiographical portions of the narrative in his massive trilogy *USA*. A camera records what it is focused upon, supposedly without commentary and without passing judgment. It represents objective perception, while the participants in the action being filmed are too caught up in the excitement and danger of the small scenes in which they play a part to perceive the entire picture of the military operations. At its worst, the camera represents voyeurism, recalling Helen Gordon's criticism of her writer husband in *To Have and Have Not* and anticipating Catherine Bourne's resentment of David's "storing away" emotional material for future use in his fiction in *The Garden of Eden.*

In both "Night Before Battle" and "Landscape with Figures," Henry feels guilt and dissatisfaction because the camera is so far removed from the action, set up in houses whose shadows will shield the camera lenses from the sunlight so that they will not reflect light and draw fire. In the former story, the very distance of the camera (and the filmmakers) from the battle gives an air of unreality to the scene filmed. Soldiers and tanks resemble insects and toys; the absence of humanity and death in the perceptions of the film crew is emphasized in the imagery the narrator employs: "if we could get the sudden fountainings of earth, the puffs of shrapnel, the rolling clouds of smoke and dust lit by the yellow flash, . . . we would have something that we needed" (111). Thus, the artist's perspective emphasizes color, shape, and movement. However, a different perspective is provided when Edwin Henry spends the evening in Chicote's with Al, an old friend in the tank corps. Perhaps because he operates from a position of relative safety behind enemy lines, Henry has deceived himself during the day, but in the evening he has to admit that his daytime optimism about the offensive has been false. Al serves as an objective correlative for the reservations Henry has begun to develop about the war.

Al is the veteran of many major engagements, but he is convinced that the next morning's offensive is suicidal and that he will be killed. Henry is placed in a position where he must unwillingly hear the last words of a man under extreme stress—the reverse of the situation that Henry Emmunds experiences in "The Denunciation," in which Emmunds set up the tragic situation at least partly out of his writer's desire to watch how someone would react under emotional stress. Edwin Henry tries to convince Al that he will not be killed the next day, but the inevitability of Al's death becomes increasingly apparent to the reader as the evening wears on.

Although Henry seems to be a writer like most of the protagonist-narrators of the civil war stories, his current inactivity as a writer is symbolized by his typewriter, which sits unused on a table in his room in the Hotel Florida, and he seems more politically interested in the outcome of the war than aesthetically interested in the conflict as a source of future material. In short, he reflects Hemingway's own involvement in the Spanish civil war and World War II, both of which curtailed his literary output while they were in progress.

If Edwin Henry is more involved in personal commitments than in his writer's craft, "Night Before Battle" does present—albeit through caricature—one writer who can write about the war even while he is participating in it. Among the visitors to Henry's room in the Florida is Baldy, an American aviator who has just that day performed a genuine act of heroism, shooting down a fascist Junker trimotor bomber and bailing out of his damaged fighter. When his friends ask the drunken flier to tell about the experience, however, his account is disappointing, ironically so, since he takes pains to identify himself as a writer as well as an aviator. He boasts that he has a newspaper clipping that praises his "fresh and original talent for description" (134), and one of his friends fleshes out his literary resume: Baldy writes for the Meridian, Mississippi, *Argus*. When he tries to tell his story, Baldy fails to capture the action as it happened because he falls back on "literary" clichés.

When he looked into the burning Junker, it was like "a blast furnace" (134) and a "raging inferno" (136); the parachutes of the crew members who escaped were like "big beautiful morning glories" (134). Like Henry, who has earlier used similar metaphorical language and viewed the war as spectacle because he is divorced from the action, Baldy has allowed himself to become distanced from the events he describes—"sightseeing" and "watching the spectacle" (135). At least temporarily, Baldy has allowed himself to be divorced from the reality of war. Baldy ignores the satirical fellow flier who tells him that he should write for *War Aces*, a pulp magazine, and admonishes him to tell what happened "in plain language." When Baldy offers additional facts about the engagement, he slips into the technical clichés of fliers' shoptalk, telling how his squadron moved from a "left echelon of V's" to a "left echelon of echelons" (135).

Juxtaposed with this talky literary flier is Al, the tank commander, who knows that he will die the next day but apologizes for "talking wet" because he has asked Henry to take charge of some personal effects and send them home after his death. Al stoically gambles away the last of his pesetas in a game with the fliers and then, to save Henry's feelings, gruffly resumes the pretense that he will meet Henry the next night at Chicote's. He insists that he's fine, now that he's regained his "perspective." The comment underscores the different perspectives that have been explored in the story. Al creates an effective counterpoint to Baldy: he is obsessed with his impending death because he is so closely in touch with reality that he cannot ignore it, while Baldy—perhaps because he is too much the man of action—fails to observe reality no matter how close to the action he comes. Together, the two illustrate reactions that are polar opposites from which the writer-observer, Edwin Henry, may learn.

Henry's epitaph for Al is so understated that Baldy and his friends would never recognize it as literary. He observes, "You get angry about a lot of things and you, yourself, dying uselessly is one of them" (139). Unlike so many of Hemingway's fallible writers, Henry reacts more strongly to his human side than to his literary side. But he pays for his humane rather than artistic orientation by his failure to write: his typewriter lies silent on the table in his hotel room.

If the problem of artistic perspective is implicit in the above stories, it is made explicit in "Landscape with Figures," where Hemingway's choice of a title underscores the relationship between reality and art and the difference that perspective can make. Unlike Baldy, most writers are spectators rather than men of action, and it is a more typical writer who is portrayed as a negative example of the writer at war in "Landscape with Figures," a civil war story that remained unpublished until it was included in the Finca Vigía edition of the short stories. The story features three writers: Edwin Henry, again working with his camera crew, narrates; a hardworking young woman correspondent named Elizabeth—a more sympathetic treatment by Hemingway of his future wife Martha Gellhorn—gets her first real view of war; and a British writer/correspondent known as the Great Authority, who always dresses like a field marshal, fills a negative role much like that of Robert Preston in *The Fifth Column*.

In the first paragraph Hemingway establishes the gap between perception and reality with Henry's description of a filming post in an abandoned apartment house; the upper floors of the ironically nicknamed "Old Homestead" offer vantage points overlooking the battleground at the edge of the city. The narrator describes an elevator that no longer runs, upper story interior doors that lead not into rooms but into space, and lower floors that are blasted away while the two top floors are unexpectedly intact. Later, the message "DEATH TO JOHNNY," which the narrator prints on an unbroken mirror as a joke, enrages Johnny the cameraman because he perceives the words as if they were reality. The Great Authority also suffers from flawed perspective; Elizabeth bitterly notes that he had told her the observation post was "quite safe." Clearly, he came only because he thought that the area was safe. Instead, the building almost becomes the grave of correspondents and film crew.

Henry and the cameramen are filming from the Old Homestead when the Great Authority brings Elizabeth there. Unlike the camera crew and Henry, who carefully shade their lenses from the sun, the Authority immediately draws artillery fire because his binoculars flash in the sun. When shells begin to hit the building, the Authority's response to real war is panicky—he leaves Elizabeth to be helped to cover by Edwin Henry and flees like a flushed rabbit. Although the Great Authority is considered an expert on war, he recalls Richard Gordon or Robert Preston by showing that he has never encountered the real thing.

Braver than the Great Authority, Elizabeth joins Edwin Henry in watching the battle through binoculars from the observation post after the artillery fire ceases. Although she has been reporting from Madrid for some time and has been sharing the dangers of the populace, she has never been the target of direct fire before. The landscape they view could be considered picturesque: in the foreground are the trenches of the friendly forces and in the background a stone farmhouse partly surrounded by trees. But for the woman, the scene is dominated by the "figures," the soldiers in the middle ground who are soon immobilized into a still life when they are killed or wounded during the ensuing Loyalist assault. She sees infantrymen shot in the back after their advance is repelled, stretcher bearers killed as they attempt to rescue the wounded, and a trapped Loyalist tank burned with the crew inside. In spite of her distance from the battle, she is upset by the scene and says that she never wants to see war again, not out of curiosity "or to make money writing about it" (Finca Vigía edition, 594). She loses her journalist's objectivity and cries for the dead and wounded.

In contrast, the narrator has viewed the scene from a reporter's perspective and sees only an offensive that has failed and a dispatch that isn't "going to be an easy one to write." An unnamed cameraman responds, " 'You must write what can be said' " (595)—one of the most succinct expressions of Hemingway's creed. Unlike a journalist, who will immediately report what he is allowed to write, the artistic writer who is true to his calling enters a war zone to serve as a witness and to write what *must* be written when the war is over—telling the story that cannot be told within the strictures of wartime censorship. Perhaps this act of bearing artistic witness to the truth is the duty of any writer at any time. The same perceptive cameraman later warns Henry not to let Elizabeth see a battle from any closer vantage point: " 'From where she saw it is only a picture' " (596). Here is the other side of the complaint Henry voices in "Night Before Battle": the professional laments his distance from the action; the amateur is horrified by war at whatever distance.

The ending of "Landscape with Figures" is unexpected. After the Great Authority drew fire and then ignominiously fled, the rest of the group snubbed him. Now, on the way back to the cars they will take to the Florida, Elizabeth decides that she doesn't "want anyone to be hurt tonight," (596) not even emotionally. She calls to the Great Authority and they make plans to meet that night with the other correspondents. Even the battle-hardened Henry accedes to the peacemaking gesture and implicitly agrees to join the group in Elizabeth's room that evening. The horror of war is so great that it awakens pity even in marginal participants.

The inept writers in "Night Before Battle" and "Landscape with Figures" recall the emotionally and artistically bankrupt writers of earlier stories such as "Mr. and Mrs. Elliot," *The Sun Also Rises*, and *To Have and Have Not*. Hemingway's last published story about the Spanish civil war, on the other hand, returns to the topic of the true writer who attempts to come to terms with the materials of war. Written in the fall of 1938, when the war was beginning to appear lost, "Under the Ridge" echoes the disillusioned mood of *A Farewell to Arms*. Its story of a principled deserter who is shot after he walks away from a hopeless battle recalls the retreat from Caporetto and Frederic Henry's separate peace. This time, however, a writer is present when the noncombatant battle police summarily execute a deserter. The crux of the story is the writer's disillusioned response to the incident, a heartfelt reaction on Hemingway's part that signals the direction he would take when he began, some six months later, to write a major novel about the war in Spain.

As in "Landscape with Figures," the writer, probably again Edwin Henry, is primarily engaged in filming the battle he witnesses. He reflects that the communist reaction to films of a battle depends on the outcome. If the action were a success, the staff at brigade headquarters would want it recorded on film, but if it were unsuccessful, they might arrest the camera crew. This attitude is similar to the reaction against honest objective writers in "The Butterfly and the Tank," where the doctrinaire communist woman in Chicote's assumes that the writer will employ only favorable aspects of the movement when he writes about the war.

The writer and his companions see two leather-coated secret policemen track down a deserter—a Frenchman in the uniform of the International Brigades who has simply walked away from a suicidal battle "with great dignity" (*Fifth Column* 147)—and hear the shots when the police execute him. A Spanish soldier from Extremadura who has previously proclaimed his hatred for all foreigners is prompted by this shooting to recall the source of his own xenophobia, and his story of harsh military discipline imposed by party members complements the central incident in "Under the Ridge."

He knew a young boy from his own province who had also evaded battle but later regretted his fear and did his best to serve in the army. Despite his return to duty, the same two battle policemen executed him on the same spot where he had previously shot himself in the hand. A third incident is briefly sketched when the writer hears of a tank commander in the present battle who had to get drunk in order to have enough nerve to lead an attack that would obviously fail. Because he got too drunk to lead the attack, he was sentenced to be shot as soon as he was sober.

The last page of "Under the Ridge" is the most important part of the story, dwelling on the writer's reaction to what he has witnessed and heard. His first reaction is the immediate response of the wartime correspondent: he asks what he can write in his dispatch and is told that he can write only about the material contained in the "official communiqué." This press release will obviously falsify the results of the battle to put the best possible face on the defeat. But the pictures in the writer's mind, unlike the film of his cameramen, tell a more truthful and timeless story. Although he complains that he cannot write his story now—the harsh censorship and the life of action he is leading conspire to stifle his creativity—his friend the general tells him to " 'write it all afterwards' " (151). Hemingway himself would write it all afterward when he composed *For Whom the Bell Tolls*, which reflected his ultimate cynicism about the war.

The films of the battle turn out to be only propaganda, not art and not truth. In spite of the ineffectiveness of the tanks in actual battle, on the screen they appear powerful and invulnerable. An "illusion of victory" is projected. The more important record of the battle, however, is not on the movie screen but in the mind of the writer-narrator. When he has the leisure to recreate the war artistically, the image he will emphasize will be a true one, like that of the only true victory achieved that day—by the Frenchman who walks away from the battle with his head held high, prepared to die but not to throw his life away foolishly in an empty gesture of loyalty to a corrupt cause.

Hemingway would use his World War II experiences in the last two books of *Islands in the Stream*, but he also used them in a short story that remained unpublished until it was included in the Finca Vigía edition of his stories. "Black Ass at the Crossroads" intensifies the disillusioned view of war that pervades the stories about the Spanish civil war. The story opens with the mistaken shooting of a French civilian and centers on the young German soldier whose death at the hand of the narrator induces "black ass," or depression. Although the narrator is never explicitly identified as a writer, his wartime activities are the same sort that led to

Hemingway's own court-martial for bearing arms as a correspondent, and it is not unlikely that the narrator's sensitivity stems from the fact that he is a writer.

The shooting with which the story opens underscores the absurdity of war. The narrator's partner, Red, shoots the man and is quite pleased with his shot until they realize the dead man is a Frenchman with impeccable papers. Red tries to justify his actions: the man failed to halt even though commanded to do so in French; most Frenchmen who flee from Allied troops have collaborated with the enemy; Red even suggests that the man has "a mean face." But none of these attempts at self-justification obscures the fact that an innocent man has been shot for no good reason. The narrator makes what amends he can by ordering his irregulars to leave the man's money on his body.

More traumatic than the Frenchman's death is that of the German boy, even though he is clearly a uniformed member of the enemy forces. After overseeing the ambush of several German soldiers on bicycles and another party in an armored personnel carrier, the narrator himself shoots another German cyclist, taking the shot at long distance and, like Red at the beginning of the story, gloating over his marksmanship. His elation disappears when he approaches the downed German and sees that he looks no more than seventeen years old; although the bullet has passed through both lungs, the boy is still alive.

In a sequence much like the story of the wounded German sailor in the "At Sea" section of *Islands in the Stream*, the narrator's companions gently move the boy out of the road and dress his wounds. The narrator feels for the boy's pulse, and then is haunted by regrets—the regret that he has shot the boy in the first place and the regret that he did not yield to the impulse to kiss him before he died as Claude, one of the more impulsive French guerrillas, had done. The story closes with Claude and the narrator "splitting [the depression] between us and neither liked our share" (Finca Vigía edition, 589). The writer who goes to war to gain experience may become the victim of that experience when it becomes more than he has bargained for.

*The Fifth Column* and this group of short stories about war, most of which were turned out quickly while Hemingway was close to the action, document what he stated in his introduction to *Men at War*: writers seldom write their best when they are too close to war. Nevertheless, the play and the stories are evidence that Hemingway's interest in writer figures, so apparent in *To Have and Have Not* and "The Snows of Kilimanjaro," continued even when he was employing most of his energies elsewhere. These works are full of writers who are actively involved in a war. Some are authors, such as Philip Rawlings, Henry Emmunds, and Edwin Henry, who may share biographical details with Hemingway himself but who are not always presented in a favorable light. Contrasted with these serious writers are journalistic or literary opportunists—like Robert Preston, the Great Authority, or Dorothy Bridges—who recall the lazy, incompetent, or self-important writers of earlier works from the 1920s and 1930s.

Good or bad, the central writers such as Rawlings share an estrangement from their peacetime literary careers. They have allowed the war to distract them, to channel their energies into helping to fight the war as Philip does, to propagandize for a chosen side as Edwin Henry does, or simply to report on the war to the noncombatant world. As Hemingway implied in *Men at War*, good men of action make bad writers. Good writers may function as men of action when it is necessary, but only by suspending their artistic detachment. They must not only become partisans of one side in the war but must cultivate the soldier's necessary disregard for morality. But the artist can never fully suspend the sensitivity that makes his art possible. When Hemingway's writers do take up arms, as the narrator of "Black Ass at the Crossroads" has done, they suffer attacks of conscience afterward.

The play and the stories about war continue a line of thought concerning the social engagement of the writer introduced in "The Gambler, the Nun, and the Radio" and *To Have and Have Not* and carry that line to its logical conclusion. If the writer becomes deeply involved in a political struggle—the most serious of which is war—he can do so only at great cost to his art. For as he becomes more and more engaged with social questions, more caught up in his role as man of action, he will lose the necessary perspective that the true artist must have. These works mark an interlude in the more explicit investigation of the artist's nature and his relationship to the rest of mankind, the problems Hemingway explored in works such as *The Sun Also Rises*, "The Sea Change," and "The Snows of Kilimanjaro." Hemingway would attempt to take up those significant problems once again in the two book-length manuscripts that he began soon after he returned from World War II.

# 4

## *Posthumous Works:* Islands in the Stream

AFTER HIS MIDCAREER exploration of the problems of the writer in the 1930s and his more fragmentary meditation in *The Fifth Column* and the civil war stories, for all practical purposes Hemingway departed from the theme in the rest of the works he published. Although Robert Jordan of *For Whom the Bell Tolls* (1940) has written a book on Spain and plans to continue to write, his problems concern his role as a partisan working with Spanish guerrillas rather than literary matters. Similarly, Richard Cantwell is an unliterary man, and *Across the River and Into the Trees* (1950) has little to do with art, although Hemingway's ill-tempered habit of sniping at his contemporaries caused him to include a gratuitous satiric portrait of Sinclair Lewis in that work. The passage returns to the theme employed in *Death in the Afternoon* of a writer's need to know his material: Lewis is represented writing travel books cribbed from tourist guidebooks while enjoying the comforts of the best hotels rather than making an effort to discover the real Venice, which the colonel knows. Finally, *The Old Man and the Sea* (1952) presents Hemingway's least literary character, Santiago, who lives his life face to face with reality. Even while he was producing these works, however, Hemingway was also struggling with the two novels that he would never finish: *Islands in the Stream* and *The Garden of Eden*.

His heavy involvement in World War II had dissipated the momentum that Hemingway might have enjoyed after completing *For Whom the Bell Tolls* and left him where he had been in the troubled decade of the 1930s. Between 1940 and 1945, Hemingway produced little writing of a literary nature. Perhaps his most thoughtful piece during the period was his introduction to *Men at War* (1942), in which he reflects on literary questions as well as on the topic of war. Other writing from this time consists of dispatches, a few short stories, and some free verse poems. After the war, returning to Cuba and to the responsibilities of a literary career, Hemingway found it hard to start a new literary project, but in the two novels he began, he again focused on the artist's problems. Both books were started shortly after Hemingway settled in Cuba after World War II.

The earliest drafts of *Islands in the Stream* and *The Garden of Eden* indicate that both novels would have shared a concern with how a writer lived his life and that they would have complemented each other. *Islands in the Stream* would have treated the midcareer problems of the mature writer who attempts to stabilize his life, balancing the conflicting demands of his work and his family while coping with the myth that has enveloped him. *The Garden of Eden* would have treated the emerging writer who attempts to deal with some of the same pressures at an earlier stage of his career. While the two books are very different, many pages in the manuscript of each are devoted to the same theme that had concerned Hemingway during the 1920s and 1930s—the necessity for the artist to balance his personal life and his artistic life. Each manuscript moves toward a tragedy that never fully materializes, since Hemingway was unable to conclude either project.

According to Carlos Baker, Hemingway began both books in 1946 and continued to work on them through early 1947, stopping when his son Patrick became ill after an auto accident in April 1947.[1] He returned to *Islands in the Stream* in 1951 but never finished the cutting of the manuscript, which had grown to unmanageable size and contained several divergent plot lines that were mutually incompatible. In the late 1950s he worked extensively on the manuscript of *The Garden of Eden* but was also unable to complete his revision of that book.[2]

Factors such as Hemingway's deteriorating health and his worries about the Cuban political situation were certainly major causes of his inability to work decisively on the manuscripts. However, the sensitive and personal nature of the material, the probing exploration of the writer's psyche, would have been difficult for Hemingway to deal with under the best of circumstances and might well have been the cause of a psychological writer's block. But it was not writer's block in the usual sense of the term. Hemingway did not find it impossible to write—as the masses of manuscript at Kennedy Library attest. Rather, he had difficulties putting the revelations in his rough drafts into publishable form. Furthermore, it seems significant that during the same period Hemingway faced no comparable challenges completing other novels that presented only the conventional difficulties with character, plot, and structure. Clearly, *Across the River and Into the Trees* and *The Old Man and the Sea* did not involve the same dilemma of identification with his characters that *The Garden of Eden* and *Islands in the Stream* did. In these two manuscripts, Hemingway returned to his own deepest conflicts for his inspiration, but this time he lacked the ability to master his material. Was it because of his own failing powers or because the revelations would be more autobiographical than any that had come before?

## The Lost Protagonist

Through the development of Roger Davis, a prominent figure in the "Bimini" section of *Islands in the Stream,* Hemingway comments on some special problems of the writer more extensively than in the novels he published during his lifetime. Moreover, Thomas Hudson, the main character of the novel, shares many artistic problems with Roger, and the two discuss their respective arts. Hemingway further draws the two together because he presents them as doubles of each other, as if one character were insufficient to carry the burden of the theme concerning the artist's plight. The closeness of the resemblance between the two characters is even more apparent in the manuscripts of *Islands.*

Even in his diminished role in the novel as edited for publication, Roger Davis is the sort of man and writer around whom legends collect. Like Hemingway himself, at various times he is rumored to be a communist sympathizer, a womanizer, a saloon brawler, and a drunk. Roger often suffers from the rumors of columnists, even the favorable rumors that suggest he is working on his masterpiece. Such rumors distract him, setting up impossible expectations and keeping him from simply doing the best work he can. Roger has a dark side: he often suffers from insomnia, frequently experiences grave doubts about his work, and sometimes hints at suicide. Yet he is an ingenuous and vulnerable person, susceptible to the charm of children and, often to the detriment of his own peace of mind, to women.

But Roger's foremost characteristic is his identity as a writer. If he has not always been completely true to his talent, he has suffered for the lapses that have caused him to write scripts in Hollywood or to publish books that are not his best work. Except for the Hollywood involvement, all of these facts about Roger are so clearly recognizable in Hemingway's own life and character that it would seem foolish to deny a further connection between Roger's inner conflicts as a writer and Hemingway's. Hemingway seems, then, to be suggesting reasons for his own faltering career in the 1940s and 1950s when he reveals that what has kept Roger from achieving literary greatness is his unwillingness to plumb the deepest recesses of his own personality. Like Roger, Hemingway was not yet ready to debunk the legend of his own invincibility. Like Roger, he found it more comfortable to play a role.

Roger is implicitly established as a double to Thomas Hudson early in the novel, when he is introduced by a description that stresses his physical resemblance to Hudson, who has been described as a big, powerful man who carries "no extra weight" at 192 pounds and who favors beachcomber clothing.[3] Roger is first introduced in similar garb and looks "awfully big" as he leaps from the dock onto the deck of Johnny Goodner's cruiser (26). Either Hudson or Davis could have been mistaken for Ernest Hemingway, who, like them, tipped the scale at slightly under 200 pounds when he was in good shape and favored Basque shirts and baggy shorts. When Roger takes part in some dockside violence, he is established as a strong man who knows how to use his fists, much in the manner of the legendary Hemingway.

Other biographical similarities continue to link Hemingway to one or both of his doubled characters: like Hudson, Roger has lived in Paris during the early years of his artistic career when each was struggling to achieve greatness in his respective art. Both men have led turbulent personal lives featuring unhappy love affairs and marriages. Both have been noted for heavy drinking and brawling. The doppelganger effect is made explicit later when Mr. Bobby, the bartender, asks Roger whether he and Hudson are related. Bobby explains that he has asked because Roger and Hudson look like "quarter brothers" and Hudson's sons resemble Roger as much as Hudson. Hudson replies that they are not related but that they " 'used to live in the same town and make some of the same mistakes' " (155). However, the manuscript shows that the relationship of the two characters is closer than even Bobby might have suspected, for they have a common origin: Hemingway split the character he originally conceived into two different creative artists. A writer in the first version of the story becomes both the writer and the painter during Hemingway's revision of the beginning of the novel.

In the first pages of the holograph manuscript of "Bimini," the main character of the novel is Roger Hancock, a writer who has three sons with whom he plans to spend some time at the home of a friend in Bimini. Thomas Hudson's earliest prototype is that friend, a man named George Davis who plays host to Roger and the boys and who narrates the story. George sketches the background of Roger Hancock in an early manuscript, Item 98, part 1, in the Hemingway Collection, which Hemingway identified as needing cutting and revision.

After beginning his career as a newspaper reporter, Roger soon began to write hardcover books.[4] George, himself an unliterary type, says that he has always liked Roger's books, although many hate them. Roger has made a great deal of money from his books and from occasional screen-writing jobs in Hollywood, but he seldom has much money because of large alimony payments to former wives.[5] Recently blacklisted in Hollywood for some unspecified reason, he jokes with George about this apparent misfortune. Like Roger Davis in the published version of the book, Hancock also laughs about his shaky literary reputation. Although in the past his novels have been critically acclaimed as well as lucrative, the consensus for years has been that his career was declining,[6] another clear parallel to Hemingway and one that must have been painful for him to acknowledge, however indirectly.

George Davis has little personality and no characteristics that suggest identification with Hemingway in this first version of the story. Definitely not an artist like Thomas Hudson, he exists mainly to tell the story and to provide places for Roger to vacation with his three sons. George owns both a ranch in Wyoming (alluded to in the published novel, where it becomes Hudson's ranch in Montana) and the house and boat at Bimini that are the settings for the first book of *Islands in the Stream*. Although he himself has no artistic aspirations, he has known other artistic people besides Roger, such as Scott and Zelda Fitzgerald. George maintains his identity in the manuscript for the first 400 pages of the holograph novel. Then, on page 401, his name is crossed out and "Tom" is substituted, after which Hemingway began to alter the manuscript from first-person narration to third-person and to alter "George" to "Thomas Hudson."[7] During a transitional period in the composition, the boys address George Davis/Thomas Hudson as a friend of the family. It was only during later revision that Hudson became the father of the boys and Roger took on the role of family friend, at the same time taking on George's surname "Davis."[8]

This curious evolution of the two characters in "Bimini" explains the similarities between Hudson and Davis as well as the similarities both have to their creator. The interchangeability of the two characters and the ease with which characteristics of one can be transferred to the other suggest that it was not important to Hemingway that the characters be decisively distinguished from one another. In fact, Hemingway seems to have consciously decided to emphasize rather than diminish the doppelganger effect, as evidenced by the changes he made when George Davis became Thomas Hudson and by the number of explicit references to similarities between Roger and Thomas Hudson in the final version. Hemingway had obviously decided that a single artist would be inadequate to convey the complexity and variety of the conflicts that plagued the author himself, and the doubling ultimately offered him two ways of exploring the resolution of those conflicts. The necessity to use both a painter and a writer emphasizes how critical the theme of the creative artist's life was to Hemingway during this period.

The fact that the split characters result in one man who is a writer (whose career experiences so often echo Hemingway's own) and a second man who is the father of three sons (like Hemingway's the products of multiple marriages) suggests that Hemingway was attempting to deal with the conflicts of the writer as artist and the writer as man by splitting an individual character who is much like himself into two parts. In one sense, the crossover of traits as well as the fact that Hudson is an artist of another kind shows the psychological impossibility of the kind of distinction that Hemingway had been trying to make between a writer's creative and personal lives in the first version of the story. Furthermore, Hemingway's reluctance to distinguish one artist completely from the other creates a psychological tension in the novel—as if parts of a multiple personality were attempting to fuse into a single personality.

One can only speculate about why Hemingway altered his plan to use Roger Hancock the writer as the protagonist of the novel, but one reason may have been the extreme closeness of the narrative to his own life and a desire to blunt what Carlos Baker would later call the "Narcissus principle." Baker notes that, even though Hudson is a painter rather than a writer, he has so much in common with his creator that readers can be excused for taking the book as thinly veiled autobiography:

> Like Hemingway at this period, Hudson had been married twice. . . . Like Hemingway, Hudson sometimes reflected that he had "behaved stupidly and badly with women"—his excuse being that he had formerly been "undisciplined, selfish, and ruthless". . . . Among the many parallels between Hudson and Hemingway were their youthful apprentice years in Paris. These years were diversified in both instances with skiing trips to Switzerland and afterwards to Austria where the child Tom, like his prototype Bumby, had a pretty, dark-haired nursemaid and a pet dog called Schnautz. . . . When Hemingway took up the second part of Hudson's story a few years later, he added other parallels in which Hudson shared Hemingway's memories of boyhood summers in Michigan.[9]

However, Hemingway also experimented with the notion of writing a novel about a painter named James Allen, who shares some of Hemingway's experiences even though he works in a different medium. (Allen's character gave way in revision to Philip Haines, a writer.) Hemingway's creation of Hudson as a pictorial artist, therefore, is not without precedent.[10]

Perhaps because he made Roger Davis a secondary character in later revisions of the novel, Hemingway used experiences that might be identified as autobiographical more freely than he had in fiction since the Nick Adams stories and *A Farewell to Arms*. In the published novel, Roger Davis, like Hemingway himself, is the sort of writer who makes good copy for the gossip columnists. Before he is introduced, Johnny Goodner asks Hudson if it is true that Roger has become a "Red" (25). He has heard that rumor on the West Coast, along with even more juicy bits of gossip. Hudson implies that the charge of communism is not true but that it might be expected. About the other rumors he knows nothing. Goodner replies that—at least this time—the trouble Roger got into has nothing to do with "St. Quentin quail" [*sic*] (25), implying that in the past Roger has been involved with underage women. Roger later tells Hudson the Hollywood story, which started with some "woman trouble" and ended with a fistfight. The fight was provoked by an aggressive stranger who was nearly killed. After the man recovered, Roger had been "framed" in some unspecified way, causing him to leave Hollywood for good (46–47).

The nature of that Hollywood fight alluded to so briefly can be inferred from an incident dramatized in *Islands*. Hudson and Roger have been drinking and talking noisily on a friend's boat when the drunken owner of a nearby cruiser comes up on the deck of his craft to try to quiet the party. Once he recognizes a celebrity—whom he loosely identifies with both Roger and Hudson, thus intensifying the doppelganger effect of the novel—he singles out Roger and tries to pick a fight with him: " 'You big fat slob,' the man almost choked. 'You phony. You faker. You cheap phony. *You rotten writer and lousy painter*' " (39; italics mine). Uncharacteristically calm, Roger reacts to more of the same insults by trying to reason with the man, saying that he knows the man is insulting him just so he can later brag about the incident in New York.

When the man climbs up on the dock to fight, Roger punishes him unmercifully, just as Hemingway had done to publisher Joseph Knapp in their 1935 bare-knuckle fight on the Bimini docks.[11] Although Roger feels guilty about the fight the next day, the story creates in the reader sympathy for a man who is unable to drink quietly at a private party without being subjected to such abuse. The incident exemplifies one view of the burdens of literary and popular fame in an era when the press sensationalized the private lives of writers. Though Roger's resentment of his notoriety reflects a Hemingway complaint, it might be countered that Hemingway himself often courted notoriety and, if he did not always welcome the attention of journalists, used the pages of *Esquire* to publicize the self-created image of himself as a virile, adventurous writer. Another kind of invasion of Roger's privacy is presented in the manuscript of *Islands*, where Helena (Audrey Bruce in the edited version of the novel) tells Roger that college professors force students to read his work and to memorize biographical misinformation.[12]

Much as Hemingway himself resorted to parody of the persona that had been created by and for him—for example, when he performed for Lillian Ross during the interview for her controversial *New Yorker* profile—Roger sometimes deliberately plays the part of the stereotype the press has created. Early in the novel his friends on Goodner's boat correct Roger's grammar and ask him how someone so ignorant of the language can write books. Roger's reply is offhand: " 'I can always hire someone to put in the grammar' " (26).

But the best example of Roger's spoofing the stereotype of the writer occurs a bit later, when Tom's sons are baiting tourists by pretending to be drunk in Mr. Bobby's bar. Roger plays along with their game and adds embellishments of his own, assuming the part of the swashbuckling author the press has portrayed, the stereotyped moody author who has to get drunk before he can write. The eldest son, Tom, attempts to dissuade Roger from drinking more by reminding him that he has to write. Roger answers, " 'What do you think I'm drinking for?' " (167). Tom argues that Roger successfully wrote an earlier novel, *The Storm*, on less alcoholic fuel and warns that if he gets blind drunk, he won't be able to write. Roger replies that, like Milton, he'll dictate if he gets blind. Then Tom turns to literary criticism: the plot of Roger's novel is good, but the heroine is the same one he killed off in a previous work. In fact, Tom's younger brother observes, Roger uses the same heroine in all his books, a criticism that echoes complaints about Hemingway's own female characters. Unlike some authors, Roger has not yet sunk to the expedient of hiring a secretary to write his books for him. Young Tom has heard " 'that novelists did that' " (168); in the manuscript of the novel, he accuses Louis Bromfield of doing just that.[13] But Roger's reason for writing his own books rather than using a secretary has nothing to do with his integrity; he maintains that a secretary would be too expensive.

As Hemingway had played a part for Miss Ross, Roger plays one for the tourists. Hemingway usually concealed his bookishness beneath an unlettered exterior and exaggerated his rough mannerisms as Roger does in the barroom scene. Roger reflects his creator's amusement over the popular notion that a writer could produce anything of value while drunk, ignoring how much hard work must go into publishable writing. Young Tom's reference to Roger's heroines suggests that Hemingway was well aware of what the critics had said about Catherine Barkley and Maria, but by alluding to the negative comments during lighthearted banter, he belittles their criticism: in effect the critics' assumptions are treated as if they are in the same category as popular myths about well-known writers.

But Roger's lighthearted role-playing, like Hemingway's own, conceals an inner life marked by gloom, guilt, insomnia, and occasional thoughts of suicide. For example, after his fight on the dock, Roger feels "low." His mood is apparently a familiar one to Hudson, who urges Roger to talk. Roger tells about the fight in Hollywood that ended his screenwriting career. In the manuscript version of this conversation, Roger Hancock jokes with George about being blacklisted by Hollywood, saying that he can no longer sell out to Hollywood because the producers are no longer interested in prostituting his literary talents.[14] The published book, however, omits these caustic allusions to the writer's conflicts and the effects of external controls on the writer; emphasis is shifted from the writer to the safer topic of world politics. Roger is less flippant and observes, foreshadowing the coming of World War II, that bullies just keep getting worse after being knocked down. Roger does not sleep at all that night.

Since Roger's pugilistic episode recalls Hemingway's, it is tempting to wonder whether Hemingway is also drawing on his own experience when he describes Roger's moodiness as it exacerbates his unreasonable feelings of guilt and has led in the past to masochistic behavior. That Hemingway is really exploring his own feelings of guilt would explain why Roger's guilt about hitting one man in Hollywood and the other man on the dock is so inexplicably out of proportion to his actions. Similarly, when a shark nearly attacks David, it is Roger, not the boys' father, who feels the most guilt for exposing the boys to danger: he terms his own recklessness with the boys' lives "irresponsible," and while his offer to drink hemlock to atone for his sin is a humorous exaggeration, it is also a sign of his own excessively guilty reaction as well a muted reminder of his suicidal impulses. In view of Hemingway's own eventual suicide, Roger's impulses provide an eerie autobiographical connection to the novelist.

Roger's extreme reaction to David's endangerment and his generally low self-esteem are attributed to feelings of guilt that arose from an accident when Roger was twelve. He had always had a foreboding of death and a fear of losing his brother. The nightmare came true when their canoe overturned and only Roger survived, leaving him with an inescapable feeling of guilt. He tells Hudson, " 'I've wished it was me every day since. But that's hardly a career' " (75). Roger explains that he tried to dive for his brother but was unable to rescue him in the deep, cold water. It is clear that, whether his father ever forgave him or not, Roger has been unable to forgive himself. This invented incident may displace Hemingway's own feeling of unresolved guilt over the death of his father, for which he felt partly responsible.

In manuscript, Roger Hancock is given more background, the most important feature of which is his hopeless love for one of his former wives, a feeling that seems to parallel Hemingway's deep regret over his divorce of Hadley, his first wife. Roger has gone through a period of extreme instability when he has drunk even more than usual and has had unspecified "woman trouble." Afterward he spends the winter in the mountains at George's ranch in Wyoming, trapping with Red, a cowhand. Roger's idyllic life that winter is based loosely on Hemingway's own summer and fall experiences at Lawrence Nordquist's L——T ranch just across the Wyoming border from Cooke City, Montana.

Separated from his artistic and personal problems and performing hard physical labor rather than sedentary literary work, Roger is able to sleep through the night, cured of his insomnia. Hemingway had acknowledged in a manuscript fragment that writing was never an unalloyed joy. The writer, he says, must "destroy himself with each book," must consider his own survival as secondary to the life of the book. He is at once the mine from which the raw materials of his work are extracted, the mill that refines the ore, and the skilled worker who turns the metal into "something of enduring worth."[15] Freed of this terrible responsibility, Roger gains a new perspective that enables him to clarify his goals and to control his excessive drinking. The idyll comes to a close, however, when he determines to reconcile with his second wife and is refused. He leaves his camp, has a final drinking party with Red, and goes to Hollywood, where he gets in trouble as in the published novel. George sums up the experience by saying that "geography" failed to cure Roger but had given him temporary respite from both mental and physical problems.[16] The "geography treatment" is an interesting response to the artist's problems, one of several put forth in the novel, but is clearly rejected because it offers no permanent cure, a judgment that might easily have resulted from Hemingway's own multiple experiences with travel and adventure as a distraction. As Jake has warned Robert Cohn, a person cannot get away from himself by changing where he lives: travel is a fool's paradise.

Roger's other vulnerable point in the manuscript novel is his love for his children. The eldest is named for his lost brother David, and Roger tries to recreate for his own children the happy early boyhood he had with his brother. The happiest times of Roger's life are those he spends with his boys; in fact, the manuscript suggests that they keep him from a more self-destructive course than he actually pursues. In the published novel, where Hemingway attempts to distance Roger's experience from his own, the children are Hudson's, but in another example of the shared characteristics of the two men, the children still have a special relationship with Roger, on whom they exert a wholesome influence. Roger is particularly close to David, Hudson's middle son, helps him in his fight against the huge fish, and consoles him when the fish is lost with a private comment that is never disclosed, even to Hudson (143). At one point, when Roger hints to Hudson that he has had thoughts of suicide, Hudson reminds him that suicide " 'would be a hell of an example for the boys' " (156).

Roger's assumption of part of Hudson's role as father figure has interesting implications. For example, Roger the writer is freed of the burden of children and can devote all his time to his work. His freedom from the responsibility of the boys allows him to relate to them naturally and affectionately—a father figure who is not a father. Hudson, on the other hand, represents the artist as father, who must protect himself from the boys behind the ruthless discipline of his work (9), which shields his vulnerable self from the boys. Yet at the subconscious level of the author creating the novel, even this distancing is not enough and the boys must be destroyed. First, David is nearly killed by a shark when Hudson, the expert marksman, unaccountably misses the shark repeatedly while shooting his Mannlicher, the most accurate rifle he has ever owned. Is this an instance of buck fever striking Hudson? Or is it a Freudian slip on the part of the author signifying that the real artist must forsake all for his art? This near disaster is merely the precursor of the real deaths of the two younger boys at the end of "Bimini." Tom, Jr., will die shortly afterward, piloting a Spitfire with the Royal Air Force.

In both the manuscript novel and the revised version, one of Roger's weaknesses, a result of his failed marriages, is his feeling that he is not worthy of the love of a good woman. This notion has led him to fall in love with evil, manipulative women. In the published novel, Thomas Hudson recalls one beautiful, healthy-looking girl with whom Roger was involved: although she drank steadily, she looked deceptively wholesome. This doomed woman "was on a very strange voyage to somewhere and for a while she took Roger with her" (102). It is this healthy-looking girl—perhaps based on Jane Mason—who grinds out cigarettes on the back of Roger's hand with Roger's masochistic approval. Eventually she kills herself, leading Roger to consider suicide also.[17]

But the very sensitivity that makes Roger a psychologically wounded personality also contributes to his development as a writer. Although he attempts to conceal his dedication to and concern for his writing behind a flippant exterior, Roger is deeply committed to his career, which has gone wrong for reasons that he does not fully understand, a feeling that Hemingway knew only too well in the years following World War II. In manuscript, Hemingway's attempt to probe beneath the exterior of a popular novelist is a principal concern, but sections cut during revision leave only a few signs of the theme in the published version of "Bimini."

One of the vestiges of this theme is the fact that Roger, like Hemingway himself, has seemed at times to be his "own goddamned hero" (154). Like Harry in "The Snows of Kilimanjaro," he has led an exciting life in exotic places and has written about the events he experienced. Yet his work seems to some critics to be repetitive—the joking of Tom, Jr., in the scene at Mr. Bobby's echoes a critical truism—and his popularity has made him suspect among the highbrows of the literary world. Hemingway intensifies the distance between Roger's artistic and popular reputations by making him a sometime screenwriter, a role Hemingway himself never played but knew secondhand because of the film treatments of his own work and the experiences of F. Scott Fitzgerald. Roger jokes about how Hollywood has corrupted him when he suggests that he would spoil even an attempt to write truly about the single greatest trauma of his life: if he were to write about his brother's drowning, he would commercialize the story into something that would sell to Hollywood, putting in a beautiful Indian girl and transforming himself into a larger-than-life frontier hero.

But irony underlies the James Fenimore Cooper parody: Roger's real problem is his failure to look deeply into his own being for his material. He writes the easy stories, but, like Harry in "Snows," he is saving the hardest yet the best of his stories—perhaps for too long. When he tells Hudson the long-suppressed story of his brother's death, Hudson remarks, " 'You told me a hell of a good novel tonight if you wanted to write it' " (77). Paradoxically, the author who is viewed as too autobiographical a writer has failed to plumb the most private recesses of his own experience, those that hold the greatest emotional power in his life and the greatest potential for powerful art. When Roger claims that he has never written the story because he doesn't know how it will end and is afraid that the ending will be tragic, he acknowledges the psychological risk in writing as introspection. Such a story, when it ventures into uncharted territory, may carry the author beyond his power to control his fiction: perhaps the face in the mirror will be so terrifying that the writer not only must hesitate to depict it but may be destroyed by it. Roger's story, for example, would be one of self-hatred that, once clarified, might lead him to kill himself. But if he is to become the best sort of artist, he must confront his own story.

Roger's fears surely reflect Hemingway's own misgivings as he worked hesitantly with his portraits of writers after the war. These misgivings probably account for his changing the original plan to make Roger the central figure of the novel. As it begins in manuscript, the novel reveals the divided commitment a writer must feel toward the demands of his art and those of his family. (When Roger is living his trapper's life in the mountains, all his writing is channeled into letters to his sons.) The commitments to art and to loved ones clash at the expense of the latter when the writer withdraws into the world of his work as David Bourne does in *The Garden of Eden*, or when he treats his own most sensitive ethical problems as Phil does in "The Sea Change," or when he employs domestic unhappiness for his material as Harry thought of doing in "Snows." To tell the story of Roger Hancock fully and honestly, Hemingway would have had to publish passages that would relinquish some of his most private experience and to delve even more deeply into his own psychology, forcing himself to acknowledge and expose some of his most closely guarded feelings about his craft and its relationship to his own life.[18]

*Islands* as published reflects Hemingway's reluctance to lay bare his inner life. For example, Roger protects his privacy as much as possible from Audrey Bruce. His suspicious attitude reflects the near paranoia of a literary celebrity who has been hounded by interviewers and camp followers—and the wariness of a man who knows his susceptibility to beautiful and ruthless women. The manuscript fills in the background reasons for Roger's caution. He broke up with his former wife, whom he now recognizes as his one true love, for the sake of a woman writer (obviously based on Hemingway's third wife, Martha Gellhorn) who pursued him to further her own literary career. Flattered by her attention, Roger left his wife and children, only to find that his new mistress loved him less than the positive reviews of her own works, which arrived regularly from her clipping service,[19] an interesting reversal of the situation in *The Garden of Eden*, in which David's press clippings come between him and Catherine. Having had this bad experience before Helena meets him, Roger is extremely cautious, especially since she tells him that she has studied his work in college, that she has come to Bimini on the yacht of a publisher, and that she is an aspiring writer herself. This last news is the most disquieting. She has worked on the staff of *New Republic*, a magazine for which Roger has little respect, and she asks him to read a couple of pieces she has written.[20]

Roger's caution turns to love, however, in both the early holograph manuscript and the later typescript followed by the editors of *Islands in the Stream*: the published novel ends optimistically, with Roger leaving for the mainland with Audrey, whom he plans to take to Thomas Hudson's ranch, where he *may* be able to regain his literary powers and his self-respect in the high country—as he had done, albeit temporarily, in the earlier version of the novel.

The ambiguous ending to Roger's story evades some of the harder questions that Hemingway would have had to ask had he continued the story. Could Audrey love a man who has so little respect for himself? Could two writers have a successful relationship that would survive the ruthlessness necessary to create art? If so, could their art survive? Could Roger look unflinchingly into his own psyche and tell his own best story? Would Hemingway have reversed himself and shown that sometimes the "geography treatment" can have lasting effects? The novel as it had evolved when Hemingway stopped work avoids such painful self-examination. In the early manuscript, however, Hemingway attempts to follow Roger and Helena, as Audrey is called in the holograph story, on an automobile trip across the South on their way to the ranch. During this trip, Hemingway expands his treatment of Roger's literary problems and the resulting psychological problems.

One section omitted in the published *Islands* but later printed in the Finca Vigía collection of stories contains some autobiographical echoes as Hemingway explains the rumor that Roger is a "red." He tells Helena that at one time he was politically involved and tried to "buck" political powers in Florida.[21] Roger does not specify what he wrote to attack Florida politicians, but the context concerns convict labor.[22] Another hint about his perceived leftist sympathies is a vague reference to his involvement in the Spanish civil war, as either reporter or participant.[23] Although he has not yet done so during the time period covered by the manuscript, Roger may go on to support the Loyalist cause in Spain, just as Hemingway did during the 1930s, in spite of his warning to Helena that it is a mistake to try to save the world through one's writing.[24] This segment of the manuscript was excised for good reason: it adds little to Roger's characterization and it suggests a clumsy attempt at self-justification on Hemingway's part.

However, Hemingway does tackle a more crucial issue in greater depth. Particularly significant in view of *The Garden of Eden* are Roger's worries about his relationship with Helena: he recognizes the loneliness necessarily felt by the mate of a writer, yet he is fiercely determined to maintain his privacy. This conflict in priorities, which foreshadows the conflict between David and Catherine Bourne, indicates Hemingway's continuing personal concern and utilizes his own experiences. Although

Helena protests that she will not be bored while Roger is writing, he cannot really believe her, and his uneasiness leads to a minor argument that interrupts their idyllic life together:

> "But you won't be bored?"
> "Of course not."
> "I work awfully hard when I work."
> "I'll work too."
> "That will be fun," he said. "Like Mr. and Mrs. Browning. I never saw the play."
> "Roger, do you have to make fun of it?"[25]

Even after Roger has reassured Helena and she begins to talk again about their writing together, Roger once again resists. His irritability and inconsistency reveal the serious nature of his conflict. When Helena asks if he minds talking about writing with her, he answers, " 'Hell no.' " She asks why he sounds so angry, and he offers to talk about writing, but Helena nevertheless feels shut out of an area of his life: " 'Now you've made me feel like a fool. You don't have to take me in as an equal or a partner. I only meant I'd like to talk about it if you'd like to. . . . [But] I suppose I wanted to be partners even though I said I didn't.' "[26]

One reason for Roger's inability to share his writing emerges when he tells Helena how a suitcase of his manuscripts—including a novel and stories on boxing, baseball, and horse racing—was stolen from Andy's mother. The incident obviously goes back to Hadley's loss of Hemingway's manuscripts in 1922—one of three versions of the loss to appear in the posthumous work.[27] Roger describes his reactions:

> "They were the things I had known best and had been closest to and several were about the first war. Writing them I had felt all the emotion I had to feel about those things and I had put it all in and all the knowledge of them that I could express and I had rewritten . . . until it was all in them and all gone out of me. Because I had worked on newspapers since I was very young I could never remember anything once I had written it down; as each day you wiped your memory clear with writing as you might wipe a blackboard clear with a sponge or a wet rag; and I still had that evil habit and now it had caught up with me."[28]

Roger says that he did not miss the novel that was in the suitcase because he knew that it was apprentice work and that he could write a better one, but he says, " 'I missed the stories as though they were a combination of my house, and my job, my only gun, my small savings and my wife; also my poems.' "[29] The suggestion is that Roger can never again trust another person enough to allow him or her to get close to his art, either physically or metaphorically. Roger and by implication other writers are the victims of an isolation that separates them from their fellow human beings. In order to create, they must establish between themselves and the rest of mankind a distance that cannot be bridged completely when working hours are over. The artist, then—like Hawthorne's Owen Warland in "The Artist of the Beautiful" or, more ominously, like Dr. Rappaccini—becomes a detached observer and manipulator of life rather than a full participant in it.

Hemingway further bares the psyche of the writer in passages that treat Roger's writer's block. Such passages represent Hemingway's most trenchant examination of the artistic problems of the writer since "The Snows of Kilimanjaro." At one point, Roger gets up early and confronts himself, taking stock of his writing career, ignoring such external elements as his seduction by Hollywood or distraction by those around him and concentrating the blame for his flagging career on himself. In a passage that is a variation on Harry's self-accusations in "The Snows of Kilimanjaro," Roger reminds himself what he must do if he is to survive as a writer:

> I know six good stories, he thought, and I'm going to write them. That will get them done and I have to do them to make up for that whoring on the Coast. If I can really do four out of the six that will pretty well balance me with myself and make up for that job of whoring. . . . The hell with these sexual symbols. What he meant was that he had taken money for writing something that was not the absolute best he could write. . . . Now he had to atone for that and recover his respect by writing as well as he could and better than he ever had. That sounded simple, he thought. Try and do it sometime.[30]

Here Roger is trying to be honest with himself rather than to impress anyone else. He realizes that simply sitting down and writing one's best is the hardest thing that any writer can ask of himself. Hemingway, who had spent much of the 1930s writing work that was not "the absolute best he could write" for *Esquire* or for the Spanish Loyalists, for *New Masses* and for *Ken*, was well aware of his own apostasy; the atonement concept which Roger introduces suggests the nearly religious images surrounding writing elsewhere in Hemingway's works. He would echo Roger's reflections on the awful loneliness of the writer years later in his Nobel Prize acceptance speech, where he would write of the awareness of facing eternity or the lack of it every time a serious job of writing is undertaken.

The third-person narrator of the novel, however, maintains an ironic distance from Roger. Although Hemingway had faced some of the same demons Roger faces and had sometimes been bested by them, through his narrator he upholds the ideals to which the writer should conform: "So having promised and decided that did he then take a pencil and an old exercise book and, sharpening the pencil, start one of the stories there on the table while the girl slept? He did not. He poured an inch and a half of White Horse into one of the enamelled cups."[31] Clearly Hemingway was as familiar with Roger's techniques of evasion as he was with the tools of his trade—the sharpened pencils and the student's exercise book. In the published version of *Islands in the Stream*, this passage is condensed into a single sentence in which Roger admits that what he really needs for his salvation is to " 'write a good straight novel as well as I can write it' " (76). There is something plaintive and hopeful about the apparent simplicity of this prescription, considering the state of Hemingway's own career as he attempted to complete the novel, but the sentence leaves out the desperation and terrible sense of failure conveyed in the full details of the original passage.

The weaknesses in Roger's character—his tendency to avoid treating the most difficult subjects and to procrastinate in order to avoid possible failure—lead him to commit one of the key sins of which a writer can be guilty. Like Harry in "The Snows of Kilimanjaro," Roger does not put off writing just because it is hard work to "bite the nail" and write but because he fears failure. As long as he does not attempt any of the six good stories, he cannot fail to do them justice; he can defer any possible artistic failure to another day. His reluctance to make a leap of faith in opening the exercise book and attempting one of the stories has transformed him from an active writer to something like the leopard on top of Harry's mountain: only a shell of Roger and his work are preserved, shrunken and desiccated, in the college classes such as those Helena has taken—where Roger's life and work are completely misrepresented.

Roger's story clarifies much of what is only implied in "The Snows of Kilimanjaro" about the disappointing nature of literary immortality: it is the act of creation, not the fact of having created in the past, that is the most precious reward of the artist. Roger also sheds further light on the life in death suffered by the writer who fails to develop his talent to its fullest extent. Unlike Harry, he has gone on using his ability to write, but he has used it to produce inferior work that has left him disgusted with himself. Hemingway had been writing with false confidence about the problems of other writers in 1935 when he stated, "Something happens to our good writers at a certain age,"[32] undoubtedly thinking of past writers such as Melville and Twain and contemporaries such as Anderson and Fitzgerald. Such American authors could be destroyed by money, which caused them to produce inferior work and to fail to use their talent wisely. By the time he was working on *Islands in the Stream*, he could see that the warning also applied to him. In "A Situation Report" (1956), for example, he complained of the time he had thrown away on the filming of *The Old Man and the Sea*—which was done at least partly for the money involved—and vowed never again to allow himself to be distracted from his real work by such projects.[33] Yet a few years later, he would interrupt his two novels in progress with the project that began as an article for *Life* and eventually became the self-indulgent book *The Dangerous Summer*.

The manuscripts of "Bimini" thus suggest that, if Hemingway had continued to develop the character of Roger Hancock, the novel might have become a brutally honest confrontation of the aging writer's life and his unique problems in living with himself, juggling artistic responsibilities that he was no longer able to live up to, and avoiding family responsibilities. However, even though the published work falls short of its potential, the manuscripts do allow the biographer or the critic to glimpse fleetingly the face that the artist sees in the mirror. Unlike the hard-boiled Roger Davis of *Islands in the Stream* as published—and unlike the public persona that Hemingway had created during the 1930s and 1940s, Roger Hancock as he exists in the holograph manuscript is a sensitive, mature, troubled artist who reflects the anguish that Hemingway himself had endured during the fallow years of the 1930s, the time when this part of the story takes place, and was still enduring as he attempted to revive his writing career after World War II. Hemingway's creation of Roger was a confessional act that tells much more about the inward terrain of the writer—his fears and cowardice and bitter hopes—than Hemingway was ever able to reveal in works published during his life.

But in an act of evasion uncannily parallel to those of Harry and Roger, Hemingway resisted the rigorous self-examination that Roger's story would have required and directed the main focus of *Islands in the Stream* toward Thomas Hudson instead. In the published novel, Roger remains an incomplete though interesting doppelganger whose enigmatic character simply hints at the parts of the iceberg beneath the surface of "Bimini." Hudson offered a safer means of commenting on the problems of the artist without the confessional sort of honesty that telling Roger's whole story would have demanded.

### Portrait of the "Ideal" Artist

In revising *Islands in the Stream,* Hemingway gave Thomas Hudson many of Roger Hancock's personal characteristics as well as his children and some of his marital history. In line with these revisions, after Roger's disappearance at the end of "Bimini," Hemingway transferred the theme of the artist's plight to Hudson, an easy transition, since Roger's experiences with painting as well as writing reinforce his role as double to Hudson. One conversation treats the differences between painters and writers: Roger reflects that painting is "fun" as compared to writing, which is agony. Hudson replies that painting has a stronger tradition than literature, so that there are "more people helping you" when you paint even if you break from that tradition. Roger suggests that the best people become painters, while less virtuous people may become writers by default. As for Roger, " 'Maybe I'm just enough of a son of a bitch to be a good writer' " (78). The passage marks a transition between Hemingway's early determination to treat Roger's problems as writer and his later effort to mask this theme by transferring the protagonist's role to Hudson.

This transfer allows Hudson to generalize on the arts and to reflect sympathetically but critically, later in the novel, on what is really wrong with Roger: there is a fatal flaw in his dedication to his art. Hudson mentally lists Roger's betrayals of his talent. He has wasted it by writing what will sell, by using formulas, and by losing his respect for craftsmanship. Roger has failed to realize that every bit of creative work the artist does is training for later and better work. To save himself as an artist, Roger must exploit his remaining talent artistically rather than commercially.

Hemingway here uses Hudson to distance himself from Roger, who, like Hemingway in so many ways, is clearly different in that he has never used his talent to write "one good novel." Unlike Hemingway, who admitted to having, by physical adventures, blunted "the instrument" that he wrote with, Roger has blunted his by abusing his talent and squandering it to obtain mere commercial success.[34] For Hudson, artistic values transcend material values—and even most human values. When Audrey Bruce plans to help Roger regain his spiritual health, Hudson states that Roger needs to " 'work well to save his soul. I don't know anything about souls. But he misplaced his the first time he went out to the Coast' " (191). Hudson thus warns Audrey not to interrupt Roger's work, the most essential part of his identity from Hudson's point of view.

Perhaps Hudson's clear vision of Roger is possible because Hudson himself is not guilty of any of Roger's sins against his talent, but there are other sins, other problems, that may afflict both painters and writers. The capsule biography of Hudson in chapter 2 suggests that when he was younger, he was much like Roger: so reckless in his personal life that his artistic life was slighted. He has had much to feel guilty about, including the breakup of his first marriage, but he has "exorcized guilt with work insofar as he could" (7), although he still maintains a sort of love for his boys and loves his first wife from afar. In "Bimini" Hudson seems superficially to represent the ideal artist: he works hard at his painting daily, and his commitment to his painting is pure. Having inherited land in Montana, he has a steady income from oil leases, and this money permits him to "paint exactly as he wanted to with no commercial pressure" (8). He keeps all business dealings at arm's length, working through a New York dealer and resisting any attempts to involve himself in the tawdry business of selling his work (8, 173).

But this apparent portrait of the ideal artist is subtly undercut throughout "Bimini." If Roger has valued his work too little, Hudson has gone to the opposite extreme. Like Phil in "The Sea Change," Hudson has placed his work above human relationships. As his life has evolved by the beginning of "Bimini," everything that he valued in the past has been replaced by work, which he views as a cure-all as well as the primary source of meaning in his life. Women in his past have criticized him for being "selfish" and "ruthless," (169) perhaps like Phil. Now that women are no longer an important part of his life, now that he has no life except in his art, Hudson has promised himself that he would be "selfish" and "ruthless" only for the sake of his painting and that he would "accept the discipline" his art demanded (9).

Such discipline means that when his sons come for their brief visits, Hudson never stops work to spend more time with them. Unlike Roger, who amuses the boys from the time they wake up in the morning, Hudson maintains his schedule of doing a day's work early in the morning and then devotes the rest of the day to his sons. He rationalizes that he is merely protecting himself against his eventual feeling of loss when the boys leave as well as against the loss of his creative ability and work habits:

[Hudson] was having a difficult time staying in the carapace of work that he had built for his protection and he thought, if I don't work now I may lose it. Then he thought that there would be time to work when they were all gone. But he knew he must keep on working now or he would lose the security he had built for himself with work. . . . It was next week when they would leave. Work, he told himself. Get it right and keep your habits because you are going to need them. [190]

Hudson's position, looking down on the boys from the high spot where he paints, offers a paradigm for the position of the artist vis-à-vis mankind: while mankind cannot reach as high as the artist, neither can the artist reconnect himself with mankind. Hudson's art has become an obsession, and he cannot bear to leave it even if his immersion in his painting means that he will be cut off from the world of humanity. Hemingway underscores the sacrifice that Hudson's obsession exacts. Two of Hudson's boys will be dead a few weeks after leaving, and the other will be killed in World War II just a few years later. Why does Hudson invest so much time and emotion in his career? Perhaps more than any other Hemingway character, Hudson views art in religious terms. The discipline of art can "save his soul" and "exorcize guilt"; it can provide him with a sense of security, a refuge from real life, just as monasticism provided its recruits with a refuge from the world. He loses himself in his art, then, even at the risk of estranging himself from those he loves.

Hudson is dragged back from the safe isolation of his artistic sanctuary, first by the deaths of his two younger sons in an accident and later by the advent of World War II. The "Cuba" section of *Islands in the Stream* might aptly be subtitled "Portrait of an Artist Without His Art." In this section Hemingway dismantles the self-assured, controlled artist that he had depicted in the first book of the novel. Hudson returns to the reckless habits of his youth and adopts the role of the absent Roger, drinking heavily when he is ashore, whoring occasionally, and suffering from insomnia. While his changed behavior could be due to the loss of his sons, it is not. Rather, he is suffering withdrawal pangs from his addiction to his art.

Hudson's meeting with his former wife, the mother of Tom, Jr., leads to this conclusion, as does later evidence in "At Sea." When she guesses that young Tom has been killed in action and asks Hudson if it is true, he answers tersely—" 'Sure' " (319), an odd word choice suggesting that the only possible outcome for hopes and love tied to living things is their eventual loss.[35] The passage recalls the conclusion of a much earlier story, "In Another Country" (1927), in which the Italian major, having just lost his wife to influenza, tells the narrator that the way to avoid loss is to " 'find things [one] cannot lose.' "[36] Hudson attempted to protect himself from disappointment, to find what he could not lose by devoting himself single-mindedly to his art, but when current events draw him out of his sanctuary, he finds that he has no center to his life.

Yet it is Hudson's capitulation to his human side that wins sympathy for him as the novel moves into its second and third books. As he loses the protective "carapace of work," he becomes more sensitive to the feelings of others. Not only must he remind himself not to think about his dead children, but he tries to be gentle with his former wife after his harsh acknowledgment that Tom, Jr., is dead. He concerns himself with the emotional well-being as well as the physical safety of the men who make up the crew of his Q-boat, sympathizes with casual acquaintances like Honest Lil, the over-the-hill whore who frequents the Floridita Bar, and worries about what will become of his pets if he is killed at sea. As he surrenders his absorption in his art, Hudson regains his humanity.

Sensing that he is close to the end of his life, in "At Sea" Hudson retreats into his art even though he can no longer paint because of his wartime activities. Like Harry in "The Snows of Kilimanjaro," who "writes" mentally by reviewing the unwritten experiences he had been saving, Hudson reverts to thinking like an artist, taking refuge in the detachment that art makes possible. For example, when he returns to his boat from a search mission, he sees his crew standing naked on the stern, bathing in the water of a tropical downpour, and something about the strange light takes him back to the world of art. He thinks of Cézanne's bathers, then imagines how Eakins might have painted the same scene, and finally decides how he himself would paint his men if art were possible in wartime.[37]

Hudson cannot return to the disengagement of the artist, but he continues to long for it, especially when death is imminent. As he lies on the bridge of his boat, fatally wounded, he tries to console himself with dreams of painting, again recalling Harry's fantasies in "The Snows of Kilimanjaro." The experiences he has gained from his wartime activities, the more intimate knowledge of the sea, and perhaps even the emotional pain he has endured could make him a better painter if he were to survive. He tells himself that "life is a cheap thing beside a man's work" (464). Other things have intruded to distract Hudson from his art, sometimes bad experiences such as the war but also positive experiences such as his emotional involvements with other human beings—lovers, wives, children, and comrades. Having suffered a similar loss of creative time to devote to his art and uncertain how to revive his career during the postwar period, Hemingway allows Hudson to express his creator's own uncertainty about his artistic and personal priorities, a problem thrown into high relief in his biography by his desertion of his work to care for his son Patrick in the spring of 1947.[38]

Just before he dies, Hudson realizes that he has just been dreaming that he will live. He was "quite sure, now, that he would never paint [the lagoon where the boat lies]" (466). His friend Willie, sensing Hudson's detachment, has the last word in the novel: " 'You never understand anybody that loves you' " (466). It is an apt indictment of Hudson or of any artist who so detaches himself from life that his work becomes more real to him than the lives of the other human beings around him.

It is not surprising that *Islands in the Stream* remained unfinished when Hemingway died. Roger Hancock/Davis's story stresses the importance of the writer's commitment to his art. As his story trails off in the manuscript fragment published in the Finca Vigía edition, Roger is determined to dedicate himself afresh to his art, yet his efforts seem doomed to failure. He lacks the ruthlessness or the single-mindedness necessary to become a great artist. On the other hand, Thomas Hudson, who took on many aspects of Roger's character during the years of rewriting and revision that Hemingway spent on the novel, illustrates exactly the opposite failing. Hudson dedicates himself so exclusively to his art that he has little room in his life for spouse, children, or comrades at arms. A success as an artist in "Bimini," Hudson loses his grasp on art when the war comes, and he finds nothing to replace it, leaving him feeling as empty when death comes as the unfulfilled Harry in "The Snows of Kilimanjaro." Neither Roger's story nor Hudson's ends positively; the best Hemingway could offer was ambiguity.

In *Islands in the Stream*, as in *The Garden of Eden*, his other posthumous novel, Hemingway addresses questions close to his own heart with a frankness not paralleled in any of the works published in his lifetime— with the possible exception of "The Snows of Kilimanjaro." Yet in *Islands*, even as he worked to clarify how he felt in his own mind about the divided loyalties of the artist, Hemingway censored his critical portrait of the artist by deemphasizing the importance of Roger's failure and probing the artist's psyche largely through a more successful surrogate who works in a different medium. In *The Garden of Eden*, on the other hand, where Hemingway again planned to pair a writer with a painter, he was clearly moving in the opposite direction as he wrote and revised his manuscript: there the major figure was to be the writer, with the painter reduced to a supporting role. Hemingway would attempt in *Garden* to depict the final confrontation between his artistic conscience and his human side, leaving behind another uncompleted manuscript that posed even greater difficulties with revision than the manuscript of *Islands in the Stream*.

## The Writer's Children: A Postscript

Two posthumously published stories have much in common with the manuscript of *Islands in the Stream*, in which Hemingway had begun to treat Roger Hancock's children. Both stories emphasize the challenges faced by the child of a famous author, making their point through the depiction of a boy, Stephen Wheeler. In the first, "I Guess Everything Reminds You of Something," the boy attempts to measure up to his father in writing as he has already surpassed him in pigeon shooting, while in the second, "Great News from the Mainland," the same boy is being treated for an undisclosed mental illness with electric shock treatments.

"I Guess Everything Reminds You of Something" begins with Stevie's winning a short story contest, a triumph to which he reacts with suspicious diffidence. In spite of Wheeler's sense that his son's story is familiar and that there are some discrepancies between the story and Stevie's experience, the father happily accepts the fact that his son writes very well— far better than he did at that early age—and attempts to help Stevie develop his talent. Wheeler unsuccessfully tries to be low-key with his efforts, saying that he does not want to make his son uncomfortable. He gives Stevie books to read, attempts to start technical discussions about them, and suggests that they engage in joint prewriting exercises—a process that Stevie interprets as unfair competition. To all his father's overtures, Stevie replies that he feels he should use the same technique he used with the first story, rejecting his father's step-by-step exercises and promising to mail the finished story to his father.

Parallel to the plot line of Stevie as an apparent literary prodigy is that of Stevie as accomplished shooter. Stevie's precocity as a shooter helps Wheeler to accept his precocity as a writer, although differences in Stevie's development in the two areas give Wheeler his first clues that something might be wrong. From the age of ten, Stevie has had an uncanny intuitive talent for wing shooting, a talent enhanced by the disciplined exercises Wheeler has designed for him. Embedded in the parts of the story that deal with Stevie's shooting are the clues the reader needs to recognize Stevie's concealed competitiveness with his father and his need to win out by fair means or foul. Already a master of the shotgun, Stevie is still subject to harsh discipline. When he wants a Coca-Cola between rounds of shooting, Wheeler allows him only half of a soft drink. The boy's apology for hitting a bird late is excessive, considering that he still shot the pigeon in plenty of time so that it fell within the fence. He reacts to earlier criticism by anticipating any critical remarks his father may make. Small wonder that he does not want to serve as his father's literary apprentice.

Meanwhile, Stevie intends to beat his father at the shooting game to which his father has introduced him. In live pigeon shooting, the birds are thrown in random order from any of five traps. The shooter must identify his target, swing, and shoot before the bird flies outside the scoring fence. Stevie makes a sensational shot, killing the pigeon just a few feet from the trap that has thrown it into the air. He tells his father he had noticed the number two trap from which the bird was thrown was louder than any other trap. Stevie seems to be giving his father a useful tip, but when Wheeler eventually gets a bird from trap two, the trap is quiet, and Wheeler barely hits the bird in time. Stevie has attempted to improve the odds in his competition with his father, just as he has improved the odds of writing a prize-winning story by plagiarizing.

Wheeler contrasts Stevie's shooting with his writing when he recalls that, as natural a wing shot as the boy was, he had needed instruction in the early stages and suffered occasional setbacks corrected by Wheeler's coaching. Unlike his apparent easy success as a writer, Stevie's improvement as a wing shot had been slow and steady. The parallel between writing and wing shooting is very close in Wheeler's mind and presumably in Hemingway's: like shooting, writing requires "good training,"[39] acute and detailed observation, a recognition of what is significant, and tedious exercises like the practice sessions with which Wheeler attempted to make Stevie "a perfect shot" (600).

Stevie leaves his father's home at the end of the vacation, and his second story never arrives in the mail, a fact Wheeler understands when he finds the original pirated story in a book in the boy's room seven years later. During these intervening years, an estrangement has developed between father and son, caused in part by Stevie's illness, to which Wheeler had attributed the "hateful" and "stupid" things the boy had done over the last five years. Wheeler is shocked by the plagiarism; nevertheless, the reader is unprepared for the harshness of Wheeler's final judgment of his son: the boy has "never been any good" (601).

Hemingway's characterization of Wheeler is perhaps the most significant thing about "I Guess Everything Reminds You of Something." In his early pride and apparent fondness for his son, Wheeler is a sympathetic father figure, obviously willing to spend time to encourage his son's interests. The clumsy attempts to teach and his excessively authoritarian approach to discipline are unattractive but understandable characteristics. Maintaining the narrative focus on the father, Hemingway wins the reader to Wheeler's point of view—until the final damning judgment. The disparity between that judgment and the harsh but sympathetic character developed in the rest of the story tells less about a father's relationship with his son than about a writer's sense of values: truth and honesty in one's métier, whether writing or shooting, are paramount measures of character and bases for evaluation. Interestingly, Hemingway provides understandable reasons and excuses for the son's behavior, as he has for the father's severity, and leaves the reader to choose between them—or to sympathize with both. Each in his own way is a victim of the demands of the writer's art.

An even bleaker picture of the writer's relationship with his son is afforded in a companion story, "Great News from the Mainland," in which Stevie is being treated for a mental illness, by implication the long-term illness mentioned at the end of "I Guess Everything Reminds You of Something." The ironically titled story opens as "The Three-Day Blow" does, with weather that reflects a yet-unspecified internal turmoil. For five days arid winds of nearly hurricane force have ravaged the trees on the grounds of Wheeler's Cuban retreat and have left the grass dry and dust covered. Wheeler phones the mainland and speaks to the artificially cheerful Dr. Simpson, who reports that he was unable to give Stephen his last electric shock treatment because as soon as he injected the boy with sodium pentothal, Stevie fought the medical personnel. One reason for Stephen's reaction might be the fact that sodium pentothal, widely used as a calming agent, is known to laymen as "truth serum." The suggestion is that there are things Stevie chooses not to acknowledge to himself, much less confess to a therapist. From the previous story it is apparent that chief among these is the deadly rivalry he perceives between himself and his father. The shallow therapist has made no progress toward discovering the roots of Stephen's disorder, though he marvels at an "interesting and significant" letter Stephen has written him. Ironically, writing, an area of conflict between Stephen and his father, has become part of the boy's therapy.

Before he places his next call to the mainland, Wheeler thinks of the windstorm that has made a wasteland of his grounds. Such winds always come during Lent, he remembers. The Lenten setting is appropriate, for Lent is a traditional time of repentance, and even though there are no overt references to Wheeler's guilt in this story, he has somehow failed as a father. That failure is implied when, even as he worries about Stevie, Wheeler is writing, working slowly in longhand, more immediately concerned with his phrasing than with his son's plight.

When his call goes through, Wheeler listens to his son's report on his own progress. In view of Stevie's claim to have faith and confidence in Dr. Simpson, who has given Wheeler no such sense of confidence, there is heavy irony in Stevie's assurance that he now has a "grasp of reality" (604). His true condition is apparent in the facts that the boy glosses over his difficulties, keeps the conversation on a superficial level, and obviously does not want to talk to his father for long. The story ends on a bitterly ironic note. After Wheeler hangs up, he passes on Simpson's easy platitudes to the inquiring houseboy: " 'Fine' " he says. " 'Everything is fine' "

(604). Wheeler's willingness to accept this fiction is yet another indictment of his failure as a parent.

Although Stevie's attitude may seem to recreate the stoicism of the son in "A Day's Wait," it is more likely, given Stevie's characterization in "I Guess Everything Reminds You of Something," that he is putting up a confident front, maintaining a fiction of progress just as he maintained the fiction that he had written the prize-winning story and was working on another. He obviously does not feel that he can confide in his father. What son of a writer could, knowing that his illness might later provide material for a story, as this story itself seems to demonstrate?

Together, these two late stories reveal Hemingway's acknowledgment that the writer who is also a father may harbor a deep-seated guilt about his treatment of his children. He may neglect them in their formative years, when his favorite children are his literary rather than his biological progeny; in "Everything Reminds You of Something," Stevie sees his father only for vacations, just as Roger Hancock's or Thomas Hudson's children do (and as Hemingway's own sons did). Another source of guilt is Hemingway's recognition in "Everything Reminds You of Something" that the child may think he must measure up to an impossibly high standard to prove himself worthy of his famous father. Finally, the mere existence of these two stories, which Hemingway chose not to publish, illustrates a third possible source of guilt: the writer-father may find the private life of his child irresistible as the raw material for fiction and may betray confidences by writing fictionalized versions of sensitive material.[40]

These two late stories combine with *Islands in the Stream* to explore the psychological division experienced by the father who is also an artist. Torn between his commitments to his art and his children, the artist chooses the former, but only at the cost of being tormented by guilt. In *The Garden of Eden* Hemingway would return to explore more fully a theme he had employed before: the divided loyalty of the artist who is also a husband.

# 5

## *Posthumous Works:* The Garden of Eden

BESIDES *Islands in the Stream*, Hemingway's chief project after World War II was a sprawling manuscript about life in the south of France between the wars. Carlos Baker was the first to examine the manuscript of *The Garden of Eden*, which he pronounced "an experimental compound . . . filled with astonishing ineptitudes."[1] In spite of that verdict—and in spite of the awesome task that editing the huge manuscript entailed—in 1986, Scribner's brought out a severely cut version of the novel, edited by Tom Jenks.

A comparison of the manuscript of *The Garden of Eden* with the Jenks edition suggests that Jenks probably performed his job as well as nearly anyone but Hemingway himself could have done. The job of the editor, like that of a novelist, was not to provide a definitive scholarly text with notes and tables of variant readings but to produce a readable story in which the major themes of the novel come together to make a coherent statement about life. Jenks selected most of the good material in the manuscript and cut many distracting elements. Yet in handling some facets of the novel, particularly its ending, Jenks departed radically from Hemingway's intentions insofar as they can be ascertained.

Anyone reading *The Garden of Eden* must be struck by the difference between the optimistic final chapter and the endings of other Hemingway novels. Jake Barnes's bitterly ironic reply to Brett Ashley in *The Sun Also Rises*, Frederic Henry's solitary walk back to his hotel through the rain in *A Farewell to Arms*, Robert Jordan's preparations for death in *For Whom the Bell Tolls*, and even Santiago's fragile moral victory in the face of ostensible defeat in *The Old Man and the Sea*—all seem to have little in common with the optimism of chapter 30 of *The Garden of Eden*, in which David Bourne discovers that the sentences of his destroyed story "came to him complete and entire and he put them down, corrected them, and cut them as if he were going over proof. Not a sentence was missing and there were many that he put down . . . without changing them."[2] This ending is the reverse of the tragic story of lost (and unrecoverable) manuscripts that Roger tells in material cut from the *Islands* manuscript. Some readers who know Hemingway's canon very well might have wondered whether Jenks had not concocted this optimistic ending himself. Such is not the case, but neither is it true that Hemingway wrote the passage as the end of the novel.

The manuscript of *The Garden of Eden* presents many difficulties for an editor, difficulties that so baffled the aging Hemingway that he was unable to complete the work to his own satisfaction. The manuscript contains three separate story lines concerning marital betrayal, sexual role-playing, and conflict between artistic commitment and human commitments. The most consistent and nearly complete of these plots was chosen by Jenks for publication. In the Jenks edition, which might be termed the Bourne plot, David and Catherine Bourne's marriage is shattered by Catherine's approaching insanity, by David's obsessive devotion to his writing, and by the introduction of a third partner, Marita, into the relationship, creating a ménage à trois. But Hemingway also wrote two variations on this marital triangle theme, and no definitive evidence in the manuscript suggests that he ever made a final decision to eliminate the two additional plots completely. Had he retained his old skill at omitting the unnecessary, he might have reduced the subplots to deft hints that would have strengthened the Bourne plot while not distracting the reader from it.

One alternative plot may be termed the Sheldon variant: the opening of book 2 introduces Nick Sheldon, a painter who knows the Bournes from Paris. He and his wife Barbara have played sexual role reversal games much like those played by the Bournes in the published novel. For example, Barbara has persuaded Nick to let his thick black hair grow as long as hers—to shoulder length—although Nick complains that he feels like a homosexual. Barbara, who has dabbled in painting, has no intellectual or artistic interests in life and displays the same sort of emotional instability that Catherine exhibits. When David and Catherine meet Nick and Barbara in Biarritz, Catherine is fascinated by the bizarre appearance of the Sheldons, especially Barbara, and David is interested enough in the pair to begin a story about them. When David encounters Barbara alone at a café, she warns him that she is infatuated with Catherine, in whom she senses lesbian tendencies, and that if he loves Catherine, he will get her out of town quickly. She also alludes to a character named Andy, who has been important to her.

Andrew Murray is a central figure in what might be called the Murray plot. His story is intertwined with both the Bourne and Sheldon plots. In the former, Andy meets Catherine and David soon after they arrive in Spain. Like David, Andy is a writer of integrity, interested in doing his best work whether or not it sells well. Having inherited a small amount of money, Andy lives frugally in Europe while he attempts to become self-supporting through his art. Andy is something of a moralist: he accuses David of "corrupting" Catherine by introducing her to Pernod and fast cars such as the Bugatti they drive.[3] Catherine likes Andy at first but later dismisses him as too wholesome an influence on David.[4] David assumes that Andy is in love with Barbara Sheldon but that she is not interested in him.

When the Sheldon plot meshes with the Murray plot, events take a tragic turn. Andy meets Nick and Barbara at Hendaye, and Barbara tries to persuade Andy to let his hair grow to match hers and Nick's. According to the symbolism throughout the novel, this is the opening ploy in a seduction. Barbara also shows signs of emotional instability: Andy thinks her paintings suggest that she is on the brink of madness,[5] while Barbara herself wonders if she is losing her mind. Like Catherine in the published novel, who encourages David to write an account of their life together, Barbara is eager for Andy to write the story of Nick, herself, and himself, and she plans to take photographs to illustrate the book, much as Catherine intends to hire painters to illustrate David's story of their marriage. One day while Nick is painting outside town, Barbara comes to Andy's room and seduces him. Afterward she displays extreme remorse, drinking absinthe and denying that the sexual encounter took place. The next time Nick is away, however, she returns to Andy's room and sleeps with him again. This time she feels less immediate remorse, but when two gendarmes come to report that Nick has been killed by a car, her latent guilt causes her to crack. These incidents form the background for a tragic conclusion in a draft ending Hemingway labeled "Provisional Ending" that Jenks ignored in his editing.

Choosing an ending would have caused any editor a good deal of trouble. None of the plot lines here summarized is as separate and distinct as the synopses might suggest. Hemingway worked through a number of variations of the three plots and experimented with the characters in different roles. For example, in the Murray plot line just summarized, Nick's wife is first named Catherine, and that name is canceled and replaced with Barbara. Later, when Barbara is talking to Andy, she mentions Catherine as a character in her own right and criticizes her destructive nature.

In one possible ending of the novel, Andy writes the story of the aftermath of Nick's death. When the gendarmes question Barbara about Nick to complete their reports, she cannot talk but is finally able to answer their questions in writing. At the funeral, she goes to the graveyard but is unable to accompany Andy to the gravesite. Afterward, she exhibits many signs of depression, refusing to speak or even to look at Andy and refusing to see her sister, who has come to Europe to help her. Andy attempts to help Barbara recover by taking her to Paris, then to Italy. Later he reflects that he should have taken her to Switzerland for psychological treatment, but Barbara has adamantly refused to enter any sort of mental institution.[6] Andy vows to take care of Barbara while his money holds out. In Italy Barbara finally seems to emerge from her depression. She talks to Andy long into the night for two weeks. When they reach Venice, Andy is confident that she is recovering.

One night, after an apparently happy day, Andy leaves Barbara alone at the hotel. When he returns, their rooms are empty, and Barbara has left him a note. Hemingway worked long and hard over the note, writing three separate versions, and two variations exist even in the typescript. In one note, Barbara discloses that she has taken an overdose of sleeping pills, while in another she has drowned herself. One letter thanks Andy for his consideration and urges him to write the story of their ménage à trois. She feels that her decision to kill herself is a sign of returning mental health, not illness: given her past, it is the only right thing to do. She wishes that she had taken pictures that could be used as illustrations for Andy's "monograph."[7] The first conclusion says that Barbara knew that she was doing the "proper" thing and hoped that the fact that she had saved up her legally prescribed sleeping pills for a month would keep the unpleasantness of the police investigation to a minimum. The second version suggests that she has drowned herself and emphasizes the cheerfulness of the day, its bright sunshine and the cleanliness of the water that day when the tides were high in Venice; Barbara had not wanted to think of drowning herself in filthy water. She hoped her suicide would not cause Venice to have unpleasant associations for Andy.

While Hemingway never put the segment of the manuscript on Barbara's suicide into final form, it is probable that at some point he considered Barbara's suicide to be a possible ending for the novel. The holograph manuscript has the name Catherine signed to the suicide note; it is crossed out and Barbara's name is substituted. In the published novel Tom Jenks retained the idea that Catherine might become suicidal. When she leaves David and Marita at the rural hotel, David insists that Catherine take the train, not the Bugatti. The recklessness of her driving has convinced David that she may kill herself on the road, either deliberately or in response to subconscious impulses. Like Barbara, Catherine is deeply committed to the idea of a written record of her love affair and to its illustrations. The two women are essentially versions of a single creation.

The passage depicting Barbara's suicide and Andy's reaction to it is in keeping with other Hemingway endings. Like Catherine Barkley at the end of *A Farewell to Arms,* Barbara dies and leaves Andy the sadder but wiser protagonist who must ponder the meaning of their love affair. But unlike Frederic Henry, Andy is a writer. Like Jake Barnes, he must attempt to write the story to gain a better perspective on what has happened. And there is a suggestion that Andy values the experience as literary capital, striking a chord that had appeared in Hemingway's previous considerations of writers.

Although Jenks was unable to use the suicide of Catherine/Barbara as an ending for the novel without violating the principle of adding nothing to the posthumous manuscripts in the course of editing them,[8] he might have considered using a short chapter that Hemingway himself had written and labeled "Provisional Ending." The main action of the novel would have concluded after Catherine has destroyed the manuscripts and left David and Marita alone; David acknowledges that, in spite of everything, he still loves Catherine and feels responsible for her well-being. Although David and Marita would prefer to go to Africa, they discuss taking Catherine to Switzerland to a mental sanitarium. At that point the manuscript does not indicate whether Catherine will actually return to David. Hemingway might have intended to write material to explain what happened next, but his labeling of the seven-page "Provisional Ending" makes it more probable that he felt that he could drop the story at the point where Catherine *might* return and then append the ending, using its abruptness for its shock value. There are, after all, similar time gaps between some of the earlier books of the novel.

This ending would have concluded the novel on an ironic note but with somber hints of tragedy to come. It begins with a man and a woman revisiting the south of France. The woman says that what happened there seems in the distant past and that they were childlike then.[9] They lie in the sun on the beach and reminisce about their trip to Madrid and the sexual games they played so that eventually the reader realizes it is Catherine, not Marita, who is with David. Attempting to blot out the tragedies the couple has endured, Catherine talks about how "comic" things were in the old days, but David responds with restrained irony.[10]

As the chapter progresses, it is apparent that David has become more caretaker than husband; he resembles Fitzgerald's Dick Diver. His ministrations to Catherine, coating her body with oil to keep her from burning and telling her when to move out of the sun or when to enter the water to cool off, are clinical. The relationship has become a parody of the one

David and Catherine shared in the early pages of the novel, furthering the theme that the discovery of evil makes it impossible to dwell in the Garden of Eden.

Other manifestations of the lost Eden are evident in this ending. David rubs oil into Catherine's breasts, a lover's action in the early chapters but a doctor's ministration in this final chapter. Catherine reflects the same clinical attitude when she looks down at her breasts and observes that while they are still "good," it is uncertain what they are good for.[11] The suggestion is that her breasts no longer attract David, nor will they ever nourish a child in this sterile marriage. Catherine acknowledges the losses they have suffered when she asks David how they managed to run through their seemingly limitless emotional riches in a single year.[12] Later she asks David if he remembers the time when it seemed as if the two of them owned their entire world.[13]

Gradually, Catherine shows alarming signs that her mental illness continues. She forgets major details of their life together, saying that it is too bad they never went to Africa, though David reminds her that they have been there. Too often she refers inappropriately to "comic" things in life: Love is a comic word, old friends are recalled as comic characters; finally she reassures David that she won't commit a certain comic act.[14] One of her "comic" tricks has obviously been a suicide attempt.

David tries to reassure Catherine. When she talks of having gone away (into the world of insanity), he tells her that she has come back. She replies that her recovery is more apparent than real. Psychiatrists claim to have all the answers but actually know nothing. She warns David to expect a worse attack next time. When he replies that advances are being made regularly in the treatment of mental illness, she dismisses his attempt to comfort her as "comic." Any advances will come too late to save her.[15] Catherine finally tells David that she loves him, then asks him to promise her something without asking what it is. Even though David knows what the promise will entail, he agrees. Catherine's request is a predictable one. She asks if David will allow her to kill herself if she again becomes ill enough to require hospitalization. When David refuses, she asks if he will join her in a suicide pact. This time he simply answers, "Sure."[16] She tries to reassure David that she will probably never ask him to join her in death, and in the end, the two agree to go for a swim, but experienced readers of Hemingway will not be reassured.

The fact that this ending was labeled "provisional" by Hemingway suggests that he had some reservations about it, but it is more artistic than the story of Barbara's suicide and more in keeping with the Hemingway canon. Rather than closing with a shocking incident involving violent death, this ending would have concluded with the sort of falling action that is consistent with the balance of the novel. Like so much of Hemingway's work, this ending would have had the advantage of leaving many important facts beneath the surface of the story like the unseen portion of the iceberg—so that the reader must infer their existence and their exact nature. Like the open ending of *The Sun Also Rises*, the provisional ending would have left many questions about the future of the major characters unanswered, perhaps a major virtue in itself.

Hemingway had deliberately constructed a tragic story with multiple tales of betrayal, jealousy, and guilt—a novel that might have given him, had he published it early in the postwar period, the sort of success that he needed to reassure himself that his career was back on track. Why was he unable to complete *The Garden of Eden*, despite the facts that he had completed so many of the essential incidents of the novel and had sketched out a suitable ending? Part of the answer to that question lies in the backgrounds of the book and part in the nature of the theme it attempted to probe. Both elements were intensely personal for Hemingway, and although he was able to write about them like "a man possessed," as Kenneth Lynn has observed,[17] publishing them was another matter.

## The Background of *The Garden of Eden*

The relationship between David, Catherine, and Marita obviously owes a great deal to that between Hemingway, Hadley, and Pauline—before, during, and after the breakup of Hemingway's first marriage in 1926. The identification of Hadley with Catherine is difficult to ignore, since Hadley had in effect "destroyed" almost all of Hemingway's literary output when she packed all of his manuscripts and carbons into a small suitcase before leaving Paris to join Ernest in Lausanne in 1922. The suitcase, which was stolen from Hadley's compartment on the train, was never recovered, and Hemingway felt the loss of his manuscripts deeply. Although there is no evidence that Hadley lost the manuscripts as an act of deliberate malice, her loss might have seemed to Hemingway like a Freudian confession of hostility toward his career.

Similarly, the triangular relationship between Hemingway, Hadley, and Pauline suggests a rough source for that depicted in the novel. During her teens, Hadley had supposedly encountered the lesbian mother of a school friend and had been convinced for a short time that she too was a lesbian.[18] Pauline's sister Ginny, whom Hemingway knew well and liked, was a lesbian, and rumors about Pauline after her divorce from Hemingway suggested that she too became involved with women. There is no evidence that Hadley and Pauline ever had any sort of sexual relationship, but Pauline was Hadley's friend before she became Ernest's lover, and the three spent vacations together in Schruns, Austria, and elsewhere.

Catherine's experiments with hair coloring recall Pauline's attempts to hold Ernest's interest by dying her hair in the 1930s, and the description of Catherine's close-cropped haircut matches photos of Pauline. Like Pauline, Catherine has sufficient wealth to support a writer who chooses to be idle. Like Pauline, Catherine takes an active interest in her man's writing career, though Pauline's interest was positive rather than negative. Overall, Hemingway had used just enough material from his personal life to excite any fledgling biographical critics who might read the books for insight into his life and personality—much as Kenneth Lynn has done in our own time. Hemingway must have felt constrained by the idea that publication of *The Garden of Eden* might cause readers to jump to conclusions about matters that he rightfully felt should be off limits.

If the plot of *The Garden of Eden* recalls Hemingway's first two marriages and his early writing career, perhaps it owes even greater debts to the real-life relationship of Scott and Zelda Fitzgerald and to the fictional triangle between Dick and Nicole Diver and Rosemary Hoyt, for in some respects *The Garden of Eden* is a literary response to *Tender Is the Night*. Over the years, Hemingway reacted both negatively and positively to *Tender Is the Night*: he criticized it in a letter to Fitzgerald in 1934, soon after he had read it for the first time;[19] however, when he reread the novel, he liked it better, as reflected in letters written between 1935 and 1950 to Fitzgerald, Maxwell Perkins, and Arthur Mizener.[20] He expressed admiration for the book, for example, in a 1939 letter to Perkins but wished that it had been better "integrated."[21] Hemingway thought that Diver and Nicole were composite characters based on Gerald and Sara Murphy as well as on Scott and Zelda. But because Fitzgerald had made Diver a psychologist rather than a writer, he had left out an important facet of his own relationship with Zelda.

As he would also suggest in *A Moveable Feast*, Hemingway believed that Zelda was extremely jealous of Scott's writing and had engaged in lesbian flirtations to distract him from his work, just as she sometimes discouraged his efforts to maintain sobriety for the same reason.[22] David Bourne's efforts to continue his writing even in a holiday atmosphere recall Fitzgerald's efforts to write during his residence in Paris and the south of France during the 1920s, and Catherine's attempts to distract David, first with idle amusements and then with sexual intrigues, parallel Zelda's assaults on Fitzgerald's career.

In *The Garden of Eden*, Hemingway in effect replied to *Tender Is the Night*, using not only the Fitzgeralds but also autobiographical material and, most importantly, his accumulated insights into the special problems faced by a literary artist. But using such material carried certain risks, particularly for a writer whose life was almost routinely confused with his fictions. Thus, treating such sensitive sexual material could be potentially embarrassing if it were associated with himself or if it undermined his public image. On the other hand, mirroring the Fitzgeralds in his characters could provoke the sort of identification and criticism caused by "Mr. and Mrs. Elliot." In an apparent attempt to forestall the identification of David as either Ernest Hemingway or Scott Fitzgerald, Hemingway wrote a passage in which he and Fitzgerald are mentioned as characters in their own right, as friends of David. Another friend has just arrived from Paris with the latest gossip. He has seen Scott in St. Raphael and reports that Zelda had " 'got in a jam' " with a French aviator and that the Fitzgeralds attempted to patch up their marriage afterward. Fitzgerald is working well but is sad. Then David asks whether he has encountered "Hemingstein." The friend gives a complete report of Hemingway's activities in 1923 and 1924. He has moved to Canada, skied in Austria, and is now living in an apartment on the rue Notre Dame de Champs.[23]

The fragment survives among the miscellaneous notes left over from the composition of *Garden*, apparently discarded, though it is impossible to know for certain whether Hemingway would have used it or not. However, the very act of introducing himself and Fitzgerald as characters in the manuscript would have had the effect of distancing the Bournes from their real-life sources, distancing them for their creator as he wrote as well as for his potential audience. Thus Hemingway—who had experienced repercussions when characters in his first novel were identified with real people—might have felt free to explore private aspects of the Bournes' life together more deeply when he did not fear that the characters would be identified with living prototypes.

In spite of Hemingway's evident wish not to be identified with David Bourne, several of the earliest responses to *The Garden of Eden* have focused on the personal and sexual dimensions of the novel. Kenneth Lynn, for example, has subjected *The Garden of Eden* to a psychological reading, finding elements of Hadley and Pauline in Catherine (and perhaps in Marita) and suggesting that the novel is a confessional work by the author, who wrote it at great speed. Lynn sees Hemingway in the grip of "a manic need to unburden himself" concerning his own "sexual duality."[24]

But *The Garden of Eden* is much more than the story of a failed marriage or of the sexual duality of three expatriates living in the south of France during the 1920s. The sexual elements of the plot have clouded the fact that the main conflict in the novel hinges equally on David's writing and its role in destroying Catherine's sanity and the Bourne marriage. Perhaps Hemingway's "confession" was written with such speed because he was "possessed" by the psychological necessity of confronting the writer's destructive power, over himself and over others. David Bourne's vocation is even more strongly emphasized in the novel's manuscript, where it is apparent that Hemingway faced and attempted to resolve serious problems encountered in his professional life.

## Faces and Mirrors

As a continuing motif to reinforce his examination of the writer and the sins that necessarily accompany the artist's obsession with his art, Hemingway employs frequent references to mirrors throughout *The Garden of Eden*. David frequently looks at his own image in the mirror, as if to seek external evidence of the depths of his own depravity; Catherine looks at herself in the mirror in imitation of David, the true artist; David and Catherine look at each other and at themselves together as a couple in the mirror they have bought for the bar at their hotel; finally, they use each other as mirrors: if husband and wife are one, each may see his or her own present state reflected in the other.

David gazes into mirrors repeatedly throughout the published novel. References to his gazing into mirrors range from relatively simple statements that he is looking into a mirror, such as the occasion in chapter 9 on which he first looks at Catherine "and then at his own face in the mirror" to compare their appearances and then "looked once more in the mirror" (82) just after having his hair cut like Catherine's. This reference appears as a superficial interest in an experiment in hair styling, but the significance increases as the tone becomes more somber in the next chapter.

The early casual comparison to Catherine gives way to David's more disapproving self-appraisal after he has allowed the barber to bleach his hair to the same color as Catherine's:

> . . . David got up and looked at himself in the bathroom mirror. . . .
> Then he came back and picked up her big hand mirror.
> . . . . . . . . . . . . . . . . . . . . . . . . . . . . . . . . . . . . . . .
> He asked the mirror. "How do you feel?"
> . . . . . . . . . . . . . . . . . . . . . . . . . . . . . . . .

He looked at the mirror and it was someone else he saw but it was less strange now.

· · · · · · · · · ·

He looked at the face that was no longer strange to him at all but was his face now and said, " . . . You know exactly how you look now and how you are."

Of course he did not know exactly how he was. But he made an effort aided by what he had seen in the mirror. [84–85]

A later passage (133) echoes and elaborates upon David's attempt to know himself and is strongly reminiscent of Hemingway's successful use of the mirror in the closing lines of "The Sea Change." David, like Phil in the short story, looks into the mirror that he and Catherine have bought for the hotel bar (as if to supply their own personal touchstone to test their own private truths). David studies his reflection, lifts his drink to his image in a mock toast, and thinks that he would have hesitated to have a drink with the person he sees reflected there if he had met him four months earlier. Superficially, David is suggesting that he appears to be a homosexual, whose company he would have avoided, but on a metaphorical level he is acknowledging a true corruption that goes deeper than surfaces. Later, sitting before the same mirror after a writing session in which he has evoked the memory of his father, David enjoys the aura of his father's lingering presence until he accidentally "glances" into the mirror and sees himself sitting alone (147). In this case, the mirror denies David a pleasant feeling, a passing fantasy, by providing a corrective image. This incident underscores the function of mirrors to provide a reflection of reality that is sometimes more accurate—if more cruel—than the unaided perceptions of the characters.

As he progresses further into the psychological experiments involving Catherine, Marita, and his own writing, David's juxtaposition of his past and present states is again conveyed by a mirror image—this time of his reflected face as he shaves: "He looked at his face in the mirror with one side shaved" (167). One side of his face recalls the old life he had lived, while the other represents his new self, corrupted by Catherine's money and the sexual experiments that she employs to hold him, and by his own narcissistic devotion to his art rather than to emotional relationships.

Catherine's habit of peering into mirrors complements David's obsession with his reflected image. Not capable of producing art herself, Catherine nevertheless can emulate the self-absorption of the true artist. At first, Catherine's self-examinations in mirrors coincide with the physical changes she makes in her appearance. However, her sense of otherness from her reflection signals the onset of her psychological breakdown. Just before David looks into the mirror at the barber shop, Catherine foreshadows his immediate action and his later reaction by looking into the same mirror: "She looked in the mirror as though she had never seen the girl she was looking at" (81).

In this instance Catherine's looking into the mirror is literally explained by the barbershop context, but her later obsession with mirrors is more symbolically significant: just after she has told David about her own earliest sexual advances toward Marita and has tried to interest him in an affair with the younger woman (and implicitly in the establishment of a ménage à trois) she goes into her bathroom and carefully examines her mirrored image (115) as she has many times, looking either for some outward sign of her moral degeneration or for features that might catch the attention of her writer husband.

Sitting with David in front of the mirror they have purchased for the bar in their hotel, Catherine both admires the new mirror and laments its accuracy in reflecting her face—and perhaps her character: " 'It's a very good one. . . . It's awfully critical though' " (133). Later she watches herself in the same mirror as she manipulates Marita and David to cause them to fall in love. Although powerless to transform into art the tragedy she is shaping, Catherine nevertheless enjoys observing the changes she sees in herself and in her lover and husband as she deliberately corrupts the other two. In this way she seems to parody the true artist as he has previously been depicted by Hemingway. The latter may sell out the lives of those closest to him for the sake of the art he will create out of their misery, but he will regret the cost to himself and to them.

In addition to the instances in which David or Catherine study their own images in mirrors, other mirror images that link the two of them abound. Catherine herself serves as a sort of mirror to David, since she looks enough like him so that people think they are brother and sister. This motif of the physical resemblance between David and Catherine is repeated throughout the novel. Catherine first attempts to mirror David by assuming his sexual role during their lovemaking and by having her hair cut like a man's. She later attempts to make David the mirror image of herself by having his hair cut and later bleached to match her own.[25] At last she tells him that she wants each of them to be exactly the same as the other (176) and rebukes him for negating her attempts to merge their identities. Her encouragement of David's interest in Marita, with whom Catherine has already begun an affair of her own, seems an attempt to seduce him into a more perfect reflection of Catherine—or to allow Catherine to reflect David more perfectly.

To this end, Catherine has insisted that she and David use some of her wealth to buy the mirror for the bar of the hotel. " 'We'll get a mirror for it. . . . And then we can all see each other when we talk. . . . You can't fool a bar mirror' " (102–103).[26] Sometimes it is used to allow David or Catherine to avoid looking directly into the eyes of the other, as when Catherine, shortly after burning all of David's manuscripts, "did not look at him, only at his reflection in the mirror" (219). A similar scene occurs between David and Marita shortly after they have made love on the beach. Embarrassed to look directly at David, Marita instead looks at his image in the mirror.

David's—and Hemingway's—obsession with mirrors in the novel marks the importance of Hemingway's most thorough and sustained examination of the role of the writer: how does he live with those about him, and how does he live with himself? As David scrutinizes himself in literal mirrors throughout the novel, Hemingway subjects his character as artist to continual scrutiny throughout *The Garden of Eden.*

## The Writer as Parasite

As if the Bourne marriage were a laboratory experiment in which only one factor—David's writing—could threaten the survival of the marriage, Hemingway grants the fictional couple an idyllic setting, ample funds, sexual and personal compatibility, love, and generous spirits. In the beginning of the novel, each of the main characters is willing, even eager, to compromise or to sacrifice for the sake of the other. Nevertheless, like the snake in the garden, David's writing will ultimately destroy the Bournes' happiness and their marriage. One source of conflict, emphasized in the manuscript, is that Catherine feels left out of David's work. David himself fears that Catherine will feel lonely while he is working, so he puts off writing early in their marriage, telling Catherine not to worry about the fact that he has not resumed his work. He can forgo his work for a little while.[27] His reason for not beginning work immediately is that it would isolate him from her.[28] To overcome this obstacle, Catherine naively suggests that his next writing project should be the autobiographical story of their life together, so that they will always have the memory. David is unwilling the first time Catherine brings it up, but when she persists, he reluctantly agrees to shelve his other work and to begin the story that both come to identify as "the narrative." Hemingway clearly disapproved of efforts to dictate the artist's subject, as he showed in "The Butterfly and the Tank," *The Fifth Column,* and *Islands in the Stream.*

When he first begins to work on the narrative, the writing goes so well that it worries David. He knows that running through their marriage is a complexity belied by the simplicity of the story he is putting on paper. Beneath the surface of his doubts there may lie a fear that through the introspection that accompanies his writing, he may discover hidden flaws. Indeed, as he continues the story, he finds that he is becoming aware of a subtext: "the sinister part [of the marriage] only showed as the light feathering of a smooth swell on a calm day marking the reef beneath" (42). The narrative is an extension of the mirror symbolism in that it will be a reflection of David and Catherine's life together. But can it be an accurate reflection? An accurate reflection would not, in fact, satisfy Catherine, whose own view of their marriage is flawed, but a less than accurate reflection would betray David's sense of honesty as a writer.

Hemingway certainly had ample personal experience on which to draw in his examination of the effects of writing on a marriage from a male writer's point of view, but one of the strengths of *The Garden of Eden* is his ability to convey the wife's feelings. His sensitivity to Catherine's emotions and reactions, both overt and subconscious, provide evidence for those who would defend Hemingway against charges of male egocentrism.[29] Catherine has difficulties with her own ambivalence about being wife and partner to a writer. Although she was the one who suggested that he write about their marriage, one side of Catherine resents David's analytical approach to their relationship. At first her resentment does not center on David but on writers in general and then, only in the manuscript novel, on a particular writer, Andy Murray. In a way, Andy is a live reflection, and the use of a double, which Hemingway used to such good effect in *Islands in the Stream*, reinforces the use of the mirror as revelation.

When David and Catherine arrive in Spain in manuscript book 2, they meet Andy, an old friend of David's and a fellow writer. Several remarks Catherine makes to David after being introduced to Andy suggest her disenchantment with writers as a class, though she qualifies her generalizations by saying that David and Andy are exceptions. Andy is surprisingly "nice" and seems more "clean" than most writers,[30] a compliment so restrained that it verges on an insult. Usually she does not like writers other than David because writers remember everything, the implication being that they will later use what they remember in their fiction. Her jealousy of writers and other artists is explicit when she says she had had no artistic ambitions of her own before coming to Spain, but that now she feels a constant hunger to express herself through writing or painting.[31]

The introduction of Andy permits Hemingway to explore writers' conflicts in dialogue as well as to show that David's problems are not isolated or idiosyncratic but generic in their relevance to all artists who must balance personal and professional lives. In the manuscript chapter that introduces Andy, he and David agree that they have too much integrity to sell their "dross," or work that is less than their best. David does not have to sell his work because he is married to a wealthy woman. Andy's father has left him enough money so that he can live carefully on it for several years while he writes. Andy feels that he can support himself if he can earn $600 per year. In his opinion, no writer of integrity can possibly earn more than that.[32] Such talk of artistic principles irritates Catherine, who is becoming increasingly aware of the conflicts an artist's wife faces.

Although Andy is a wholesome influence on the Bournes, Catherine soon decides that she does not like him. Andy, she thinks, is too analytical, an accusation that might apply to all writers.[33] Later, she relents in her dislike of Andy, suggesting that her feelings toward writers are more ambivalent than hostile.[34] Although Hemingway eventually dropped the character from the Bourne plot, Andy's identification with David in the early version of the manuscript gives some clues to the underwater part of the iceberg in the published novel. Catherine's early interest in Andy, her later dislike of his traits as a writer, and her final ambivalence are displaced indications of the latent hostility Catherine feels for David in the published novel, where these feelings come to the surface only briefly and occasionally.

Another section of the manuscript that illuminates the writer's problems deals with writer's block, which surely plagued Hemingway in his later years when he struggled to complete his postwar novels. When David has difficulty resuming his writing, he asks himself why he should care if he is not writing when life with Catherine is so pleasant, rationalizing his inability to work.[35] Yet he realizes that for a writer, experience is meant to be used, and that he will eventually have to "bite on the nail" and resume his work. He tries to believe that his inactivity is no cause for concern, but it is obvious that he is concerned. His ambivalence about using his life with Catherine as subject matter has caused a conflict between his artistic conscience and his moral conscience. Catherine, too, feels ambivalent about being used in the fiction even though she offered her life to David as material: at the close of their stay in Madrid, Catherine is talking wildly while David merely listens; she breaks off suddenly because she has seen David "storing" up her conversation for use in his fiction.[36] She asks if she has helped David as a writer by giving him new material, a comment that reminds the reader of the woman in "The Sea Change." While Catherine does not accuse him of invading her privacy, her undirected anger is evident in the passage. Probably, like Harry's wealthy friends in "The Snows of Kilimanjaro," Catherine would be more comfortable if David chose not to work.

Catherine's feelings about David's writing are emphasized in the published novel. When David begins work on the narrative, things go well at first, as Catherine feels that she is involved. But she soon becomes disenchanted with her merely inspirational role. Attempting to involve herself more deeply with the creative process, she supplies new material for the narrative by bringing Marita into their life together. The narrative, she tells David, will be improved once it has a "dark girl" in it as well as the blond Catherine (188). Also, knowing something of business, she plans to have the narrative illustrated by prominent painters and tries to engage David in publication plans, but he puts her off by telling her that he has not thought about publication, only about the writing problems involved—problems that he will not discuss with her. Similarly, he refuses to allow Catherine to read the work in progress until he feels satisfied with it.

Outwardly, Catherine accepts David's exploitation of her and of their life together. She seems unaware of the extent of her hostility toward David and his role as writer and eavesdropper. Hemingway captured her underlying feelings neatly, however, in a manuscript incident involving an unidentified writer she has seen in St. Raphael. Although the man looks as attractive as a model in a collar ad, his handsome face and sporty clothing conflict with his "sly" look, which suggests the detached observer who spies on the people around him. Although no specific part of the man is actually physically deformed, he gives Catherine the impression that he is grotesque in some way as he "peers" at her.[37] This writer recalls Richard Gordon of *To Have and Have Not* in his physical attractiveness, which conceals a corrupt nature (suggested here in the writer's apparent undefinable deformity), and in his compulsion to study the lives of others. He also anticipates the old writer of *Across the River and Into the Trees*, who sits "peering" at Venice society. With both writers, the "peering" marks one who is a spectator of life, gathering impressions by watching the emotions and actions of people who are more actively engaged with life. At first Catherine does not connect her negative attitude toward other writers such as Andy and the man at St. Raphael with her attitude toward David, but she will as the tragedy progresses.

David is far from blameless. Especially in the manuscript portions cut from this segment of the novel, it is clear that he uses Catherine, not just as raw material for his narrative but as a diversion in his off hours, yet he conveys to her that she is secondary to his work and will be deserted for it when it suits him to leave her. Here, as elsewhere, Hemingway may be drawing on his own experience of the writer's ruthlessness. As he pointed out in an interview, if the writer's imagination is to be replenished and his subconscious is to be allowed to work, he must stop thinking about his writing when he is done working for the day.[38] When Marita joins the couple, David is happy enough to divert himself with both women even though he worries about Marita's effect on his marriage. His work comes first, and he now has two women to exploit rather than one.

In manuscript this notion of the writer coolly exploiting his relationships with other people is even more prominent than it is in the published novel. For example, David finds that he writes best in the morning because of the alertness and mental focus he always experiences after intercourse.[39] Sex, then, is valued more for its side effects than for itself. David's love life is again subordinated to his artistic life when Catherine tells David that she plans to have an affair with Marita. Unlike Scott Fitzgerald, who allowed Zelda to distract him by associating with lesbians,[40] David remains more interested in his writing than in the two women. Does he feel that their story too will provide him with further grist for his mill?

In a plot development reminiscent of "The Sea Change," Catherine attempts to capitalize on this possibility: she talks to David about the beginnings of a lesbian relationship with Marita. David urges her to stop, and when she says that she plans to develop the relationship, he tells her that he'll leave them alone and return to Paris. Catherine, like the young woman in "The Sea Change," asks for his understanding: " 'Please try. You always understood before. You know you did' " (114). As a writer, David has to understand human nature, but now as a man he is unable to extend the same sympathetic understanding to his wife. Catherine must feel that she has the worst of both worlds. Her husband exploits their relationship by using it as the basis for his fiction but hides himself from her in the detached world of his creative work. Yet when the insightfulness and sensitivity of his imaginative life might work to her advantage, he reverts to the status of an ordinary man and condemns what he cannot understand. He will neither draw her back from the dangerous game she is playing by giving himself wholly to her nor tolerate her new nature and try to understand it. But David's exploitation of Catherine and his marriage is only one of the essential elements for the building tragedy.

## The Writer as *Isolato*

If the exploitation of others is a major sin of the writer, perhaps even more important is his inhuman isolation from the rest of humanity. Both the writer's status as celebrity and his need for privacy to practice his craft influence him to withdraw from the rest of mankind. In a late story, "Get a Seeing-Eyed Dog" (almost certainly written during the fifteen years during which he struggled with *The Garden of Eden*), the relationship between a blinded writer and his wife forms an interesting contrast to the writer-wife relationship in *The Garden of Eden*. In the novel, David is whole, while Catherine is not. In the story, on the other hand, the wife is whole, while Philip, the writer, is not. In both the novel and the story, the writer-protagonist distances himself from his mate, who wishes to help him with his writing. It is certainly significant that the writer in the story bears the same first name as the protagonist of "The Sea Change," of *The Fifth Column*, of *The Garden of Eden* in its earliest draft, and of the posthumously published sketch about Philip Haines.[41] For Hemingway, Philip (or Phillip) was a writer's name. The late story also bears some resemblance to "The Snows of Kilimanjaro."

Like Harry in "The Snows," Philip spends much of his time recalling events from his past, intending to use them in his writing. He and his wife have recently returned from a safari where Philip presumably suffered the injury that cost him his eyesight. His wife assists his attempts at total recall, supplying facts that Philip cannot remember. In this way she achieves what Catherine Bourne can only wish to accomplish: she is a sort of partner in a creative act—at least for the present. Unlike David Bourne, however, Philip is unable to write. Although he claims that he intends to use a tape recorder, his despair over not being able to write is evident.

Julian Smith has suggested that Philip's blindness "is the metaphor for Hemingway's own creative difficulties,"[42] but it might also be a metaphor for what had worried Hemingway for some time: the self-imposed isolation of the writer. Hemingway's writers are usually unaware of anything that does not concern their art, including the needs of a spouse, a child, or a friend. At its best, this tendency can be described as tunnel vision, the necessary concentration that allows Andy to write his best work while he is desperately worried about Barbara or that allows Thomas Hudson to continue his painting while his children are visiting him in Bimini. At its worst, the extreme concentration becomes an utter disregard for anything that is not his work—a blindness to the needs and wishes of others. Ironically, the perceptiveness that makes an individual *see* the true nature of his fellows and become a writer in the first place is lost as he withdraws into his art; thus the blindness metaphor is singularly appropriate.

Both the title and verbal repetitions in the story call attention to the metaphorical blindness of the writer. A writer must possess not only a physical "seeing eye" capable of recording external details but a mind's eye that helps him to empathize and achieve insight into the lives of others. Throughout the story, Philip repeatedly employs the phrases "you see" and "you know"; the interchangeability of the verbs emphasizes the dependent relationship between the two capabilities. For the artist to know enough about the human heart to project his own artistic "vision," he must see others truly, perceive them more fully than the nonartist is able to do. This artist has lost his metaphorical vision as well as his eyesight, as is proved by his inability to continue sharing his life with his wife.

Delbert Wylder has stated that Philip needs the cooperation of his wife to write,[43] but the story concludes with his determination to "get her away as soon as I can."[44] In the context of the story, his resolve seems an unselfish desire to spare his wife the pain that she would share if she stayed. However, this may be a fiction that Philip has created to put the best face on a selfish act: if he is like Hemingway's other writers, writing is a private thing for him, a temple to which he can admit no one else. From that point of view, it would be better, as Philip suggests, to use a tape recorder rather than a human amanuensis. Perhaps he thinks that banishing his wife will revive his moribund creativity. But to modify Wylder's contention, what Philip needs from his wife is not secretarial help but the bridge that she offers to the rest of humanity. If Philip could share with her, he could rejoin the human race and regain his artistic ability. By choosing further isolation, Philip will lose his grasp of his art.

If viewed in this way, the story is incredibly compact, even for a Hemingway story. It both documents, in metaphorical form, the major difficulty of the writer, his insensitivity to others, and shows a writer impaled on one horn of the classic dilemma all writers must face: they need their fellows in both a personal and an artistic sense, yet they must secede from human relationships during their working hours and view humanity with Promethean detachment. Philip is a man who finds himself unable to return to previous human relationships and unable even to recognize what has gone wrong with his life. While "Get a Seeing-Eyed Dog" is not completely successful, it complements the major conflict inherent in *The Garden of Eden.* Stripped of the sexual subplots of the novel, the story succinctly attacks the chief concern that informs the novel.

Like Philip, David Bourne illustrates the artist's tendency to isolate himself by his treatment of Catherine. Early in their marriage, David and Catherine have an argument that seems to be precipitated by a minor event—the arrival of some clippings forwarded by David's publisher. At first Catherine is proud of the positive reviews, which affirm David's skill as a writer. Soon, however, she begins to feel threatened by the clippings, telling David, " 'They could destroy you if you thought about them or believed them. You don't think I married you because you are what they say you are in these clippings do you?' " (24). Catherine's part in the argument over David's literary reputation seems petty and shallow. A wealthy young woman, she is used to owning and controlling things, and she seems to resent David's having a life in which she does not participate fully.

The published novel, however, omits some features of the manuscript novel that more fully explain David's reaction to his literary fame and Catherine's concern about his growing status. David feels himself taking on a new role as the clippings establish a more prestigious identity for him. Catherine perceptively notes this change and worries that he will be estranged from her by his literary reputation.[45] She suggests that the clippings have been an intoxicating drug for David.[46] Catherine is somewhat off the mark. She assumes that David is motivated by a desire for literary fame, but the clippings, which come long after the creative process itself, have only a minor appeal to him. David's true addiction is to his writing itself.

Even in its truncated form in the published novel, however, this scene is pivotal. With dramatic irony, the scene illuminates the beginnings of a gap between David and Catherine; now a minor irritant, their differences of opinion about writing will increase in time, as David's obsession with his art intensifies. Catherine says that she would have been just as happy and as proud of David if the reviews had been bad and the book had not made money, but David secretly realizes that he would not have been either happy or proud. The disparity between David's and Catherine's reactions to the clippings epitomizes their relationship as it will develop later in the novel: the more positive David feels about his career, the more negative Catherine feels as she sees his identity as writer taking precedence over his identity as her husband. As if on a seesaw, husband and wife are unable to balance; they are doomed to a relationship where only one can be fully satisfied or happy at a time. Catherine is right to sense foreboding: David's dedication to writing will threaten not only their marriage but her sanity.

The argument over David's press clippings is merely the opening skirmish of what will become a bitter war between the Bournes over David's devotion to his writing rather than to Catherine and the marriage. Even in book 1, which might be subtitled "Eden before the Fall," there are ominous hints of trouble to come. In an early scene David thinks that "it would be good to work again" but that, when he does resume his writing, "he must remember to be unselfish about it and make it as clear as he could that the enforced loneliness was regrettable and that he was not proud of it" (14). In addition to feeling ambivalent about his writing, which he misses despite the isolation it entails, he obviously anticipates trouble with Catherine: the "regrettable" and "not proud of it" suggest a shift in point of view. The adjectives are not true expressions of his own feelings but a rehearsal of the defenses he will use to justify what Catherine might be expected to view as his selfish withdrawal. By anticipating Catherine's negative reaction but not confronting it directly, David is beginning to avoid unpleasant reality in their relationship.

In the manuscript, David's dissatisfaction about suspending his work during the honeymoon is more apparent. Lying on the beach with Catherine, David thinks with traces of bitterness that his writing career is now behind him. He cynically reflects that their sexual experiments interest him more than his writing, but the assertion is hollow.[47] Even while obviously enjoying himself, David is haunted by the nagging of his artist's conscience, which tells him that a writer must work regularly to maintain his ability. Like Thomas Hudson in *Islands in the Stream,* who must work even during his sons' brief visit, David cannot merely abandon his work for a few days without feeling guilty for doing so. In manuscript David lets Catherine know about his dissatisfaction, thus providing a context for her jealousy and alienation, which seem unmotivated in the published novel. At one point, he suggests that she should be the writer in the family, and when she lovingly tells him that there is going to be just one writer in the family, he petulantly answers that there may not even be one,[48] as if fearful that he may never succeed in resuming his work. In another sentence omitted by the editor, Hemingway even suggests that David's personality is so intricately bound to his writing that the loss of his artistic persona would be tantamount to loss of his identity: David feels a shock of recognition while reading his own name in the reviews, as if he would be nameless without their printed affirmation. It is small wonder that, in response to one of David's complaints about not being able to write, Catherine tells him that he hasn't signed his soul away to the devil.[49] The irony is, of course, that David will sell his soul to be a writer. But he will sell out to his art, not to any person, no matter how much he loves her. Catherine's remark is the part of the iceberg underlying David's mental note in the published novel that "somewhere something had been said [about his not writing] and now he could not remember it" (27).

Although David wants to get back to work, he realizes the dangers his writing may pose to his marriage, dangers Catherine does not recognize early in the novel when she assures him that she is not worried: she will amuse herself when he begins to write again. After all, she says, she won't have to leave him so that he can write. Ironically it is David who will leave *her*, retreating into the cold chamber of his artistic privacy; it is this desertion that Catherine will attempt to counter, first by her sexual play, eventually by her lesbian affair with Marita, and later by her own retreat into another world—that of insanity.

David's hesitancy to get back to work is further emphasized in a passage cut from the published version of his catching the huge fish (8–10). In this omitted section of the first chapter, Catherine actually urges David to resume his writing and taxes him with the fact that he hasn't written at all since their marriage. His reason for not starting to write immediately is that he would have to spend too much time away from Catherine. He avoids explaining his fear of thus isolating himself, but later it becomes obvious that what David dreads is the habit-forming nature of his artistic isolation. In the published novel he avoids the problem, telling himself, " 'When I have to work I will. Nothing can stop that' " (31). The last sentence ominously underscores the nature of the writer's compulsion: his motivation is an irresistible urge that Hemingway himself knew well, a drive the writer is helpless to deny regardless of consequences. David's awareness of this obsession accounts for the feeling of malaise underlying the Bournes' seemingly carefree marriage, for he understands that once he immerses himself in his work, he may find himself addicted to isolation, even from Catherine.

Although Catherine does not understand the exact anatomy of David's malaise, she intuitively perceives a dark side to David's nature and fears that it may threaten their relationship. As a way of sidestepping the loneliness of his writing, David adopts Catherine's plan that he should work on the account of their life together. This scheme presents problems of its own, but it has the virtue of keeping the Bournes together. Even while David is writing about her, however, Catherine resents the activity that keeps him isolated so much of the day.

In the manuscript of *Garden,* David attempts to label what is happening as mere boredom on Catherine's part, saying that life with a working writer is dull. Only the writer himself feels the excitement of creativity.[50] He realizes the source but not the nature and extent of the problem: Catherine is not only bored but pathologically jealous of David's artistic life—from which she is excluded. Moreover, so great are the excitement and joy David experiences in his writing that he could hardly give it up even if he realized the risk he was running.[51]

The rift between the Bournes widens when David abandons the sanctioned "narrative," which he regards as a tour de force, and embarks on a story that will test all his powers as an author. He had always put off writing this story about his life with his father, the hardest story that he can think of to write. Writing about a period of his life in which Catherine had no part takes David further from her, and as her resentment grows, David talks less with her about his work. Catherine begins to feel that her chief rival, David's writing, is stronger than she and will always triumph.

The sense of rivalry is exacerbated when David, Catherine, and Marita talk about the story he has begun. Unlike Catherine, Marita draws David out about his early life, his novel about life with his father in East Africa, and his great love for his father. Catherine jealously remarks that David has never talked to her about his father:

> "You never asked me."
> "Would you have?"
> "No," he said. [111]

In manuscript, Hemingway added a telling reply by Catherine, who tells Marita that being kept at an emotional distance is the customary lot of the writer's wife.[52] Catherine's remark—perhaps too obvious a signpost for Hemingway to have left it in his final draft—is a reminder that nowhere else in his work has he told the reader so explicitly what living with a writer is like—nor what living *as* a writer is like.

When Catherine and Marita begin their love affair, David lives more exclusively within the story he is writing, so much so that, at the beginning of chapter 15, he is startled by the sound of the Bugatti because where he is living imaginatively, there are no cars. He is detached from the problems of real life, concerned only with the creative problems to be solved as he writes his story. During working hours his emotions are those that he is portraying in his father. Only when he quits for the day and feels loneliness, not because he desires human companionship but because he cannot go back to his work until the next day, does he think about Catherine and Marita.

In the manuscript Hemingway enlarged upon this sense of detachment and how it affected David's literary fortunes. David dwells on the ruin his private life has become but comforts himself with the observation that literary ability is the only asset he has left but that it is improving in the midst of tragedy.[53] On the verso of that same page, David—echoing Catherine's earlier comment—reflects on the Faustian nature of the bargain he has made with life, selling his soul, if not to the devil, to art. He links his moral failure to the improvements he has seen in his writing.[54] In spite of this knowledge, which is like Phil's in "The Sea Change,"

David continues to retreat into his writing even as the situation involving Catherine, Marita, and himself grows more forbidding. No matter what the cost to the people around him, the writer's obsession with his art is strong enough to override love or even common decency.

Hemingway reveals the psychological effects that accompany the physical effects of David's obsession: in manuscript David leaves his writing room aware that he is "groggy" and "dopy,"[55] like a man emerging from a trance or from an encounter with a powerful drug. When David tells Marita that this state is a result of his work, she replies that such work must be "terrible." Agreeing, David says that it is nevertheless his only real interest in life.[56] He later apologizes to Marita for hurting her feelings with this remark, saying that he had gone away into his writing and was not fully back to the world of reality when he said it, but the statement reveals a significant truth. David is willing to leave not only his current wife but his new mistress for the sake of something that means more to him than his relationships with others—his writing. In the published novel, all that remains of this disquieting conversation is David's mental note, when Marita offers to help him in things other than his writing, that "there are no other things" (140), and he keeps this harsh observation to himself. In this instance, as in others noted above, Hemingway's harsh judgments of the selfish, egocentric nature of the writer are moderated in the published novel.

As David sinks deeper into the fictive world of his African story, Hemingway underscores the ill effects of the writer's immersion in his art by suggesting an ominous allegorical connection between the work and the author. Having forgotten Catherine and Marita, David empathizes with his father—both with his real father as he remembers him and with the fictional persona he is creating from his memory. His father had taken evil too lightly, too casually, treating it like a friend. However, David uses his knowledge of evil (recently derived from his marital experience) as an abstraction that underlies the story, a technique that Hemingway himself employed. David believes that evil's unseen presence strengthens the story but ignores the fact that, like his father (and like Phil in "The Sea Change"), he may find himself "poxed" by the evil with which he is becoming all too familiar.

The relationship between the characters of Phil in "The Sea Change" and David (who was called Phil during the earliest stage of the composition of *Garden*, when Hemingway clearly recognized their kinship) becomes even more evident: concentrating on the artistic difficulties of treating the story he has put off writing for so long, David fails to recognize the psychic danger the story represents for him. By leaving real life

behind in order to live in this world of his own creation, David is guilty
of a perversion greater than the one Catherine has been acting out in her
attempt to awaken him from his inhuman absorption in his writing. His
insistence on the privacy of his internal world signals a destructive withdrawal from the world of human relationships, a withdrawal that renders
him less human.

The destructive effects of David's withdrawal move outward like rip-
ples in a pond to affect those around him, most notably Catherine. Psychologically unstable, she eventually abandons her attempts to bring David
back to real life and instead attempts to become a part of his fictive world.
Just as writing is the most important thing in David's life, David as writer
becomes more important to Catherine than David as husband or lover, so
she is more concerned with being part of his creative life than with being
his sexual partner. Her jealousy of Marita's share in David's writing is
apparent at the end of chapter 17, when Marita curses Catherine for distracting David when he is in the middle of a story. The manuscript speci-
fies that Marita calls it an "important" story, and Catherine asks whether
she has read the story. David has to reassure Catherine that Marita has
not seen it.[57] Allowing Marita to read the story before Catherine would
be the worst sort of betrayal.

The manuscript version of chapter 18 provides an illuminating analysis
of the feelings of a writer upon completing a major manuscript. David is
proud of the finished story but also misses his work on it, almost as a
former addict might long for a drug from which he is withdrawing. The
psychic strain caused by David's devotion to his work and by the breakup
of his marriage paradoxically adds to the value of the story, as David realizes that the psychological pressure he had been under during its composition had strengthened the story[58] and later reflects that perhaps he
should thank Catherine for the strength of another story that has come
out even better than he had expected.[59] Andy Murray felt the same way
about Barbara's breakdown, during which he had written better than he
could write during untroubled times.[60] In contrast to this full treatment
of the writer's postpartum emotions—Hemingway's fullest examination
of the writer's feelings at this stage of the creative process—the published
novel briefly acknowledges David's reaction to the story itself and not his
emotional response to leaving his fictive world. Only one phrase concerning David's "cold, hard part" (his critical faculty) hints at the manuscript
details that underlie this scene (153).

Hemingway's analysis of the reactions of the writer's wife is perceptive
and sympathetic. From Catherine's point of view, David first deserted her
by seeking the privacy of his fictive world, a world she cannot enter and

into which he allowed her no glimpse while he worked on the story, claiming that it is "bad luck" to let anyone read a work in progress.[61] Then he wrote about a private experience that antedates their life together, thus shutting her out of his imaginative life just as he has shut her out of the writing room. Finally, he compounded the offense by allowing her rival to read the finished story first. Thus, it is not surprising that Catherine reacts to the story by tearing the little notebook in which it is written in half, an action that foreshadows her later destruction of all of David's manuscripts. (Another pointed foreshadowing appears in the manuscript: after Marita compliments David on his writer's memory, he replies that he forgets stories once he has written them.)[62]

Before the desperate act of destroying David's manuscripts, Catherine makes some final attempts to share his creative process. First she reads the next story David has begun, filching his keys to unlock the suitcase in which he keeps his work; then she tries to influence the course of the story by suggesting that nothing bad should happen to the dog in it. But David has already been won over by the support of Marita, the rival muse, who confines herself to praising David's finished story and encouraging him to choose another difficult subject he has avoided and begin a new story the next day.

Emphasizing the writer's problems in the manuscript, Hemingway wrote much more on David's feeling of isolation than appears in the published version of *The Garden of Eden.* Manuscript chapter 29, for example, recalls Hemingway's Nobel Prize statement when David tells himself that in writing about Africa, he has no precedent for his stories set on that continent, no previous tradition to "guide" him.[63] He realizes also that he can omit nothing because he is ashamed of it or because it might not be understood. The writer's emotional life must be an open book to his readers—an ideal Hemingway himself had not been able to fulfill easily in his later years. Thus in some ways the reader is closer to the writer than those who live with him day to day, from whom he withholds his true self while revealing it to his readers. Even sexual intimacy may detract from an author's writing. When Marita asks him whether lovemaking is bad for his writing, David answers that both sex and writing employ the same vitality. Too much sexual activity might make him artistically impotent.[64]

In the manuscript, the theme of David living a dual life, poised between his writing and real life, deepens as David becomes increasingly estranged from Catherine. Retreating into the safe haven of his self-created literary world to escape from Catherine, he eventually finds that Marita has come to share his obsession. She tells him that like himself, she is willing to sacrifice everything for his writing. She feels they are both "servants" to David's work.[65] Marita becomes so close to David that she is like an overzealous votary or an artistic conscience, defending his selfish concentration and warning him of the danger to his writing that Catherine represents. She tells him that Catherine is jealous of his work, and, when David excuses Catherine, claims that Catherine used her money to keep David from working.[66] Unlike Catherine, Marita loves his work because it is his best feature.[67] Her empathy with David's creative nature is so extreme that at times it is easier to view her as a symbolic alter ego than as a realistic character in her own right. Like Renata of *Across the River and Into the Trees*, who represents the rebirth of Colonel Cantwell's youth, Marita seems to serve as an incarnation of David's creative self—with all of its weaknesses as well as its strengths.

A symbolic rather than realistic interpretation of Marita answers some of the critical objections that she is in many ways a much less fully realized character than Catherine. Her inner life, her life before she arrives fullblown in the setting of *The Garden of Eden*, is somewhat of a mystery. Her motivations and thoughts are obscure: at times she seems almost a creation of David's imagination—or of his imagination coupled with Catherine's. Does she represent idealized womanhood or personify David's devotion to his art? Or is she yet another reflection of the writer—the one in the mirror: pragmatic, self-centered, and ruthless?

As Marita supports David's withdrawal into the private world of his work, Catherine attacks it. She resents and ridicules his African tales. In manuscript, this argument is even more virulent. Catherine calls David a conceited "poseur" and a "scribbler," terms that recall Hemingway's early critical portraits of Robert Prentiss and Hubert Elliot. She implies that he is a mere hack whom she is attempting to help. She taunts him about her financial support and the "Bohemian" life from which she has rescued him.[68] The manuscript version of this attack thus helps to explain David's motivation in shifting his allegiance to Marita late in the book.

As this shift progresses, David finds himself sharing his writing with Marita in a way that is completely foreign to his nature as a private and withdrawn writer. He allows her to read the story he has just finished. Marita's plea to be allowed to share his creative act has moved David enough so that he shares "what he had believed could not and should not be shared" (203). The manuscript is even more explicit about the significance of Marita's expanded relationship with David: by asking if she approves of the story, David violates his code as writer—to be true only to his own vision.[69] He can share his work with Marita and not with Catherine because the latter was jealous of his work, while Marita is proud of it and feels about it the same way David does: "Marita there with no damned jealousy of the work and have her know what you are reaching for and how far you went. She really knows and it's not faked" (204). To Catherine, writing is something David does to occupy himself, to keep from becoming one of the idle rich now that he has married money. To Marita, writing is a priestly occupation, a vocation to which one dedicates one's self.

Book 4 is the culmination of a pattern that has been building through the first three books of the novel. Although Catherine's mental illness is now unmistakable, David cannot resist the attraction of his work, for he now recognizes that he cares more about his writing than about anything else. All the arguments in the final part of the book concern literary topics: Catherine calls Marita a whore, not because she has been sleeping with David, but because she has been responding to his stories. Similarly, Catherine attacks David, not for his shortcomings as a husband but for his perceived failures as a writer. She attacks the stories' subject matter—especially his father—and their technique: she says that they are not real stories at all but " 'pointless anecdotes' " (210). She ridicules David's spelling and grammar, which are bad in English and even worse in French. No insult is too trivial for Catherine: even David's handwriting is messy. Her madness gives her an uncanny ability to hurt David by attacking his integrity as a writer, the trait he prizes most highly. He has said that a wastebasket is the most important thing a writer can own, so that he can throw away bad work. Now Catherine tells Marita that David never discards a bad manuscript.

Clearly, if David must choose between Catherine and his work, he will choose the latter. And Catherine, through the clairvoyance of her insanity, perceives this truth about David, saying that he has " 'traded everything he had in on those stories' " (214). Even though he resolves to help Catherine to overcome her mental illness, David retreats to his own addiction, comforting himself with the recognition that, however bad real life becomes, he has his story to return to the next day. Thus, Hemingway has established two parallel neuroses that have a symbiotic relationship: Catherine's insanity is analogous to and intensified by David's monomaniacal devotion to his art, which is in turn intensified by Catherine's madness. Mad Catherine forcefully draws the parallel between her case and David's with the clinical nature of the vituperation with which she assails David. She accuses him of sexual perversions connected with his writing. His press clippings are like obscene postcards that he carries around for his titillation.

The assault on David as writer continues until David tells Catherine that she should burn the press clippings, which mean nothing to him since they do not touch the reality of his writing. When Catherine slyly asks how he knew that she had already done so, David immediately divines that she has burned more than the clippings. In manuscript, David simply asks what else she has burned,[70] but in the published novel he appears to assume that the stories have also been destroyed because merely burning the reviews would not have been enough to express Catherine's hostility and fury. David's feelings about the loss of the manuscripts highlight his dependency on his art, as he now faces a void, a universe without meaning: "He felt completely hollow. It was like coming around a curve on a mountain road and the road not being there" (216–217).

Like a theologian witnessing the proof of the death of God, David is left with an "empty and dead" heart (219) as he checks the suitcase in which the stories have been locked, then compulsively searches the other rooms of the hotel and examines the barrel in back of the hotel where Catherine has made the fire. In manuscript, Hemingway draws on his own feelings at the accidental loss of his own manuscripts in 1922 when he describes David's reaction to the devastating loss. David's use of a suitcase to store his manuscripts recalls Hadley's accidental loss of the suitcase of Hemingway's manuscripts, and Catherine's deliberate destruction of David's work suggests that Hemingway might have suppressed the suspicion that Hadley had deliberately lost his writing so that she could again have all of his attention. This account of the missing manuscripts differs markedly from Roger's story in the manuscript of *Islands in the Stream*. There Andy's mother is absolved of blame: the manuscripts are unequivocally "stolen."

In the published novel, David first has no hope of recreating the stories, echoing an almost mystical belief Hemingway himself had expressed many times. David tells Marita, " 'When it's right you can't remember. Every time you read it again it comes as a great and unbelievable surprise. . . . you never can do it again' " (230). The optimistic ending Jenks chose for the novel, then, contradicts David's own assertion a few pages earlier, contradicts Hemingway's own personal experience, and seems too easy a solution to satisfy the demands of artistic truth.

Jenks's ending is derived from the manuscript, where Hemingway experiments in detail with the possibility that David might be able to recover the stories. Marita says that if the stories are to come back, they will do so first through David's creation of specific, "concrete" details rather than major themes and abstractions.[71] David attempts to recreate the stories, but his first attempts are futile, and Hemingway likens them to the torment of a sexually impotent male. And when David does break through, the manuscript contains disquieting notes that Jenks omitted from the published novel.

When David recovers and emerges from his first successful writing session, he tells Marita that the rewritten story is better than before in some ways. But Marita no longer shares his writer's world. She feels his detachment and distance, enforced by the artistic discipline he has imposed on himself.[72] David is aware of the problem—if not of its magnitude—and apologizes. He tells Marita that he always experiences this difficulty bringing himself back into reality after writing.[73] It is clear that David is already on his way to isolating himself from Marita as he has from Catherine. The manuscript, then, holds out the prospect of a recurrent pattern—a cycle in which women are taken up, used, and then shut out of the writer's life—and suggests a grim future for David, a grim existence for any writer.

Most at odds with the optimistic ending of the published novel is the manuscript Hemingway labeled "Provisional Ending." Ultimately, David's loyalty to Catherine—and his guilt for exacerbating, if not causing, her breakdown—would have led him to become her permanent caretaker, but after sacrificing his work to care for Catherine, his life is not worth living. The suicide pact with Catherine is a way out of his now meaningless existence. Significantly, in a long line of writers who put their art first, before wife or parent or child, David—in this bit of manuscript—is the first to reverse his course, to forsake his writing for the human needs of someone close to him. The nature of this sacrifice and its implications for Hemingway himself might have been a source of difficulty for the author, one possible reason for his inability to bring the novel to a conclusion which would have satisfied both the artist and the man.

# Conclusion: A Self-Portrait Versus the Face in the Mirror

WHEN HE DIED in 1961, Hemingway was working on *A Moveable Feast*—a book that would be a frantic exercise in self-creation. In the 1920s he had surprised the literary world by coming out of nowhere to win international praise as a bold new American writer who would dominate the styles of a generation. Although in his later years his avowed goal was to live forever because of his literary works,[1] in the 1930s and 1940s he had instead become famous among people who seldom read books, first as a columnist for *Esquire* and then as a much-publicized war correspondent whose own life story overshadowed the war stories he reported. In the 1950s he had lost his reputation as possibly the leading novelist of his generation by publishing *Across the River and Into the Trees* (1950) and then—improbably—had regained and even strengthened that reputation by publishing *The Old Man and the Sea* (1952) and winning the Nobel Prize for Literature in 1954.

At the end of that same decade, unable to finish either of the novels on which he had been working for over ten years, unable even to complete the relatively simple reporting job that grew into *The Dangerous Summer*, published posthumously in 1985, he felt the need to cap his career with a final statement of who he was. A prefatory note to *A Moveable Feast* warns the reader that the book is highly selective, that "many places, people, observations and impressions have been left out" and that "if the reader prefers, this book may be regarded as fiction" (vii). In a recent study of the book, Jacqueline Tavernier-Courbin has demonstrated that the preface to *A Moveable Feast* is a synthesis of several rough drafts totaling approximately thirty pages that Hemingway wrote for use in the book's preface or conclusion. Edited into the brief preface after his death,[2] these fragments reveal that Hemingway returned almost obsessively to the question of whether the book should be regarded as fact or fiction. In fact, as Tavernier-Courbin points out, in the manuscript drafts, Hemingway "had stated unequivocally at least eighteen times that the book is fiction,"[3] a view of the book that the editors chose to deemphasize.

*A Moveable Feast* is indeed fiction—although it is peopled by many of Hemingway's friends of the Paris years and even by a character named Ernest Hemingway (the last in the series of characters bearing the initials

EH or HE). Nevertheless, as the last sentence of the prefatory note asserts, a book of fiction can "throw some light" on factual material. In the case of *A Moveable Feast*, the self-portrait is designed to mislead in the sense that it puts its subject, the youthful Hemingway, in the most favorable light possible. Except for a few pages in the final chapter, the book denies the dangers and the self-destructive behavior to which a writer can be subject, a topic that Hemingway had long been documenting in his fiction. *A Moveable Feast* was then, as Hemingway had told Mary, an example of the use of *remate*—a sophisticated two-wall shot in jai alai—rather than "the true gen" about his Paris years.[4]

Partly because the self-portrait he was creating mattered so much to Hemingway, its composition was marked by uncertainty and false starts. Probably he began work on the book—before he had any clear idea of the scope of the project—in response to a request by the *Atlantic Monthly* for a contribution to their 1957 centenary edition. He soon changed his plans and sent the *Atlantic* two short stories instead. The sketch about Fitzgerald that he had drafted with the *Atlantic* in mind eventually evolved into a more ambitious work that would set the record straight on the Paris years by reflecting the history of that period as Hemingway perceived it—or, as he recollected it much later, his memory influenced by everything that had happened in the intervening years.

Like Hawthorne explaining the origins of *The Scarlet Letter* in "The Custom House," Hemingway seems to have invented the story of his finding what Carlos Baker has described as a "Hemingway treasure trove" in the basement of the Ritz Hotel in Paris.[5] According to this myth, porters at the Ritz called Hemingway's attention to two trunks of typescripts and notebooks that had been stored in the hotel since the late 1920s. So powerful was this myth that some reviewers implied that Hemingway had merely rewritten *A Moveable Feast* from sketches that he found in the trunks. After Hemingway's death, Mary Hemingway continued to elaborate on the find. But Tavernier-Courbin, after having attempted to track down the manuscripts from the two trunks among the Hemingway papers and studying the contradictions among the statements made about their contents, concludes that the manuscripts found in the Ritz existed only in Hemingway's imagination.

The real composition of *A Moveable Feast* was far more difficult than merely retouching earlier material. Both Gerry Brenner and Jacqueline Tavernier-Courbin have written about the chaotic state of the manuscripts. The disorder suggests that Hemingway had had numerous problems with the structure of the book. In a 1961 letter, he wrote about ruthlessly eliminating certain material to strengthen the book and about the need for a better title than *The Paris Stories*. He had trouble writing an introduction and a conclusion and repeatedly shuffled chapters in an attempt to find an ideal sequence. Gerry Brenner's question, "Are We Going to Hemingway's *Feast?*" must ultimately be answered negatively. The feast never emerged from the kitchen. But *A Moveable Feast* as published is probably closer to the author's intention than the other posthumous books. And at the center of that intention was the creation of a flattering self-portrait of Hemingway as the young artist and the creation of a myth about the literary life that would balance the previous negative depictions of writers and their lives. Read in those terms, *A Moveable Feast* complements the fiction its author had been producing during the previous four decades.

## The Supporting Cast

Up to a point *A Moveable Feast* recapitulates the pattern found in Hemingway's fiction. A number of the book's anecdotes and stories illustrate, by *remate*, what the ideal writer is by showing what he or she is not, and the chapters that focus on other writers are most obviously biased. What is conspicuously absent, especially in the chapters that focus on Hemingway himself, is the vein of self-criticism apparent in Hemingway's fiction from the 1930s on: Hemingway the protagonist of *A Moveable Feast* does not share the negative qualities, the problems, or the self-doubt of such fictional writers as Phil, Harry, Roger Davis, and David Bourne. Readers familiar with the Hemingway success story, and the persona created by journalists with Hemingway's grudging cooperation, have perhaps been too ready to accept at face value the idealized self-portrait of the young writer. Actually that portrayal is as deceptive as the revisionist history of any Soviet historian of the Stalin era.

Providing a background for the carefully airbrushed self-portrait of the dedicated, self-assured writer is a rogue's gallery of imperfect writers, treated in brief vignettes or even in whole chapters. These negative examples range from minor charlatans, such as Ernest Walsh, through a major fake, Gertrude Stein, to F. Scott Fitzgerald—a highly skilled, gifted writer who allows money, critical acclaim, and the demands of his neurotic wife to deflect him from the true course of his art.

Ernest Walsh, "the man who was marked for death," is one of the figures in Hemingway's mock pantheon. Possessing a small, if genuine, talent, Walsh parlays a few poems in *Poetry, A Magazine of Verse* and a case of tuberculosis into a lifetime of support by women who are as much impressed by his persona as by his writing. Hemingway's story about Walsh is a highly selective version of the facts. In the 1920s Walsh and his coeditor Ethel Moorhead published Hemingway in their literary journal *This Quarter* and paid him well.[6] This fact is, however, barely acknowledged in Hemingway's acidulous sketch, which emphasizes Walsh's posturing, his bragging about the money he makes through his poetry, and his ingratiating behavior toward the major talents of Paris: Joyce, Pound, and Hemingway himself.

Like many of the literary characters discussed in chapter 2, Walsh is more in love with the role of writer than with the act of writing itself. Except for the early mention of the work he had published in *Poetry*, Walsh is never depicted as working on any writing. Like Robert Cohn, he enjoys the authority of editing and the powerful advantage editing gives him over more talented writers. He is impatient, however, with the details of editing and leaves Hemingway to "see his magazine through the printers" (128), a formidable task, since the printers do not read English. Walsh dies of his tuberculosis but elicits no sympathy from Hemingway.

A variation on the mediocre writer type is Ford Madox Ford. Few readers would guess from the chapter in *A Moveable Feast* that Ford was one of the major British writers of the postwar period, a former friend of Henry James, a collaborator with Joseph Conrad, and a mentor to Hemingway, whose work he had published in the *transatlantic review*.[7] Ford's kindness was poorly repaid: Hemingway offered Ford his services as assistant editor and then embarrassed Ford—who had entrusted the journal to his assistant—by the stridency of his editorial attacks on significant literary figures of the day.[8] As portrayed in *A Moveable Feast*, Ford is as self-centered as Ernest Walsh and as obtuse as Hemingway's earlier fictional portrait of him in the character of Braddocks, Robert Cohn's "literary friend" in *The Sun Also Rises*. In fact, Jacqueline Tavernier-Courbin has suggested that in writing the Ford chapter, Hemingway probably used discarded portions of his "Fiesta" manuscript as the basis for the anecdote about Ford's "cutting" of the man he believes to be Hilaire Belloc.[9] The earlier manuscript might have recalled for Hemingway real or imagined slights by the older author that would help to account for the malicious tone of the treatment of Ford in *A Moveable Feast*.

Gertrude Stein is treated more severely than Walsh or Ford. Having traded insults in *The Autobiography of Alice B. Toklas* (1933) and *Green Hills of Africa* (1935), Stein and Hemingway had allowed their feud to lapse. After Stein was dead, however, Hemingway reevaluated their relationship in terms that were quite critical of Stein as writer and as mentor. In *A Moveable Feast*, begun some eleven years after Stein's death, he points out that he had the last laugh over his story "Up in Michigan," which Stein had pronounced "inaccrochable" when she read it in manuscript. He offers cautious praise for Stein's experiments with rhythm and repetition in her fiction but also accuses her of one of the sins he considers most inexcusable in a writer. Having achieved a certain reputation, Stein, like Hemingway's fictional Harry Walden, grew lazy. Thus, although her masterpiece *The Making of Americans* started out well and was sometimes brilliant, it was finally ruined by "repetitions that a more conscientious and less lazy writer would have put in the waste basket" (18).[10] Unlike Harry's laziness, Stein's is exacerbated by the same sort of pompous attitude that is attributed to Ford Madox Ford as well as by vicious jealousy toward her betters, particularly James Joyce, whose name was not to be mentioned in Stein's salon.

But F. Scott Fitzgerald receives more complete treatment than any other flawed writer. In his character as depicted in *A Moveable Feast* appear most of the failings that Hemingway had been examining in his fictional writers during the previous forty years—and some faults that he had not treated before. A closer rival to Hemingway in popularity and achievement than either Stein or Ford, Fitzgerald served as the ideal foil for the persona through whom Hemingway chose to present himself to the world in what he must have realized might be his last book. In fact, Fitzgerald might be compared with the doubles Hemingway created in *Islands in the Stream* and *The Garden of Eden*: so emphatic is Hemingway's delineation of exemplary writer versus faulty writer that he sets up a Dr. Jekyll/Mr. Hyde relationship wherein Fitzgerald takes on all those characteristics of which the idealistic Hemingway disapproves, all those for which he is reluctant to admit guilt. No longer willing to acknowledge his own faults straightforwardly, Hemingway deals with them obliquely, condemning them in the author most similar to himself. Fitzgerald is accorded three chapters near the end of the book,[11] a climactic position where his story has a major impact.

As recreated by Hemingway, Fitzgerald is an alcoholic and a voyeur who peers into the private lives of his acquaintances. Motivated too strongly by money to devote himself wholly to his art, he paradoxically worries so much about his critical reputation that he is reluctant to write serious work lest he damage that reputation. He allows his wife to dominate him to the point of literary as well as physical impotence. Fitzgerald's character as sketched in some forty pages epitomizes the negative aspects of writers, aspects that Hemingway had fictionally treated in *The Sun Also Rises*, "The Sea Change," and "The Snows of Kilimanjaro" and that he had incorporated into the early drafts of *Islands in the Stream* and *The Garden of Eden*.

Hemingway's account of his first meeting with Fitzgerald emphasizes

Scott's susceptibility to alcohol and his tendency to pry into the lives of others, especially when he was under the influence. Soon after being introduced to Ernest in the Dingo bar, Fitzgerald offended Hemingway by asking him whether he had slept with his wife before marriage. The abruptness and rudeness of the question were soon accounted for when Fitzgerald collapsed in an alcoholic stupor, his girlishly beautiful face symbolically transforming itself into a death's head. Talking to him later, Hemingway found that Fitzgerald remembered nothing of the episode, having suffered from a blackout.

When he got to know Fitzgerald better and the two talked about writing, Hemingway was disturbed by the established writer's commercialism. Money was so important to Fitzgerald that he would prostitute himself to cash in on his talent, recalling both Richard Gordon of *To Have and Have Not* and Harry Walden of "The Snows of Kilimanjaro":

> He had told me at the Closerie des Lilas how he wrote what he thought were good stories . . . for the *Post*, and then changed them for submission, knowing exactly how he must make the twists that made them into salable magazine stories. . . . I said I thought it was whoring. He said it was whoring but that he had to do it as he made his money from the magazines to have money ahead to write decent books. I said that I did not believe anyone could write any way except the very best he could write without destroying his talent. [155–156]

Hemingway finishes off this paragraph by explicitly contrasting Fitzgerald's practice with his own method of writing: his description demands the reader's admiration for having deliberately rid himself of too-great "facility" and persisted in so "wonderful" though "difficult" a task, even though this practice meant that it often took him an entire morning to produce a paragraph. The criticism of Fitzgerald is implicit, as it is when Hemingway recalled his amazement when he read *The Great Gatsby* after this conversation with Fitzgerald and realized that the latter's great talent had enabled him to write such a good book after having spent so much of his energy on hack work.

Hemingway further documents Fitzgerald's interest in money by describing Fitzgerald's display of his ledger listing the stories and books published and the prices or royalties he had received for each. But in Hemingway's eyes even this commercialism was not as serious a fault as Fitzgerald's tendency to take himself too seriously as an author. He recalled with disdain that Fitzgerald carried around a review of *The Great Gatsby* by Gilbert Seldes and was pleased by other favorable reviews. He also wrote that on his first visit to Fitzgerald's apartment, he had seen copies of his host's early books specially bound in blue leather with gilded titles. To Hemingway, at least in the persona he had created in *A Moveable Feast*, such attention to the trappings of authorship seemed an unhealthy sign, a misplaced emphasis on the wordly rewards for writing rather than on the task of writing itself.

Hemingway's most serious criticisms were reserved for Scott's relationship with Zelda. With the benefits of hindsight, Hemingway thought he detected in Zelda a jealousy for Scott's work that boded ill for Fitzgerald's future as author and as husband. He claimed that when Fitzgerald tried to curtail his drinking in order to continue his work, Zelda implied that Scott was being a "kill-joy" or a "spoilsport" (179). When sulking failed, Zelda could easily entice Scott to accompany her on her debauches by threatening to go out alone. Fitzgerald's jealousy was too great to allow her to do that. In *A Moveable Feast*, Hemingway thus presents the obverse of the situation he had been struggling with in *The Garden of Eden*. The idealistic young Hemingway persona of *A Moveable Feast* faults Scott for allowing Zelda to distract him from his work, while the aging author of *The Garden of Eden* seems to fault David, morally, if not artistically, for neglecting his wife for his work. In creating his portrait of the ideal artist in *A Moveable Feast*, Hemingway deliberately denied and reversed the serious theme of the writer's failed relationships, a notion that had haunted his last two unfinished novels.

In his last chapter on Fitzgerald, "A Matter of Measurements," Hemingway tells a story the literal truth of which is almost impossible to believe. Fitzgerald reportedly confided in Hemingway that Zelda had told him that his penis was too small to satisfy her sexually. Hemingway tried unsuccessfully to reassure Scott, comparing sexual equipment with him, taking him to the Louvre to view nude male statues, and knowledgeably offering him a variety of sexual tips. If the chapter is to be taken seriously at all, it is as a metaphor for Hemingway's frequently asserted belief that Zelda dominated Scott and induced artistic rather than physical impotence in her husband. For example, Fitzgerald, struggling between 1925 and 1934 to complete *Tender Is the Night*, was repeatedly distracted by Zelda, not only by the minor family fights Hemingway described but by Zelda's growing insanity and especially by her use of the basic materials of *Tender Is the Night* in her own novel, *Save Me the Waltz* (1932).[12] Although Fitzgerald finally completed the book, according to Hemingway's jaundiced view, Zelda had "unmanned" Scott during what might have been one of the most productive periods of his career.

Ostensibly presented as a memoir, *A Moveable Feast* persuades most general readers to accept the work as fact, but the more one learns about

Hemingway, the more one realizes how much the artist dominated the reporter. The accounts of Hemingway's fellow artists in *A Moveable Feast* must be read with extreme caution as the work of a writer of fiction rather than a reporter. All of the other writers who appear serve merely as a supporting cast for the star, Ernest Hemingway, who would appear all the brighter to readers who saw him framed by his competitors—all drawn in the most unflattering terms. When Mary supposedly protested that there was too little of Hemingway in the book, she was overlooking a fact that should be obvious: Hemingway is omnipresent in the book—grudges, prejudices, pride, and all.

## Portrait of the Artist as a Perfect Man

Among the literary characters in Hemingway's memoir of his Paris years, one admirable person—the young Ernest Hemingway himself—stands out. If the other characters of the book are treated in the manner of a caricaturist who captures a person by exaggerating his or her prominent—and often negative—features, Hemingway's self-portrait might be compared to the sort of idealization painted to secure a commission from a patron seeking flattery. As viewed by the aging artist, the young Hemingway, in spite of his inexperience, can do no wrong. Although his artistic career has barely begun, he displays the confidence of a veteran author; he is the opposite of the man Hemingway had become during his postwar struggles to complete new fiction.

Perhaps Gerry Brenner best sums up this aspect of the work when he characterizes Hemingway as he appears in *Feast* as a

> self-disciplined, diligent apprentice whose commitment to exacting standards of artistic excellence—read responsibility, please—enables him to become a major writer. . . . Only to him will Pound entrust Dunning's jar of opium. Only to him will Walsh entrust the publication of an issue of *This Quarter*. Only to him will Stein entrust the typing and proofreading of the early serialized sections of *The Making of Americans*.[13]

The Hemingway of *A Moveable Feast* has no visible faults. When something goes wrong, even when his first marriage breaks up, it is because of external factors, never through his own fault.[14]

This "Hemingway" exhibits his greatest sense of responsibility when it comes to his art. In "A Good Café on the Place St.-Michel," the first chapter of the book as assembled by Mary Hemingway, Hemingway nostalgically recreates the monastic life of a priest of literary art. The cheap hotel room that he rents as a studio is either on the sixth or eighth story above the street, and once there, the fledgling artist nearly freezes in the unheated room. When the room becomes too cold for even the most devoted artist to work in, the young Hemingway moves to a relatively quiet café. There his concentration on the creation of "The Three-Day Blow" is intense enough not only to permit him to ignore the ordinary distractions of café patrons coming and going, ordering their drinks and conversing, but also to resist the appeal of a beautiful woman who enters the café and waits, perhaps in vain, for a man.

This same idealized youth has already learned how to deal with professional difficulties such as writer's block. Although sometimes when he was beginning a story, he "could not get it going," he knows how to handle the problem: "I would stand and look out over the roofs of Paris and think, 'Do not worry. . . . All you have to do is write one true sentence. Write the truest sentence that you know.' So finally I would write one true sentence, and then go on from there. It was easy then" (12). Isn't it pretty to think so? This confident passage was written by a man who had failed to complete two of his latest three full-length novels, whose last completed full-length novel had been acknowledged to be his weakest. The *then* of "It was easy then" draws attention to the difference between that golden age and the present. This elegiac passage emphasizes the ease, confidence, and ability of the youthful writer. It not only serves to gain the reader's admiration for Hemingway—past and present—as the pure avatar of art but also expresses the writer's poignant view of a less complex past when problems were simply solved, no writer's block lasted long, story ideas were unlimited, rules for writing well and truly were clear, and a sense of joy and accomplishment accompanied the labor of love.

The aging Hemingway embodies his artistic ideals in his youthful persona. Unlike many of the more established writers with whom he associates, young Hemingway knows that the true worth of a work of art lies in the act of creating it, not in seeing it published or being paid for it. In contrast to Gertrude Stein, his sometime mentor, Hemingway realizes that his stories are worth writing for themselves, even if they might never be published, as Stein had told him "Up in Michigan" would not be. He sagely counsels himself not to worry about publication, which would come in time when the editors of magazines were prepared to understand the value and complexity of his stories.

The fledgling author takes a similar long view of the financial side of his writing career. Remuneration should not be the creative artist's major concern. Journalism, in which he had already served an apprenticeship, was different: for writing such ephemeral work, the reporter should insist on being well paid. But unlike his friend Fitzgerald, who had allowed money to become an obsession, the young Hemingway worries little about money even though he often lacks the price of a lunch. Sylvia Beach, one of the few characters in *Feast* who shares Hemingway's prescience, encourages Hemingway in his noble desire to write well whether or not he will be paid for his work, and when he follows her advice and his own inclination, skipping lunch in favor of walking through the Luxembourg Museum, he is rewarded by the sort of semimystical experience that is associated with fasting for spiritual purposes: he notices that the pictures seem more sharp and clear to a viewer with an empty stomach (69–71). He also prepares for a time when he will be published by admonishing himself not to allow the opinions of others to sway him from the path of artistic integrity. Again the negative example is Fitzgerald, who allows the reviews of *The Great Gatsby* to influence him unduly (154).

The real value of work is suggested by some of the most moving passages in *Feast*. Although much of the book serves to construct a mask behind which Hemingway hides his true concerns and his true personality, these passages seem heartfelt and of a piece with the concerns of his best fiction. Near the end of the second chapter, "Miss Stein Instructs," Hemingway, disturbed by the conversation he has just had with Stein, decides that "I would have to work hard tomorrow. Work could cure almost anything, I believed then, and I believe now" (21). His acknowledgment of the separation between the then youthful artist persona and the now mature writer looking back serves to underscore the continuity of his faith even though it must seem to readers to reflect Hemingway's growing desperation toward the end of his career.

Elsewhere in the book, he becomes more expansive, writing of the positive feelings he had after concluding a good day's work and depicting himself as being so immersed in his writing at times that even the most persistent hanger-on could hardly recall him from the fictional world he was creating (12, 92–93). Sometimes he became so involved in his created world that it was almost a shock to return from the Michigan woods to a café on the Left Bank (6). The nostalgia of the aging writer for an earlier self whose work went so well dominates his reminiscences. If there was an Edenic period in Hemingway's life, it must have been the Paris years in the 1920s.

In another example of fictionalizing the past, Hemingway reflects on the metaphysics of writing in insights that he attributes to the Hemingway of the 1920s but that were more probably attitudes that had evolved during a lifetime of writing. For example, he insists that after the day's work is done, the conscious mind must be distracted from its task rather than allowed to dwell on the fiction that had occupied it, a notion that appears in the manuscript of *To Have and Have Not*. According to his memory, when Hemingway was not working during the Paris years, he devoted himself to reading, not so much to learn as to distract himself from the literary problems that he had been attempting to solve. He also found physical exercise helpful on that same count, because the mind could better relax if the body was physically tired (25). Much of the public image of Hemingway the sportsman, which grew up a decade after the Paris period, is thus fortuitously explained by suggesting that his outdoor activities were simply an adjunct to his life as an artist. The purpose of turning off the conscious mind was to allow the subconscious mind to do its work. Hemingway learned that he should allow his works to surprise him rather than attempting to force the process.

*A Moveable Feast* is the final statement about his life and art by a man who wished to appear as an assured, successful public figure, a man of letters who had learned his craft and devised his philosophy early in life and then unswervingly followed it through good reception and bad—a priest devoted to his art. Hemingway's success enabled him to offer his ideals, his goals, his values, and even his personal habits, as if they were tenets of a holy faith—as to some extent they were. In one sense *A Moveable Feast* served as a litany, a paean of praise to the art that he had served and to the youthful acolyte whom he had been, even as in another sense his reminiscences surely served, if only unconsciously, as an attempt to recapture that youthful, self-confident believer in a simple unambiguous faith. However, almost ignored in *A Moveable Feast* is the serpent in this garden, the dark side of the artist's credo: the doubts, the flaws, the sins, the heretical tendencies that he feared might lurk in his own character and that he criticized in others or perhaps even projected onto them. One rare instance of such a doubt is the passing acknowledgment in the final chapter that "when the husband is a writer and doing difficult work so that he is occupied much of the time [he] is not a good companion or partner to his wife for a big part of the day" (209–210). This passage, a distillation of the central conflict of his unfinished *The Garden of Eden*, lets the writer off far too easily. In its creation of an idealized youthful artist, a sympathetic and admirable figure who seems too perfect to be a true portrait, *A Moveable Feast* recants the message of the dark side of the writer's nature, a story Hemingway had been trying to tell all his life.

## The Face in the Mirror

The happy myth of the writer that Hemingway attempted to create in his last years does not obscure the fact that throughout most of his career he suffered from a deep conflict about his writing. The root of the conflict was the division of his loyalties between devotion to his art and his need for ties to the rest of humanity. Determined to devote his life to his writing, Hemingway had lifted himself above the limitations of his education and his conventional Oak Park surroundings to become a major writer of fiction. Nevertheless, from the time he began his career in Paris, in those good years that he would recall nostalgically in *A Moveable Feast*, he had harbored reservations about the role of the writer vis-à-vis his fellow human beings.

While he successfully pursued his writing career, Hemingway's personal life grew increasingly complex: he added to his commitments as son and brother those of husband and father. In the 1930s, when his second marriage seemed destined to end in failure like his first, this feeling of conflicting or divided loyalties intensified, causing him to reevaluate his commitments. In his last two decades, which saw the end of a third marriage and troubled relationships with his fourth wife and his sons, he attempted to create two major works centered on the artist's conflicts. As therapy the writing went well—the manuscripts of *The Garden of Eden* and *Islands in the Stream* grew at a surprising rate—but he was never able to put either into a condition that he regarded as publishable or to clarify his final thoughts on the problems they treated.

One of Hemingway's early reactions to the internal struggle between the demands made upon him by his art and those made by intimate relationships with others was to avoid or ignore the conflict. Thus, a class of Hemingway's works features protagonists who are men of action rather than men of letters—characters such as Manuel Garcia of "The Undefeated," Jack Brennan of "Fifty Grand," Harry Morgan of *To Have and Have Not*, and Santiago of *The Old Man and the Sea*. However, Hemingway's dependence on his own emotions and inner experiences for the raw material of his fiction led him, very early in his career, to begin creating what would become a long series of writer figures. These figures—from the early depictions of superficial writers in works such as "Mr. and Mrs. Elliot" and *The Sun Also Rises* through the more probing analyses in short stories of the 1930s such as "The Sea Change" and "The Snows of Kilimanjaro" to his final unpublished novels *Islands in the Stream* and *The Garden of Eden*—chart the course of Hemingway's reservations and fears about what his art was doing to his private life.

The story of Hemingway's internal conflict as portrayed in his fiction ends with the publication of his posthumous works. It was a story that Hemingway was unable to conclude because he was never able to resolve the conflict from which it emerged. To the end of his life, he remained divided between feeling as a man and acting as a writer. That division in his loyalties is perhaps the most important continuing creative conflict that runs through his artistic career and is largely responsible for the loneliness that he identified as one of the chief occupational hazards of the writer when he accepted the Nobel Prize for Literature in 1954:

> Writing, at its best, is a lonely life. Organizations for writers palliate the writer's loneliness but I doubt if they improve his writing. He grows in public stature as he sheds his loneliness and often his work deteriorates. For he does his work alone and if he is a good enough writer he must face eternity, or the lack of it, each day. . . .
>
> How simple the writing of literature would be if it were only necessary to write in another way what has been well written. It is because we have had such great writers in the past that a writer is driven far out past where he can go, out to where no one can help him.[15]

These paragraphs could not have been written by the successful young Hemingway described in *A Moveable Feast*. But the mature Hemingway might well have added that confronting the face one sees daily in the mirror can be as frightening as facing eternity and that the voyage inward can be as lonely and as hazardous as any outward quest.

# Notes

## Introduction: An Unliterary Writer

1. James N. Westerhoven, "Autobiographical Elements in the Camera Eye," *American Literature* 48 (1976): 340–64.

2. Carlos Baker, ed., *Ernest Hemingway: Selected Letters, 1917–1961* (New York: Scribner's, 1981), 579.

3. Kurt Bernheim, "*McCall's* Visits Ernest Hemingway," *McCall's*, May 1956, p. 6.

4. An earlier instance of this theme in the fiction would have occurred had Hemingway not cut the "On Writing" section from the manuscript of "Big Two-Hearted River." This fragment makes it clear that Hemingway was thinking of Nick as a writer even before 1930. As it is, however, Nick Adams is explicitly identified as a writer only in four words of "Big Two-Hearted River" and in the last story that employs him as a protagonist, "Fathers and Sons" (1933). Debra Moddelmog, however, argues that Nick should be regarded as the narrator of *In Our Time*. See "The Unifying Consciousness of a Divided Conscience: Nick Adams as Author of *In Our Time*," *American Literature* 60 (1988): 591–610. A deleted passage from the manuscript of "An Alpine Idyll," often identified as a Nick Adams story, would also have identified the protagonist as a writer. After they hear the old peasant's story about the mutilation of his wife's body, John says to the protagonist, " 'There's a good story for you.' " The protagonist replies, " 'It's no good. . . . Nobody would believe it.' " From Item 244, pp. 11–12, Hemingway Collection, John F. Kennedy Library, Boston, Massachusetts. Unless otherwise noted, all manuscript "Items" are from this collection.

5. Wyndham Lewis, *Men Without Art* (London: Cassell, 1934), 17–40.

6. Ernest Hemingway, *By-Line: Ernest Hemingway*, ed. William White (New York: Scribner's, 1967), 216–17.

7. Ernest Hemingway, *Death in the Afternoon* (New York: Scribner's, 1932), 278.

8. "A Visit with Hemingway: A Situation Report," *Look*, 4 September 1956, pp. 24–25.

9. Ernest Hemingway, *Green Hills of Africa* (New York: Scribner's, 1935), 23–24.

10. Ernest Hemingway, *A Moveable Feast* (New York: Scribner's, 1964), 92–96.

11. Ibid., 180–83, 209–10.

12. John Raeburn, *Fame Became of Him: Hemingway as Public Writer* (Bloomington: Indiana University Press, 1984).

13. "Back to His First Field," *Kansas City Times*, 26 November 1940, pp. 1–2.

14. "Hemingway Is Bitter about Nobody—but His Colonel Is," *Time*, 11 September 1950, p. 110.

15. Mary Harrington, "They Call Him Papa," *New York Post Week-End Magazine*, 28 December 1946, p. 3.

16. "Stalking Lions Was 'Exciting' to Hemingway," *New York Herald Tribune*, 4 April 1934, p. 4.

17. "Indestructible," *New Yorker*, 4 January 1947, p. 20.

18. See, for example, "Hemingway in the Afternoon," *Time*, 4 August 1947, p. 80; "Notes from a Novelist on His System of Work," *New York Times Book Review*, 31 July 1949, p. 1; and Bernheim, "*McCall's* Visits," 8.

19. Ernest Hemingway, *The Complete Short Stories of Ernest Hemingway: The Finca Vigía Edition* (New York: Scribner's, 1987), 597–604.

20. Lillian Ross, "Profile: How Do You Like It Now, Gentlemen?" *New Yorker*, 13 May 1950, p. 42.

21. Harvey Breit, "Talk with Mr. Hemingway," *New York Times Book Review*, 17 September 1950, p. 14.

22. Bernheim, "*McCall's* Visits," 8.

23. See James A. Michener, "Introduction," *The Dangerous Summer* by Ernest Hemingway (New York: Scribner's, 1985), 11–14; Carlos Baker, *Ernest Hemingway: A Life Story* (New York: Scribner's, 1969), 553–54; A. E. Hotchner, *Papa Hemingway: A Personal Memoir* (New York: Random House, 1966), 236–44.

24. Ernest Hemingway, *The Short Stories of Ernest Hemingway* (New York: Scribner's, 1967), 210.

25. See "On Writing," in *The Nick Adams Stories*, ed. Philip Young (New York: Scribner's, 1972), 233–41.

26. *Short Stories*, 491.

27. Hemingway was himself a journalist when he wrote of Barnes the journalist, but the attitudes of the author and his protagonist are diametrically opposed. Hemingway was attempting to escape journalism on the advice of Gertrude Stein. Jake regards journalism as honest work—when he is not referring to it deprecatingly as gossip—and believes that as an honest workman, he is superior to the self-aggrandizing writers he meets in the Quarter.

28. Ernest Hemingway, *The Sun Also Rises* (New York: Scribner's, 1970), 175. Page numbers provided parenthetically in the text below refer to this edition.

29. *Green Hills*, 7.

30. Richard M. Ludwig, ed., *Letters of Ford Madox Ford* (Princeton, N.J.: Princeton University Press, 1965), 162.

31. Morley Callaghan, *That Summer in Paris* (Toronto: Macmillan of Canada, 1963), 30.

32. *Selected Letters*, 408. For an extensive analysis of the Hemingway-Fitzgerald friendship, the standard reference is Matthew J. Bruccoli, *Scott and Ernest: The Authority of Failure and the Authority of Success* (New York: Random House, 1978).

## 1. A Gallery of Flawed Writers

1. Michael Reynolds, *The Young Hemingway* (Oxford: Basil Blackwell, 1986), 48.

2. Charles A. Fenton, *The Apprenticeship of Ernest Hemingway: The Early Years* (New York: Compass Books, 1958), 15.

3. See especially "Portrait of the Idealist in Love" and "The Ash Heel's Tendon," in Peter Griffin, *Along With Youth: Hemingway, the Early Years* (New York: Oxford University Press, 1985), 161–64, 174–80.

4. On Davis, see Griffin, *Along With Youth*, 29. On Hemingway's high school journalism, see Fenton, *Apprenticeship*, 22–26. The early works themselves are reproduced in Matthew J. Bruccoli, ed., *Ernest Hemingway's Apprenticeship: Oak Park, 1916–1917* (Washington, D.C.: NCR Microcard Editions, 1971).

5. "The Ash Heel's Tendon," for example, suggests a debt not only to O. Henry for its surprise ending but also to Bret Harte's "The Outcasts of Poker Flat" for its demotic rendering of "Achilles." For a more sympathetic view of the work produced during this period, see Paul Smith, "Hemingway's Apprentice Fiction, 1919–1921," *American Literature* 58 (1986): 574–88.

6. Alson J. Smith, *Chicago's Left Bank* (Chicago: Regnery, 1953), 3–20. See also Dale Kramer, *Chicago Renaissance: The Literary Life in the Midwest, 1900–1930* (New York: Appleton-Century, 1966).

7. Kramer, *Chicago Renaissance*, 242.

8. On the first meeting between Anderson and Hemingway, see Baker, *Life Story*, 78–79, and Reynolds, *Young Hemingway*, 181–84.

9. Sherwood Anderson, *Sherwood Anderson's Memoirs* (New York: Harcourt, Brace, 1942), 294.

10. Ernest Hemingway, *Dateline Toronto: The Complete Toronto Star Dispatches, 1920–1924*, ed. William White (New York: Scribner's, 1985), 115.

11. Nicholas Joost, *Hemingway and the Little Magazines: The Paris Years* (Barre, Mass.: Barre Publishers, 1968), 52.

12. Baker, *Life Story*, 133, 181, 585. See Items 585–587 in the Hemingway Collection.

13. Chard Powers Smith, *Where the Light Falls: A Portrait of Edwin Arlington Robinson* (New York: Macmillan, 1965).

14. Jeffrey Meyers, *Hemingway: A Biography* (New York: Harper and Row, 1985), 144.

15. Carlos Baker, *The Writer as Artist*, 4th ed. (Princeton: Princeton University Press, 1973), 27n.

16. *Selected Letters*, 153.

17. Ernest Hemingway, "The Art of the Short Story," *Paris Review* 23:79 (Spring 1981): 93.

18. *Selected Letters*, 161. See also Baker, *Life Story*, 141, and Allen Shepherd, "Taking Apart 'Mr. and Mrs. Elliot,' " *Markham Review* 2 (September 1969): 15–16.

19. Incoming Letters file, Hemingway Collection.

20. *Selected Letters*, 242.

21. For the best discussion of the story as art rather than biographical evidence, see Paul Smith, "From the Waste Land to the Garden with the Elliots," *Hemingway's Neglected Short Fiction: New Perspectives*, ed. Susan F. Beegel (Tuscaloosa: University of Alabama Press, 1992), 123–29. See also Paul Smith's treatment of the story in his *Reader's Guide to the Short Stories of Ernest Hemingway* (Boston: G. K. Hall, 1989), 75–80, where he draws some biographical parallels between the Elliots and Ernest and Hadley Hemingway.

22. Louis Broussard, "Hemingway as Literary Critic," *Arizona Quarterly* 20 (Autumn 1964): 197–204; Sheldon Norman Grebstein, *Hemingway's Craft* (Carbondale: Southern Illinois University Press, 1973), 82.

23. George Plimpton, "An Interview with Ernest Hemingway," in *Hemingway and His Critics*, ed. Carlos Baker (New York: Hill and Wang, 1961), 31.

24. *Death in the Afternoon*, 54.

25. *Short Stories*, 161. Page numbers provided parenthetically in the text below refer to this edition (see Introduction, n. 24, above).

26. Fenton, *Apprenticeship*, 154. See also Gertrude Stein, *The Autobiography of Alice B. Toklas* (New York: Harcourt, Brace, 1933), 266. Marjorie Perloff has suggested that the story is "modeled" on Stein's "Miss Furr and Miss Skeene," composed in 1908 and published in 1922. See " 'Ninety Percent Rotarian': Gertrude Stein's Hemingway," *American Literature* 62 (1990): 668–83.

27. See Item 585, p. 6, for Hemingway's work on this brilliant choice of phrases.

28. On this question, see Joseph DeFalco, *The Hero in Hemingway's Short Stories* (Pittsburgh: University of Pittsburgh Press, 1963), 157.

29. *By-Line*, 183.

30. *Green Hills*, 27.

31. *By-Line*, 215.

32. One reason for Hemingway's bias was Stein's having published parts of *The Autobiography of Alice B. Toklas*, in which she attacked Hemingway, in the *Atlantic*.

33. See DeFalco, *The Hero*, 155; Grebstein, *Hemingway's Craft*, 181; and Smith, *Reader's Guide*, 77–78.

34. George Monteiro, "The Writer on Vocation: Hemingway's 'Banal Story,' " in *Hemingway's Neglected Short Fiction*, 141–47.

35. On the history of the *Forum*, see Wayne Kvam, "Hemingway's 'Banal Story,' " *Fitzgerald/Hemingway Annual 1974*, ed. Matthew Bruccoli and C. E. Frazer Clark, Jr. (Englewood, Colo.: Microcard Editions, 1975), 182–84.

36. Phillip R. Yanella, "Notes on the Manuscript, Date, and Sources of Hemingway's 'Banal Story,' " *Fitzgerald/Hemingway Annual 1974*, 178.

37. Smith, *Reader's Guide*, 112.

38. Kvam, "Hemingway's 'Banal Story,' " 184–87; Monteiro, "Writer on Vocation," 143–44.

39. Yanella, "Notes," 175–76; Kvam, "Hemingway's 'Banal Story,' " 182.

40. The short paragraph "It was a splendid booklet" and the sentence "He laid down the booklet" (361) were added to the *Little Review* version of the story.

41. See Kvam, "Hemingway's 'Banal Story,' " 182.

42. Monteiro, "The Writer on Vocation," 146.

43. *Selected Letters*, 62, 161–62.

44. Irving Howe, *Sherwood Anderson* (New York: William Sloane Associates, 1951), 186–87.

45. Sherwood Anderson, *Dark Laughter* (New York: Boni and Liveright, 1925), 13.

46. Ernest Hemingway, *The Torrents of Spring* (New York: Scribner's, 1972), 11. Page numbers provided parenthetically in the text below refer to this edition.

47. Anderson, *Memoirs*, 194.

48. Sherwood Anderson, *Letters to Bab: Sherwood Anderson to Marietta D. Finley, 1916–33* (Urbana: University of Illinois Press, 1985), 265.

49. Ernest Hemingway, "Monologue to the Maestro: A High Seas Letter," in *By-Line*, 215. Originally published in October 1935. Like all of Hemingway's comments on writing from the 1930s, this should be read cautiously, as Hemingway was under attack from the Left during that decade. His public statements from the period are often intended to refute charges that he was out of touch with current social realities or that he simply did not care about them. What better defense could he offer than the statement that one had a sacred obligation to tell the truth?

50. *Death in the Afternoon*, 2.

51. Reproduced in Frederic J. Svoboda, *Hemingway and "The Sun Also Rises": The Crafting of a Style* (Lawrence: University Press of Kansas, 1983), 135.

52. Ibid., 134.

53. Ibid.

54. Perhaps the best accounts of Fitzgerald's criticism and Hemingway's reaction to it are in Bruccoli, *Scott and Ernest*, 44–55.

55. For a brief sketch of the Hemingway-Wescott relationship, see Bertram D. Sarason, *Hemingway and the "Sun" Set* (Washington, D.C.: NCR Microcard Editions, 1972), 75–78.

56. Svoboda, *Hemingway and "The Sun,"* 136.

57. Compare Robert Cohn's assertion that he wants to go to South America to see the "real" South Americans. Those he sees in Paris are too much like him (9–12).

58. *Green Hills*, 21. Hemingway would return to the same theme in his Nobel Prize acceptance statement, in which he wrote that writers' organizations merely "palliate" the writer's feeling of isolation and actually do more harm than good, for as the writer becomes less isolated, he loses his ability to project a unique vision.

59. *Death in the Afternoon*, 2.

60. Svoboda, *Hemingway and "The Sun,"* 135. Loeb's reply, written some thirty years later, appears in Harold Loeb, *The Way It Was* (New York: Criterion, 1959).

61. Robert O. Stephens, *Hemingway's Nonfiction: The Public Voice* (Chapel Hill: University of North Carolina Press, 1968), 135–36.

62. *By-Line*, 218.

63. *Conversations*, 196.

64. Hemingway has been demonstrated to have read and/or owned some fifteen books by Hudson; his library at Finca Vigía included a copy of *The Purple Land*. See Michael S. Reynolds, *Hemingway's Reading, 1910–1940: An Inventory* (Princeton: Princeton University Press, 1981), 138–39, and James D. Brasch and Joseph Sigman, *Hemingway's Library: A Composite Record* (New York: Garland Press, 1981), 181.

65. *Short Stories*, v–vi. First published in 1938.

## 2. A Closer Look at the Face in the Mirror

1. Archibald MacLeish, "Years of the Dog," in *Actfive and Other Poems* (New York: Random House, 1948), 53.

2. On Hemingway's changing concept of himself during this crucial period, see Raeburn, *Fame Became of Him*, 38–72.

3. One of the most typical notes to himself was Hemingway's musing that he intended to ignore Gertrude Stein's proscription of "remarks" and would include them in his first novel (Item 194—1, p. 9). The note was, of course, cut during revision.

4. *Death in the Afternoon*, 182.

5. Baker, *Life Story*, 227.

6. See, respectively, DeFalco, *The Hero*, 177; J. F. Kobler, "Hemingway's 'The Sea Change': A Sympathetic View of Homosexuality," *Arizona Quarterly* 26 (1970): 318–24; H. Alan Wycherley, "Hemingway's 'The Sea Change,' " *American Notes and Queries* 7 (1969): 67–68; Grebstein, *Hemingway's Craft*, 114; and Warren Bennett, " 'That's Not Very Polite': Sexual Identity in Hemingway's 'The Sea Change,' " *Hemingway's Neglected Short Fiction*, 225–45.

7. "The Art of the Short Story," 88. On Hemingway's application of the iceberg principle, see Julian Smith, "Hemingway and the Thing Left Out," *Journal of Modern Literature* 1 (1970): 169–82.

8. Item 422.1, book 1, chap. 1, p. 1.

9. Item 422.1, book 1, chap. 4, p. 4.

10. Philip Young, *Ernest Hemingway: A Reconsideration* (University Park: Pennsylvania State University Press, 1966), 178–79.

11. Nathaniel Hawthorne, *The American Notebooks*, ed. Randall Stewart (New Haven: Yale University Press, 1932), 106.

12. Plimpton, "An Interview," 23–24.

13. Alexander Pope, *An Essay on Man*, in *The Poems of Alexander Pope*, ed. Maynard Mack (New Haven: Yale University Press, 1964), III, 81–82, ll. 217–21.

14. *Short Stories*, 400.

15. DeFalco, *The Hero*, 176.

16. Kobler, "Hemingway's 'The Sea Change,' " 322; Wycherley, "Hemingway's 'The Sea Change,' " 68.

17. Bennett, " 'That's Not Very Polite,' " 237–38.

18. Item 681.

19. William Shakespeare, *The Tempest*, I, ii, ll. 396–401, in *The Complete Plays and Poems of William Shakespeare*, ed. William Allan Neilson and Charles Jarvis Hill (Cambridge, Mass.: Houghton Mifflin, 1942), 546.

20. *Selected Letters*, 333.

21. Ibid., 330.

22. Baker, *Life Story*, 217.

23. Ibid., 219–20.

24. *Selected Letters*, 330.

25. Baker, *Life Story*, 231.

26. *Selected Letters*, 363–64.

27. Item 230.

28. Item 417, p. 18.

29. "Give Us a Prescription, Doctor," *Scribner's Magazine*, May 1933, p. 278.

30. See Robert E. Fleming, "American Nightmare: Hemingway and the West," *Midwest Quarterly* 30 (1989): 361–71.

31. Sister Cecilia's prayers are not always effective: in 1930 the Athletics defeated the Cardinals in six games, but in 1931, the Cardinals won in a tense seven-game series. Hemingway was in the hospital during the 1930 season, but because it took him a long time to recover from his injuries, he probably wrote the story after the 1931 season. In that case, Mr. Frazer's hospitalization might just as well have occurred during the year the Athletics lost.

32. *Selected Letters*, 331.

33. "Old Newsman Writes," *By-Line*, 183.

34. Plimpton, "An Interview," 36.

35. Callaghan, *That Summer in Paris*, 30.

36. For one discussion of the question, see Robert E. Fleming, "Hemingway's Treatment of Suicide: 'Fathers and Sons' and *For Whom the Bell Tolls*," *Arizona Quarterly* 33 (1977): 121–32.

37. Plimpton, "An Interview," 34.

38. "Art of the Short Story," 88.

39. Item 384, p. 5.

40. Among the things Nick leaves behind as he goes fishing is "the need to write." *Short Stories*, 210.

41. *Nick Adams Stories*, 217.

42. Item 385a, p. 3.

43. Ibid., p. 4.

44. Item 222–2, p. 4.

45. Ibid.

46. On these reactions to his father's suicide, see Baker, *Life Story*, 198–200, and Leicester Hemingway, *My Brother, Ernest Hemingway* (Cleveland: World, 1961), 110–11.

47. Item 617, p. 1.

48. Item 617, p. 2. This sense that the manuscript is bulking up without catching fire and beginning to "move" foreshadows Hemingway's postwar problems with *Islands in the Stream* and *The Garden of Eden*.

49. Baker, *Writer as Artist*, 212.

50. Ernest Hemingway, *To Have and Have Not* (New York: Scribner's, 1937), 196–97. Page numbers provided parenthetically in the text refer to this edition.

51. Plimpton, "An Interview," 22.

52. Ibid.

53. Item 204—6, p. 129.

54. Item 204—6, p. 130.

55. Item 204—7, p. 164.

56. Item 205, pp. 454–55.

57. Item 209, p. 2.

58. Item 204—7, pp. 179–80.

59. Item 204—7, p. 183.

60. Item 204—6, p. 130.

61. Item 205, p. 449.

62. Item 205, p. 472.

63. Ibid.

64. Item 205, p. 474.

65. On Dos Passos as a model for Gordon, see, for example, Donald Pizer, "The Hemingway-Dos Passos Relationship," *Journal of Modern Literature* 13 (1986): 111–28; Baker, *Life Story*, 298–99; Arthur Waldhorn, *A Reader's Guide to Ernest Hemingway* (New York: Farrar, Straus, and Giroux, 1972), 247; Meyers, *Hemingway*, 294; and Townsend Ludington, *John Dos Passos: A Twentieth Century Odyssey* (New York: E. P. Dutton, 1980), 333. In opposition to this point of view, see Robert E. Fleming, "The Libel of Dos Passos in *To Have and Have Not*," *Journal of Modern Literature* 15 (1989): 597–601.

66. Item 204—8, pp. 230–32.

67. Item 204—7, p. 203 and insert to 203.

68. Item 204—6, p. 148.

69. Baker, *Life Story*, 249–52.

70. Ibid., 286–87.

71. See Robert W. Lewis, Jr., and Max Westbrook, " 'The Snows of Kilimanjaro' Collated and Annotated," *Texas Quarterly* 9 (1966): 71–74.

72. Ibid., 81.

73. Ibid., 82.

74. Item 704, p. [2].

75. "The Art of the Short Story," 96.

76. See also Hemingway's much later memory of Fitzgerald's reaction to a piece of favorable criticism of *The Great Gatsby* by Gilbert Seldes, in *A Moveable Feast*, 154.

77. Lewis and Westbrook, " 'The Snows of Kilimanjaro,' " 103.

78. Matt. 25: 14–30.

79. *Selected Letters*, 678–79; Bruccoli, *Scott and Ernest*, 150.

80. On Compton as Charon, see Caroline Gordon and Allen Tate, " 'The Snows of Kilimanjaro': Commentary," in *The House of Fiction* (New York: Scribner's, 1950), 422.

81. Wirt Williams, *The Tragic Art of Ernest Hemingway* (Baton Rouge: Louisiana State University Press, 1981), 134–35.

## 3. The Writer at War: An Interlude

1. Ernest Hemingway, *Men at War* (New York: Crown Publishers, 1942), xv. Page numbers provided parenthetically in the text below refer to this edition.

2. Baker, *Life Story*, 321.

3. Ernest Hemingway, *The Fifth Column and Four Stories of the Spanish Civil War* (New York: Scribner's, 1969), 20. Page numbers provided parenthetically in the text below refer to this edition.

4. William Braasch Watson, " 'Old Man at the Bridge': The Making of a Short Story," *Hemingway Review* 7:2 (Spring 1988): 155.

5. Kenneth G. Johnston, "Hemingway's 'The Denunciation': The Aloof American," in *Fitzgerald/Hemingway Annual 1979*, ed. Matthew J. Bruccoli and Richard Layman (Detroit: Gale Research, 1980), 382.

6. Paul Smith, *A Reader's Guide*, 370.

7. Johnston, "Hemingway's 'The Denunciation,' " 372, 374.

8. Martin Light, "Of Wasteful Deaths: Hemingway's Stories About the Spanish Civil War," in *The Short Stories of Ernest Hemingway: Critical Essays*, ed. Jackson J. Benson (Durham, N.C.: Duke University Press, 1975), 71–72.

## 4. Posthumous Works: *Islands in the Stream*

1. Baker, *Life Story*, 460.

2. On the dates of composition for *Islands*, see Baker, *Writer as Artist*, 379–81, and *Life Story*, 494, 497. On the composition of *Garden*, see *Writer as Artist*, 386n, and *Life Story*, 454–55, 460, 540. In the manuscript of *Garden*, the date 19/11/58 appears in the margin near the beginning of Item 422.1, book 3, chap. 24, probably indicating that Hemingway had made revisions on the chapter that day.

3. Ernest Hemingway, *Islands in the Stream* (New York: Scribner's, 1970), 12. Page numbers provided parenthetically in the text below refer to this edition.

4. Item 98—1, p. 3.

5. In spite of her own wealth, Pauline's divorce settlement with Hemingway had been vindictive in Hemingway's eyes. He had agreed to pay substantial child support—not alimony. See Meyers, *Hemingway*, 347.

6. Item 98—1, p. 5.

7. See Item 98—9, p. 401.

8. On the differences between the manuscript novel and the final version, see Robert E. Fleming, "Roger Davis of *Islands*: What the Manuscript Adds," in *Hemingway: Essays of Reassessment*, ed. Frank Scafella (New York: Oxford University Press, 1990), 53–60, and Robert E. Fleming, "The Hills Remain: The Mountain West of Hemingway's *Islands* Manuscript," *North Dakota Quarterly* 58 (1990): 79–85.

9. Baker, *Writer as Artist*, 386–87.

10. See Item 648b. The Allen manuscript and its relationship to the story of Philip Haines are discussed by Donald Junkins in "Hemingway's Paris Short Story: A Study in Revising," *Hemingway Review* 9:2 (Spring 1990): 10–48, especially "Appendix A," 22–31, which transcribes the James Allen ms.

11. Baker, *Life Story*, 273, 286. Baker reports that the black dock singers commemorated the fight in a calypso song about the "big fat slob in Bimini Harbor" who turned out to be a real fighter. For Hemingway's firsthand account, see *Selected Letters*, 414. Although Roger's fight is recounted in almost epic terms, the novel follows the facts quite closely.

12. Item 102—3, chap. 4, pp. 19–20.

13. Item 98—12, p. 559.

14. Item 98—1, p. 4.

15. Item 845, p. 1.

16. Item 98—7, pp. 316–22.

17. Jane Mason once attempted suicide by jumping from a second floor balcony. A beautiful woman, she enjoyed fishing and sailing. See Meyers, *Hemingway*, 245–46.

18. *Islands in the Stream* was edited into publishable form by Mary Hemingway and Charles Scribner, Jr., but Hemingway had already made most of the changes relevant to the issues raised here, such as Roger's demotion to secondary status and the transfer of the children to Thomas Hudson.

19. Item 98—7, pp. 304–305. As an attempt at self-justification, this manuscript passage is obviously in the same class as several episodes in *A Moveable Feast*, especially the final chapter, in which the author explains how Pauline—aided by Dos Passos, the "pilot fish"—stole a helpless Hemingway from his one true love.

20. Item 98—13, p. 527.

21. *Complete Short Stories, Finca Vigía*, 631.

22. Compare Hemingway's own "Who Murdered the Vets?" *New Masses*, 17 September 1935, 9–10, involving veterans of World War I who lived in C.C.C. camps much like southern prison camps during the depression and worked under conditions not too much better than those associated with convict work gangs. *New Masses*, of course, could easily be interpreted as a "red" journal. *To Have and Have Not*, with its allusion to Marxism in the title, also depicts the vets from the C.C.C. camps.

23. Item 98—16, p. 754.

24. Item 102—3, chap. 4, p. 23. Roger's comment echoes Hemingway's statement in *Death in the Afternoon*: "Let those who want to save the world if you can get to see it clear and as a whole" (278). However, opinions can change: after making that statement, Hemingway wrote distinctly partisan works such as *The Spanish Earth* and *The Fifth Column* before producing a more balanced view of both sides of the conflict in *For Whom the Bell Tolls*.

25. *Complete Short Stories, Finca Vigía*, 644.

26. Ibid., 644–45.

27. The other treatments are in *A Moveable Feast*, where the loss is treated straightforwardly as a regrettable accident, and *The Garden of Eden*, where Catherine's destruction of David's manuscript is a hostile act.

28. Ibid., 649. In "Fathers and Sons" Hemingway had shown the positive side of forgetting what was written, by indicating that Nick believes memories may be purged of their bad feelings if he writes about them. The *Islands* manuscript shows him considering the other side of the same proposition.

29. Ibid., 650.

30. Ibid., 620–21.

31. Ibid., 621.

32. *Green Hills*, 19.

33. *By-Line*, 470–71.

34. Introduction to *Short Stories*, v–vi.

35. Hudson's estrangement from meaningful human contact is evident

throughout the novel in the references to his wives: None of them is mentioned by name.

36. *Short Stories*, 271.

37. On Hudson's own painting style, see Stephen Mathewson, "Against the Stream: Thomas Hudson and Painting," *North Dakota Quarterly* 57:4 (1989): 140–45.

38. Baker, *Life Story*, 460. For Patrick Hemingway's version of this incident, see his "*Islands in the Stream*: A Son Remembers" in *Ernest Hemingway: The Writer in Context*, ed. James Nagel (Madison: University of Wisconsin Press, 1984), 13–18.

39. *Complete Short Stories, Finca Vigía*, 598. Page numbers provided parenthetically in the text below refer to this edition.

40. To Hemingway's credit, it must be noted that neither "I Guess Everything Reminds You of Something" nor "Great News from the Mainland" was published during the author's lifetime; however, this very restraint suggests that Hemingway recognized the gravity of a writer's violating the privacy of his relationship with his sons.

## 5. Posthumous Works: *The Garden of Eden*

1. Baker, *Life Story*, 454.

2. Ernest Hemingway, *The Garden of Eden* (New York: Scribner's, 1986), 247. Page numbers provided parenthetically in the text below refer to this edition. Hemingway was not usually so sanguine on the subject of lost manuscripts. In *A Moveable Feast* he laments Hadley's loss of a suitcase full of manuscripts and recalls that he had been unable to rewrite the stories, or indeed to write anything at all for some time after the loss (73–75).

3. Item 422.1, book 3, chap. 11, pp. 1, 9.

4. Item 422.1, book 3, chap. 13, p. 3.

5. Item 422.2, Story—Redo, p. 19.

6. Item 422.7, p. 47.

7. Item 422.7, p. 49.

8. See the headnote to *Islands in the Stream*, [vii], and Mary Hemingway, *How It Was* (New York: Knopf, 1976), 599–600. Whether Mary Hemingway scrupulously followed her own principles in the editing of *A Moveable Feast* has been questioned by Gerry Brenner in "Are We Going to Hemingway's *Feast*?" *American Literature* 54 (1982): 528–44.

9. Item 422.6, p. 1.

10. Ibid.

11. Ibid., 2.

12. Ibid., 3.

13. Ibid., 4.

14. Ibid.

15. Ibid., 5.

16. Ibid., 7.

17. Kenneth Lynn, *Hemingway* (New York: Simon and Schuster, 1987), 540.

18. Griffin, *Along With Youth*, 142–43; Lynn, *Hemingway*, 143; Meyers, *Hemingway*, 58.

19. *Selected Letters*, 407–409.

20. Ibid., 425, 483, 527–29, 695.

21. Ibid., 483.

22. *Moveable Feast*, 180–83.

23. Item 422.4, book 3, chap. 25, pp. 24–25.

24. Lynn, *Hemingway*, 541.

25. The insistence on Catherine as physical counterpart to David might suggest a Jungian encounter of the artist with his anima. Kenneth Lynn comes close to this notion in his discussion of the novel (*Hemingway*, 539–44), although his approach is basically Freudian.

26. The mirror above the bar, already mentioned, figures prominently throughout the novel. See *Garden*, 110, 126, 133, and 144 for brief mentions that are not otherwise discussed.

27. Item 422.1, book 1, chap. 1, p. 10.

28. Ibid., 11.

29. Hemingway had, of course, shown comparable sensitivity to the woman's point of view in earlier works such as "Hills Like White Elephants," "Cat in the Rain," and *To Have and Have Not*.

30. Item 422.1, book 3, chap. 9, p. 1.

31. Ibid., 10.

32. Item 422.1, book 3, chap. 11, p. 1.

33. Ibid., 11–12.

34. Item 422.1, book 3, chap. 14.

35. Item 422.1, book 3, chap. 13, p. 8.

36. Item 422.1, book 3, chap. 15, p. 12.

37. Item 422.1, book 3, chap. 16, p. 15.

38. Plimpton, "An Interview," 22.

39. Item 422.1, book 3, chap. 19, p. 3.

40. *Moveable Feast*, 180–82.

41. *Hemingway Review* 9:2 (1990): 2–9.

42. Julian Smith, "Eyeless in Wyoming, Blind in Venice—Hemingway's Last Stories," *Connecticut Review* 4:2 (1971): 15.

43. Delbert Wylder, "Internal Treachery in the Last Published Short Stories of Ernest Hemingway," *Hemingway in Our Time*, ed. Richard Astro and Jackson J. Benson (Corvallis: Oregon State University Press, 1974), 61.

44. *Complete Short Stories, Finca Vigía*, 491.

45. Item 422.1, book 1, chap. 2, p. 6.

46. Item 422.1, book 1, chap. 3, p. 1.

47. Item 422.1, book 1, chap. 2, p. 3.

48. Item 422.1, book 1, chap. 3, p. 1.

49. Ibid., 7.

50. Item 422.1, book 3, chap. 16, p. 10.

51. Compare Hemingway's own references to the pleasure he derived from

writing in his interviews with Harvey Breit—esp. "Talk with Ernest Hemingway," *New York Times Book Review*, 7 September 1952, p. 20—and with George Plimpton.

52. Item 422.1, book 3, chap. 21, p. 14.

53. Item 422.1, book 3, chap. 23. p. 9.

54. Ibid., 9 bis.

55. Item 422.1, book 3, chap. 24, p. 4.

56. Ibid., 8.

57. Item 422.1, book 3, chap. 25, p. 27.

58. Item 422.1, book 3, chap. 26, p. 1.

59. Item 422.1, book 3, chap. 29, pp. 10–11.

60. Item 422.2, story 4, p. 25 bis.

61. Item 422.1, book 3, chap. 27, p. 3. Significantly, while Hemingway was working on *Garden of Eden* he did not "invite" Mary Hemingway to read the manuscript "each evening, as [she] had done with other books, and [she] did not press him about it" (Mary Hemingway, *How It Was*, 521).

62. Ibid., 7.

63. Item 422.1, book 3, chap. 29, p. 9. Compare the words of the Nobel Prize statement: "[The writer] should always try for something that has never been done or that others have tried and failed. . . . It is because we have had such great writers in the past that a writer is driven far out past where he can go, out to where no one can help him."

64. Item 422.1, book 3, chap. 32, p. 15.

65. Ibid., 16.

66. Item 422.1, book 3, chap. 33, pp. 25–26.

67. Ibid., 26.

68. Item 422.1, book 3, chap. 38, p. 2.

69. Item 422.1, book 3, chap. 37, p. 25.

70. Item 422.1, book 3, chap. 39, p. 16.

71. Item 422.1, book 3, chap. 42, p. 16.

72. Item 422.1, book 3, chap. 46, p. 8.

73. Ibid., 14–15.

## Conclusion: A Self-Portrait Versus the Face in the Mirror

1. EH to Harvey Breit, quoted in Baker, *Life Story*, 487.

2. Jacqueline Tavernier-Courbin, *Ernest Hemingway's "A Moveable Feast": The Making of a Myth* (Boston: Northeastern University Press, 1991), 136–37.

3. Ibid., 137.

4. Mary Hemingway, "The Making of a Book: A Chronicle and a Memoir," *New York Times Book Review*, 10 May 1964, p. 27.

5. Baker, *Life Story*, 536.

6. *This Quarter* published "Big Two-Hearted River," "The Undefeated," and "The Sea Change" as well as a profile of Ezra Pound. "Big Two-Hearted River" earned Hemingway 1,000 francs, approximately one month's living expenses. See Baker, *Life Story*, 140; Michael Reynolds, *Hemingway: The Paris Years* (Oxford:

Basil Blackwell, 1989), 263, 284–85, 325; Humphrey Carpenter, *Geniuses Together: American Writers in Paris in the 1920s* (Boston: Houghton Mifflin, 1988), 154–56.

7. The *transatlantic review* published "Indian Camp," "The Doctor and the Doctor's Wife," and "Cross-Country Snow" as well as a number of pieces of nonfiction by Hemingway.

8. See Reynolds, *Paris Years*, 198–201.

9. Tavernier-Courbin, *Hemingway's "A Moveable Feast,"* 111–13.

10. Although she was not a commercial success, Stein had a considerable reputation among the avant-garde when Hemingway first went to call on her in 1922. She had already published *Three Lives* (1909) and *Tender Buttons* (1914), experiments in prose and poetry, respectively. Hemingway did, however, help her to publish much of *The Making of Americans* in the *transatlantic review* after a series of American publishers had rejected the novel.

11. On the sequence of the chapters of *A Moveable Feast*, see Brenner, "Are We Going to Hemingway's *Feast*?" 528–44. Brenner suggests that Mary Hemingway did more to structure the book than she claimed at the time of its publication. For Mary Hemingway's own statement, see "The Making of a Book," 26–27, and *How It Was*, 600.

12. For an account of Fitzgerald's struggle to complete *Tender Is the Night*, and especially Zelda's role in its composition, see Scott Donaldson, "A Short History of *Tender Is the Night*," in *Writing the American Classics*, ed. James Barbour and Tom Quirk (Chapel Hill: University of North Carolina Press, 1990), 177–208.

13. Gerry Brenner, *Concealments in Hemingway's Works* (Columbus: Ohio State University Press, 1983), 221–22.

14. Hemingway had created a similar persona in the manuscript of *The Dangerous Summer*. There, of course, the idealized writer is an elder statesman of letters, roughly based on Hemingway's own wishful concept of himself. But the emphasis in the character created for the bullfight book is on nonliterary characteristics—his knowledge of the bullring, of the medical treatment of wounds, and of life in general.

15. Bruccoli, *Conversations*, 196.

# Bibliography

## Works by Ernest Hemingway

"The Art of the Short Story." *Paris Review* 23:79 (Spring 1981): 85–102.

*By-Line: Ernest Hemingway*. Edited by William White. New York: Scribner's, 1967.

*The Complete Short Stories of Ernest Hemingway: The Finca Vigía Edition*. New York: Scribner's, 1987.

*The Dangerous Summer*. New York: Scribner's, 1985.

*Dateline Toronto: The Complete Toronto Star Dispatches, 1920–1924*. Edited by William White. New York: Scribner's, 1985.

*Death in the Afternoon*. New York: Scribner's, 1932.

*Ernest Hemingway: Selected Letters*. Edited by Carlos Baker. New York: Scribner's, 1981.

*The Fifth Column and Four Stories of the Spanish Civil War*. New York: Scribner's, 1969.

*The Garden of Eden*. New York: Scribner's, 1986.

"Give Us a Prescription, Doctor." *Scribner's Magazine* 93 (May 1933): 272–78.

*Green Hills of Africa*. New York: Scribner's, 1935.

"Hemingway in the Afternoon." *Time*, 4 August 1947, p. 80.

"Hemingway Is Bitter About Nobody—But His Colonel Is." *Time*, 11 September 1950, p. 110.

*Islands in the Stream*. New York: Scribner's, 1970.

*Men at War*. New York: Crown Publishers, 1942.

*A Moveable Feast*. New York: Scribner's, 1964.

*The Nick Adams Stories*. Edited by Philip Young. New York: Scribner's, 1972.

"Notes from a Novelist on His System of Work." *New York Times Book Review*, 31 July 1949, p. 1.

*The Short Stories of Ernest Hemingway*. New York: Scribner's, 1967.

*The Sun Also Rises*. New York: Scribner's, 1970.

*The Torrents of Spring*. New York: Scribner's, 1972.

*To Have and Have Not*. New York: Scribner's, 1937.

"A Visit with Hemingway: A Situation Report." *Look*, 4 September 1956, pp. 24–25.

## Secondary Sources

Anderson, Sherwood. *Dark Laughter*. New York: Boni and Liveright, 1925.

———. *Letters to Bab: Sherwood Anderson to Marietta D. Finley, 1916–1933*. Urbana: University of Illinois Press, 1985.

————. *Sherwood Anderson's Memoirs*. New York: Harcourt, Brace, 1942.

Astro, Richard, and Jackson J. Benson. *Hemingway in Our Time*. Corvallis: Oregon State University Press, 1974.

"Back to His First Field." In *Conversations with Ernest Hemingway*, edited by Matthew J. Bruccoli, 21–24. Jackson: University Press of Mississippi, 1986.

Baker, Carlos. *Ernest Hemingway: A Life Story*. New York: Scribner's, 1969.

————, ed. *Ernest Hemingway: Selected Letters, 1917–1961*. New York: Scribner's, 1981.

————, ed. *Hemingway and His Critics*. New York: Hill and Wang, 1961.

————. *The Writer as Artist*. 4th ed. Princeton: Princeton University Press, 1973.

Barbour, James, and Tom Quirk, eds. *Writing the American Classics*. Chapel Hill: University of North Carolina Press, 1990.

Beegel, Susan F., ed. *Hemingway's Neglected Short Fiction: New Perspectives*. Tuscaloosa: University of Alabama Press, 1992.

Bennett, Warren. " 'That's Not Very Polite': Sexual Identity in Hemingway's 'The Sea Change.' " In *Hemingway's Neglected Short Fiction*, edited by Susan F. Beegel, 225–45. Tuscaloosa: University of Alabama Press, 1992.

Benson, Jackson J., ed. *The Short Stories of Ernest Hemingway: Critical Essays*. Durham, N.C.: Duke University Press, 1975.

Bernheim, Kurt. *"McCall's* Visits Ernest Hemingway." In *Conversations with Ernest Hemingway*, edited by Matthew J. Bruccoli, 105–108. Jackson: University Press of Mississippi, 1986.

Brasch, James D., and Joseph Sigman. *Hemingway's Library: A Composite Record*. New York: Garland Press, 1981.

Breit, Harvey. "Talk with Ernest Hemingway." *New York Times Book Review*, 7 September 1952, p. 20.

————. "Talk with Mr. Hemingway." *New York Times Book Review*, 17 September 1950, p. 14.

Brenner, Gerry. "Are We Going to Hemingway's *Feast?*" *American Literature* 54 (1982): 528–44.

————. *Concealments in Hemingway's Works*. Columbus: Ohio State University Press, 1983.

Broussard, Louis. "Hemingway as Literary Critic." *Arizona Quarterly* 20 (Autumn 1964): 197–204.

Bruccoli, Matthew J. *Scott and Ernest: The Authority of Failure and the Authority of Success*. New York: Random House, 1978.

————, ed. *Conversations with Ernest Hemingway*. Jackson: University Press of Mississippi, 1986.

————, ed. *Ernest Hemingway's Apprenticeship: Oak Park, 1916–1917*. Washington, D.C.: NCR Microcard Editions, 1971.

Bruccoli, Matthew J., and C. E. Frazer Clark, Jr., eds. *Fitzgerald/Hemingway Annual 1974*. Englewood: Microcard Editions, 1975.

Bruccoli, Matthew J., and Richard Layman, eds. *Fitzgerald/Hemingway Annual 1979*. Detroit: Gale Research, 1980.

Callaghan, Morley. *That Summer in Paris*. Toronto: Macmillan of Canada, 1963.

Carpenter, Humphrey. *Geniuses Together: American Writers in Paris in the 1920s*. Boston: Houghton Mifflin, 1988.

DeFalco, Joseph. *The Hero in Hemingway's Short Stories*. Pittsburgh: University of Pittsburgh Press, 1963.

Donaldson, Scott. "A Short History of *Tender Is the Night*." In *Writing the American Classics*, edited by James Barbour and Tom Quirk, 177–208. Chapel Hill: University of North Carolina Press, 1990.

Fenton, Charles A. *The Apprenticeship of Ernest Hemingway: The Early Years*. New York: Compass Books, 1958.

Fleming, Robert E. "American Nightmare: Hemingway and the West." *Midwest Quarterly* 30 (1989): 361–71.

———. "Hemingway's Treatment of Suicide: 'Fathers and Sons' and *For Whom the Bell Tolls*." *Arizona Quarterly* 33 (1977): 121–32.

———. "The Hills Remain: The Mountain West of Hemingway's *Islands* Manuscript." *North Dakota Quarterly* 58 (1990): 79–85.

———. "The Libel of Dos Passos in *To Have and Have Not*." *Journal of Modern Literature* 15 (1989): 597–601.

———. "Roger Davis of *Islands*: What the Manuscript Adds." In *Hemingway: Essays of Reassessment*, edited by Frank Scafella, 53–60. New York: Oxford University Press, 1990.

Gordon, Caroline, and Allen Tate. " 'The Snows of Kilimanjaro': Commentary." In *The House of Fiction*. New York: Scribner's, 1950.

Grebstein, Sheldon Norman. *Hemingway's Craft*. Carbondale: Southern Illinois University Press, 1973.

Griffin, Peter. *Along With Youth: Hemingway, the Early Years*. New York: Oxford University Press, 1985.

Harrington, Mary. "They Call Him Papa." *New York Post Week-End Magazine*, 28 December 1946, p. 3.

Hawthorne, Nathaniel. *The American Notebooks*, edited by Randall Stewart. New Haven: Yale University Press, 1932.

Hemingway, Leicester. *My Brother, Ernest Hemingway*. Cleveland: World, 1961.

Hemingway, Mary. *How It Was*. New York: Knopf, 1976.

———. "The Making of a Book: A Chronicle and a Memoir." *New York Times Book Review*, 10 May 1964, pp. 26–27.

Hemingway, Patrick. "*Islands in the Stream*: A Son Remembers." In *Ernest Hemingway: The Writer in Context*, edited by James Nagel, 13–18. Madison: University of Wisconsin Press, 1984.

Hotchner, A. E. *Papa Hemingway: A Personal Memoir*. New York: Random House, 1966.

Howe, Irving. *Sherwood Anderson*. New York: William Sloane Associates, 1951.

"Indestructible." *New Yorker*, 4 January 1947, pp. 20–21.

Johnston, Kenneth G. "Hemingway's 'The Denunciation': The Aloof American." In *Fitzgerald/Hemingway Annual 1979*, edited by Matthew J. Bruccoli and Richard Layman, 371–82. Detroit: Gale Research, 1980.

Joost, Nicholas. *Hemingway and the Little Magazines: The Paris Years*. Barre, Mass.: Barre Publishers, 1968.

Junkins, Donald. "Hemingway's Paris Short Story: A Study in Revising." *Hemingway Review* 9:2 (Spring 1990): 10–48.

Kobler, J. F. "Hemingway's 'The Sea Change': A Sympathetic View of Homosexuality." *Arizona Quarterly* 26 (1970): 318–24.

Kramer, Dale. *Chicago Renaissance: The Literary Life in the Midwest, 1900–1930.* New York: Appleton-Century, 1966.

Kvam, Wayne. "Hemingway's 'Banal Story.' " In *Fitzgerald/Hemingway Annual 1974*, edited by Matthew J. Bruccoli and C. E. Frazer Clark, Jr., 181–91. Englewood, Colo.: Microcard Editions, 1975.

Lewis, Robert W., Jr., and Max Westbrook. " 'The Snows of Kilimanjaro' Collated and Annotated." *Texas Quarterly* 9 (1966): 67–143.

Lewis, Wyndham. *Men Without Art.* London: Cassell, 1934.

Light, Martin. "Of Wasteful Deaths: Hemingway's Stories about the Spanish Civil War." In *The Short Stories of Ernest Hemingway: Critical Essays*, edited by Jackson J. Benson, 64–77. Durham, N.C.: Duke University Press, 1975.

Loeb, Harold. *The Way It Was.* New York: Criterion, 1959.

Ludington, Townsend. *John Dos Passos: A Twentieth Century Odyssey.* New York: E. P. Dutton, 1980.

Ludwig, Richard M., ed. *Letters of Ford Madox Ford.* Princeton, N.J.: Princeton University Press, 1965.

Lynn, Kenneth. *Hemingway.* New York: Simon and Schuster, 1987.

MacLeish, Archibald. "Years of the Dog." In *Actfive and Other Poems.* New York: Random House, 1948.

Mathewson, Stephen. "Against the Stream: Thomas Hudson and Painting." *North Dakota Quarterly* 57:4 (1989): 140–45.

Meyers, Jeffrey. *Hemingway: A Biography.* New York: Harper and Row, 1985.

Michener, James A. "Introduction," *The Dangerous Summer* by Ernest Hemingway. New York: Scribner's, 1985.

Moddelmog, Debra. "The Unifying Consciousness of a Divided Conscience: Nick Adams as Author of *In Our Time.*" *American Literature* 60 (1988): 591–610.

Monteiro, George. "The Writer on Vocation: Hemingway's 'Banal Story.' " In *Hemingway's Neglected Short Fiction: New Perspectives*, edited by Susan F. Beegel, 141–47. Tuscaloosa: University of Alabama Press, 1992.

Nagel, James, ed. *Ernest Hemingway: The Writer in Context.* Madison: University of Wisconsin Press, 1984.

Perloff, Marjorie. " 'Ninety Percent Rotarian': Gertrude Stein's Hemingway." *American Literature* 62 (1990): 668–83.

Pizer, Donald. "The Hemingway-Dos Passos Relationship." *Journal of Modern Literature* 13 (1986): 111–28.

Plimpton, George. "An Interview with Ernest Hemingway." In *Hemingway and His Critics*, edited by Carlos Baker. New York: Hill and Wang, 1961.

Raeburn, John. *Fame Became of Him: Hemingway as Public Writer.* Bloomington: Indiana University Press, 1984.

Reynolds, Michael S. *Hemingway: The Paris Years.* Oxford: Basil Blackwell, 1989.

———. *Hemingway's Reading, 1910–1940: An Inventory.* Princeton: Princeton University Press, 1981.

———. *Young Hemingway.* Oxford: Basil Blackwell, 1986.

Ross, Lillian. "Profile: How Do You Like It Now, Gentlemen?" *New Yorker*, 13 May 1950, pp. 36–62.

Sarason, Bertram D. *Hemingway and the "Sun" Set*. Washington, D.C.: Microcard Editions, 1972.

Shepherd, Allen. "Taking Apart 'Mr. and Mrs. Elliot.' " *Markham Review* 2 (September 1969): 15–16.

Smith, Alson J. *Chicago's Left Bank*. Chicago: Regnery, 1953.

Smith, Chard Powers. *Where the Light Falls: A Portrait of Edwin Arlington Robinson*. New York: Macmillan, 1965.

Smith, Julian. "Eyeless in Wyoming, Blind in Venice—Hemingway's Last Stories." *Connecticut Review* 4:2 (April 1971): 9–15.

———. "Hemingway and the Thing Left Out." *Journal of Modern Literature* 1 (1970): 169–82.

Smith, Paul. "From the Waste Land to the Garden with the Elliots." In *Hemingway's Neglected Short Fiction: New Perspectives*, edited by Susan F. Beegel, 123–29. Tuscaloosa: University of Alabama Press, 1992.

———. "Hemingway's Apprentice Fiction, 1919–1921." *American Literature* 58 (1986): 574–88.

———. *Reader's Guide to the Short Stories of Ernest Hemingway*. Boston: G. K. Hall, 1989.

"Stalking Lions was 'Exciting' to Hemingway." In *Conversation with Ernest Hemingway*, edited by Matthew J. Bruccoli, 6–7. Jackson: University Press of Mississippi, 1986.

Stein, Gertrude. *The Autobiography of Alice B. Toklas*. New York: Harcourt, Brace, 1933.

Stephens, Robert O. *Hemingway's Nonfiction: The Public Voice*. Chapel Hill: University of North Carolina Press, 1968.

Svoboda, Frederic J. *Hemingway and "The Sun Also Rises": The Crafting of a Style*. Lawrence: University Press of Kansas, 1983.

Tavernier-Courbin, Jacqueline. *Ernest Hemingway's A Moveable Feast: The Making of a Myth*. Boston: Northeastern University Press, 1991.

Waldhorn, Arthur. *A Reader's Guide to Ernest Hemingway*. New York: Farrar, Straus and Giroux, 1972.

Watson, William Braasch. " 'Old Man at the Bridge': The Making of a Short Story." *Hemingway Review* 7:2 (Spring 1988): 152–65.

Westerhoven, James N. "Autobiographical Elements in the Camera Eye." *American Literature* 48 (1976): 340–64.

Williams, Wirt. *The Tragic Art of Ernest Hemingway*. Baton Rouge: Louisiana State University Press, 1981.

Wycherley, H. Alan. "Hemingway's 'The Sea Change.' " *American Notes and Queries* 7 (1969): 67–68.

Wylder, Delbert. "Internal Treachery in the Last Published Short Stories of Ernest Hemingway." In *Hemingway in Our Time*, edited by Richard Astro and Jackson J. Benson, 53–65. Corvallis: Oregon State University Press, 1974.

Yanella, Phillip R. "Notes on the Manuscript, Date, and Sources of Hemingway's

'Banal Story.' " In *Fitzgerald/Hemingway Annual 1974*, edited by Matthew J. Bruccoli and C. E. Frazer Clark, Jr., 175–79. Englewood, Colo.: Microcard Editions, 1975.

Young, Philip. *Ernest Hemingway: A Reconsideration*. University Park: Pennsylvania State University Press, 1966.

——, ed. *The Nick Adams Stories*. New York: Scribner's, 1972.

# Index

# About the Author

Robert E. Fleming is Associate Dean of Arts and Sciences and Professor of English, University of New Mexico. He received his bachelor's and master's degrees from Northern Illinois University and his doctorate from the University of Illinois. He is the author of *Willard Motley* (1978), *James Weldon Johnson & Arna Wendell Bontemps: A Reference Guide* (1978), *Sinclair Lewis: A Reference Guide* (1980), *Charles F. Lummis* (1981), and *James Weldon Johnson* (1987).